The Electronic Christian

The
ELECTRONIC

105 READINGS FROM

CHRISTIAN

Fulton J. Sheen

MACMILLAN PUBLISHING CO., INC.

NEW YORK

COLLIER MACMILLAN PUBLISHERS

LONDON

Macmillan Publishing Co., Inc.
866 Third Avenue, New York, N.Y. 10022
Collier Macmillan Canada, Ltd.

Library of Congress Cataloging in Publication Data

Sheen, Fulton John, 1895–
    The electronic Christian.

        Bibliography: p.
        1. Catholic Church—Doctrinal and controversial
works—Catholic authors—Collected works. I. Title.

BX1751.2.S458   230'.2   79-10853
ISBN 0-02-610050-9

First Printing 1979

Printed in the United States of America

Contents

Foreword

THE CANDLES ON THE ALTAR—that's about all he can remember of the first religious service broadcast on television. Under the ferocious heat of the klieg lights, they
"sank in utter despair" three or four minutes after the program began. There were only forty television sets on Long
Island that Easter Sunday; perhaps only one hundred people saw the telecast; but electronic evangelization was eas-
tering in the United States, and in barely a dozen years Fulton J. Sheen would be its zenith.

As a student Sheen acquired degrees the way an Olympic
athlete amasses medals. In 1917, from St. Viator's College
and Seminary in Illinois, he earned a B.A. and in 1919, the
year of his ordination, an A.M. In 1920, from Catholic University in Washington, D.C., he won the S.T.B. and J.C.B.;
in 1923, from the University of Louvain in Belgium, he was
awarded a Ph.D. and in 1925 the Agrege en Philosophie. He

knew he had passed the examination for the latter when he was invited to dinner by the examiners, but how well did he do? If the waiters served water, then he had barely passed. If they served wine, he had passed with distinction. But they served champagne!

Sheen's thesis was published in both London and New York under the title *God and Intelligence in Modern Philosophy;* it had an introduction by that paradoxical Christian, G. K. Chesterton. On returning to the United States he served as a curate in St. Patrick's parish, Peoria, for a year. Then he joined the philosophy department of Catholic University, where for the next twenty-five years everything he taught seemed to turn to books. In 1928 there was *Religion Without God;* in 1934 there was *Philosophy of Science;* in 1948 there was *Philosophy of Religion: The Impact of Modern Knowledge on Religion.*

Sheen took every opportunity to polish his speaking voice. Walking to a convent or orphanage in Washington where he would celebrate morning Mass, he would preach to telephone poles, homilize and sermonize, until his coppery tones became golden, his rhetoric tending more to rose than purple, with a timbre that could shatter souls.

Almost every Good Friday during this period found Sheen in the pulpit of St. Paul's Church and later St. Patrick's Cathedral, New York, preaching during the three hours commemorating Christ's death on the cross. Many of these sermons were memorialized in small devotional volumes. In 1932 there was *The Way of the Cross;* in 1937 there was *The Cross and the Beatitudes;* in 1938 there was *The Rainbow of the Cross.*

Half the Sundays from 1930 to 1952, one might hear Sheen preaching the word of God on radio. He had made the first network religious radiocast; it was sponsored by the National Council of Catholic Men; and in the years that Sheen was the mainstay of "The Catholic Hour," the station received more than 700,000 letters. Not a few of these series of talks appeared later in book form. In 1930 there was *The Divine Romance;* in 1939 there was *The Eternal Galilean;* in 1952 there was the *Life of Christ.*

In 1952 Sheen left Sunday afternoon radio for prime-time television. Although such religious programming was a first, network executives did not expect it to survive. In competing time-slots on the other networks were Milton Berle acting skits with a blueish tinge and Frank Sinatra singing songs of a blues-ish caste; on ''Life Is Worth Living,'' however, Sheen told jokes of a different color—the color of the Emerald Isle—and taught orthodox Christian doctrine and solid Christian spirituality.

The program not only survived, it flourished. At the end of the first season, Sheen won an Emmy, television's highest award. Bob Hope had won an Emmy that season too and, when presented with the statuette, he felt compelled to thank his writers. Statuette in hand, Sheen thanked his writers too: Matthew, Mark, Luke, and John. By 1954 an estimated twenty-five million viewers were watching the program each week.

In 1950 Sheen had moved from Washington to New York, where he was consecrated auxiliary bishop of New York and appointed national director of the Society for the Propagation of the Faith. In this position for the next sixteen years he collected and distributed more than two hundred million dollars to missionaries around the world who were spreading the gospel mainly through non-electronic means. To the Society he also gave his television income, which at its lowest was $260,000 for a twenty-six week season and at its highest was $429,000.

Eventually and indeed inevitably, the ''Life Is Worth Living'' transcripts appeared in book form. And there were other books during this time. In 1951 there was *Three to Get Married;* in 1960 there was *Go to Heaven;* in 1963 there was *Missions and the World Crisis.*

From the television camera Sheen went to the still camera. With Yousuf Karsh, the portrait photographer from Ottawa, he produced lavishly illustrated books entitled *This Is*

Rome in 1960, *The Is the Holy Land* in 1961, *These Are the Sacraments* in 1962, and *This Is the Mass* in 1967. In 1966 he was appointed Archbishop of Rochester, where he served until the beginning of his seventy-fifth year.

Sheen has had two great passions in life. First is opposition to communism. He railed against the intellectuals in the thirties who thought kindly of the Marxian philosophy. He equated Stalin's pogroms with Hitler's atrocities; Stalin persecuted the New Testament; Hitler persecuted the Old Testament; one can be distinguished from the other only if genocide is different from murder. In *Communism and the Conscience of the West,* which was published in 1949, he attacked communism as a religion that could have grown only out of the evils of western civilization—surely a provocative statement from a man whom many hoped would be the first pope from a capitalist country.

His second great passion is love for Mary the mother of Jesus. All of his books have been dedicated to one or another of her virtues, and this one is no exception: "To Mary, virgin mother of Christ, to whom every written line of my life has been dedicated since I first scribbled J.M.J. on a page in kindergarten." *The World's First Love,* although it was written by an American bishop in 1956, thrums like a medieval ballad, its sentiments appearing extravagant only to those who know the woman less well than he.

If there is one word to describe Sheen's apostolate, it is *electronic*. Radio is like the Old Testament, he once said; listening to it, one can hear the word of God. And television is like the New Testament; one can not only hear the word of God but also see it incarnated before one's very own eyes. If there is truth in simile, then in his more than fifty years of electronic evangelization he has brought the Old Testament to millions and the New Testament to billions.

Although Sheen's radio audience was largely Catholic and his television audience mostly Jewish and Protestant, his appeal did not follow exclusively sectarian lines. The faithful of various Christian communions he encouraged to become even more faithful. The lapsed from one communion or another he coaxed to return. The unchurched of whatever persuasion he encouraged to convert. And among the converts of his own electronic evangelization he numbered the communist editor Louis Budenz, playwright Clare Boothe Luce, Russian spy Elizabeth Bentley, violinist Fritz Kreisler, and manufacturer Henry Ford II. For every celebrity conversion, however, there were a hundred more whose notoriety was known only by the Lord. After open-heart surgery in 1978, while confined to bed, he managed to instruct five converts in the faith.

What one Christian of the electronic era believes is the subject of this anthology. Selections have been taken from twenty-two of Fulton J. Sheen's more than seventy works. The readings are thematically arranged, informally systematized, and devotionally styled. Sources of the readings are given at the end of the book.

—WILLIAM GRIFFIN
Macmillan Publishing Co., Inc.
April 1, 1979

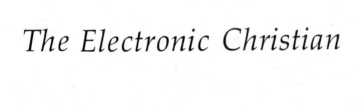

The Electronic Christian

The Thrill of Orthodoxy

WHY DO CHILDREN LIKE TO PLAY cops and robbers, walk picket fences, tramp into thick woods, play along banks of deep rivers, throw stones at vicious dogs, listen to blood-curdling ghost stories, walk on roofs? Is it not because each and every child has deep-rooted in the heart, as the foundation for adulthood, and as the very condition for enjoying life, the love of danger and the thrill of being near it, and yet never falling completely into it? Why do children, when they grow up, love to play games of chance, hunt wild beasts, explore the icy extremities of the earth, fly over trackless seas, speed at the rate of four miles a minute over land, and five miles a minute in the air if it is not because, as adults, they too love the thrill that comes with danger, and love still more the glorious escape from that to which they had so often exposed themselves?

And what is true of children and true of adults is true of

1

the Church. It is extremely thrilling to belong to the Church. It is exhilarating to be orthodox. It is romantic to be poised on the Rock of Peter that could fall into a thousand pitfalls, and yet never falls.

Every person has an instinctive desire to witness a storm at sea, providing he or she could be sure of reaching port. We who ride in Peter's bark witness such a storm and know we will reach port. For twenty centuries the bark of Peter has been riding, riding the seas, and for twenty centuries we who have been on board know the romance of the seas and its dangers, but also the romance of a port. Sometimes that bark has come within a hair's-breadth of dashing against the rocks, of saying that Christ was man and not God, and then again it has suddenly had to swerve to avoid crashing into the opposite rock and saying the Christ is God but not man.

At other moments in her voyage, Peter's bark has come within a razor's edge of being stranded on the sands of humanism and saying that man does everything, and God does nothing. And then, by an equally dexterous move, she saves herself from the sand bars by declaring with the Oriental mystics that God does everything and man does nothing. It would have been extremely easy for Peter and his successors to have sunk their ship in the depths of determinism, just as it would have been very easy for the ship to have capsized in the shallow waters of sentimentalism in the twentieth century. But it is wonderfully thrilling to have avoided both.

It would have been very easy for the bark of Peter to have been lost in the fogs of modernism, just as it would have been easy for it to have lost its course in the mists of fundamentalism. But to have avoided both of these snares, not by mere chance, but by intellectual direction, is thrilling. If one small blunder, concerning the doctrine of original sin, were made in her twenty centuries of charting the course of men to God, huge blunders would have been made in human happiness. A mistranslation of a single word one thousand years ago might have smashed all the statues of Europe. A false move in the Council of the Vatican might have impoverished reason. By one single slip, the Church might have stopped all the dances, withered all the Christmas trees, and broken all the Easter eggs.

But the Church has avoided all these pitfalls and all these errors and, as the bark of Peter, with sails flying high, cuts the waters of the sea, she looks before and aft. Behind her she can see the shriveled hulks of a thousand heresies and mental fashions that were suited to their times and died because that is all they were suited for—their times. Before her she can see the shipwrecked rafts of masterless men looking for the master Peter, who is not for one time but all time.

And now its future will be just as thrilling as the past. Always in danger, always escaping it; always threatened, always conquering; always enjoying the romance of avoiding extremes, the bark is destined to go on through all the storms and tempests of the world until one day it checks pace at the hidden battlements of eternity, and there as the children disembark from the ship of Peter, they will understand why it avoided the snares and pitfalls—because as Peter stood at the helm of his bark, there rested on his hands the invisible, eternal hands of Christ, whom the winds and seas obey; Christ, who steers the sun and moon and stars in their courses.

The Trinity

THREE IN ONE—Father, Son and Holy Spirit—three Persons and one God: such is the mystery of the Trinity, such is the Life of God. How can this be? There are some faint vestiges of this life in our own soul. I know and I love. What is knowing? It is the soul acting in a certain way. What is love? It is the soul acting in another way. Though I am, though I think and though I love, my soul remains substantially one; and although God thinks and loves, the thought and the love remain perfectly within Himself, never passing outside like the fruit of a tree or the progeny of an animal. There is perfect immanent activity; therefore perfect life. God is life. The Blessed Trinity is an impenetrable mystery, not contrary to reason, but above it.

Should we, however, desire some reasoned analysis demonstrating that there is no contradiction between reason and revelation, then we may take the explanation current among Western theologians since St. Augustine. As the trunk, the leaves, and the branches go to make up but one tree; as the three angles of a triangle go to make up but one triangle; as the direction, the brightness, and heat of the sun go to make up but one sun; as the length, breadth, and thickness of a room make up but one room; as water, ice, and steam are the three manifestations of one and the same substance; as movement, limpidity, and fluidity of water do not make up three rivers but one; as the form, color, and perfume of the rose do not make up three roses but one; as our soul, our intellect, and our will do not make up three substances but one; as $1 \times 1 \times 1 = 1$ and not 3, so too, in some more mysterious way there are three Persons in one God and yet only one God.

Creation

WHY . . . DID GOD CREATE A WORLD? God created the world for something like the same reason that we find it hard to keep a secret! Good things are hard to keep. The rose is good and tells its secret in perfume. The sun is good and tells its secret in light and heat. Man is good and tells the secret of his goodness in the language of thought. But God is Infinitely Good, and therefore Infinitely Loving. Why therefore could not He by a free impulse of His Love let love overflow and bring new worlds into being? God could not keep, as it were, the secret of His Love, and the telling of it was Creation.

Love overflowed; eternity moved and said to time, "Begin." Omnipotence moved and said to nothingness, "Be." Light moved and said to darkness, "Be light." Out from the fingertips of God there tumbled planets and worlds. Stars were thrown into their orbits and the spheres into space. Orbs and brotherhoods of orbs began to fill the heavens. The great march of the world began, in which planet passes by planet and sphere by sphere, without ever a hitch or a halt. In that long procession of the unfolding of the Creative Power of God, there first came matter, then palpitating life and the Paradise of Creation with its four-fold rivers flowing through all lands rich with gold and onyx, and finally those creatures made not by Fiat but by a Council of the Trinity—the first man and woman.

Quite naturally the mind of that Great Architect might have conceived ten thousand other possible worlds than this. This is not absolutely the best world that God could have made. But it is the best world for the purpose that He had in mind in making it. Almighty God chose to make a universe in which not all the creatures would be like sticks and stones, trees and beasts, each of which is impelled by a law of nature or a law of instinct to a determined rigorous end, without the slightest enjoyment of freedom. He willed to place in Paradise a creature made to His own image and likeness, but a creature different from all others, because endowed with that glorious gift of freedom, which is the power of saying yes or no, of choosing to sacrifice oneself to duty or duty to oneself, and forever remaining master and captain of one's own fate and destiny. In other words, God willed to make a moral universe, and the only condition upon which morality is possible is freedom.

In the very nature of things, ethics and morality can exist

only upon the condition of a veto. Bravery, for example, is possible only in a world in which a person may be a coward. Virtue is possible only in a world where a person may be vicious. Sacrifice is possible only in an order in which a person may be selfish. Love is possible only when it is possible not to love. Cold statues cannot love. It is the possibility of saying no that gives so much charm to the heart when it says yes. A victory may be celebrated only on those fields in which a battle may be lost. Hence, in the divine order of things, God made a world in which man and woman would rise to moral heights, not by that blind driving power that makes the sun rise each morning, but rather by the exercise of that freedom in which one may fight the good fight and enjoy the spoils of victory, for no one shall be crowned unless he has struggled.

God in His Goodness did not choose simply to make a person moral and then give him or her merely the moral rewards to which he or she is naturally entitled. He willed to do more than this. When a person becomes a parent, is he or she content merely to give the child only that which is necessary? Does the parent not rather give to the child even more than that which is due? So, in like manner God willed to give man certain gifts of body and soul that far exceeded the nature or the capacity of man. Imagine a wealthy banker who would form a trust fund for a foundling baby, in which a vast sum of money was to be paid to the child at twenty-one, provided that during that time the child had led a good moral life. Now God established some such trust fund. He willed to give to the first man and woman certain gifts that would be theirs permanently, and for their posterity, provided that they proved faithful in their love. Among these gifts were immunity from disease and death, freedom from the rebellion of flesh over reason, and above all a gift of *knowledge* that far surpassed reason and enabled man to grasp divine truths in a far greater way than a telescope reveals to the eye the distant stars and planets; and a gift of *power* or *grace* that made the first man and woman not mere creatures of the handiwork of God, but God's own children, and coheirs with Him in the Kingdom of Heaven.

The Fall

THE STORY OF THE FALL as recorded in Genesis is known to all. Satan, appearing in the form of a serpent, tempted Eve with the question that destroyed confidence, which is the root of all love. "Why has God commanded you that you should not eat of every tree of Paradise?" Eve looks at the forbidden fruit; it is beautiful to behold. More and more she turns herself from the voice and thought of God to the fragrancy and imagined sweetness of the forbidden fruit. The lingering thought passes into a vivid imagination, the vivid imagination into a burning wish, the burning wish into a half-formed purpose, the half-formed purpose into a hasty act. Swiftly the crisis is upon her, as all such crises are, and the deed was done irrevocably until time shall be no more.

She gave the forbidden fruit to Adam, and Pride and Self-Will entered into his heart. He wanted to show he *did know* what was good for him, and that his mind need not be kept obscured on any one point, nor his will reserved by any one condition. He wanted to be independent and show that he could do what he liked. And so he ate the fruit that he was forbidden to eat, because it was fair, and still more to show his own independence. Surely, this is understandable. Have we not done the same thing in our own lives over and over again? When we were children, were we not forbidden to do something we wished to do? Did we not long for it and determine to have it all the more because it was forbidden? Adam did it for the very same reason, and that act of disobedience by which Adam failed the test of love is the first sin of this created universe, the sin that infected humanity in its origin and the sin that, for that reason, has been called original sin.

The whole trial was perfectly reasonable. Imagine a wealthy man who owns a beautiful estate. He tells his chauffeur and the chauffeur's wife that he will permit them to live in his mansion, ride in his motorcars, use his servants, enjoy his yacht, play about his spacious gardens, eat at his expense. In a word, they are to enjoy everything provided they do not touch a certain oil painting that hangs in one of his drawing rooms. Now, if the lady persuaded the gentleman to touch that painting, she would not be a lady, and if the gentleman touched the painting at the suggestion of the lady, he would not be a gentleman. By doing the one thing forbidden, they would lose all the things provided, and who would accuse the master of the house of injustice if he no longer permitted them to enjoy his gifts?

The doctrine, then, of the Fall of man is far from the travesty made upon it by frivolous minds who make the ordinance of God repose solely on an apple, for to do this is to miss the point of the whole story. To speak of the Fall does not mean merely a garden and a serpent; to say that it is much more than any garden or any snake is not the same as saying there was no garden and there was no snake. It is simply saying what is of primary and what is of secondary importance; what is primary is the respect due to God, the fruit of the tree being the symbol of that respect.

To make light of the fruit of a tree under such circumstances is just as rash as to make light of the flag of our country, as a symbol of our country's sovereignty. A flag stands for a nation, and the hand that carries it would retain it at the cost of a thousand deaths rather than let it be seized and desecrated by the enemy. It may be a small thing to violate a cloth that is red and white and blue, but it is no small thing to desecrate that for which it stands.

So, likewise, in the terrestrial Paradise, the famous tree in which God summarized all the knowledge of good and evil was a symbol, a moral limit that God imposed on the sovereignty of man to prove his obedience and his love. To say it was only a fable is to miss the great truth that things—a handshake or a smile, for example—may not only be, but may also signify.

There are three points that I would make in conclusion concerning the Fall of man. The first is that by this act of disobedience, which is called original sin, man lost nothing that was due to him or to his nature. He lost only gifts, and became, as St. Augustine has said, "just mere man." On Christmas, when you distribute gifts to your friends, a person with whom you are unacquainted would not dare come to you and argue that you had refused to give him gifts as you had given them to your friends. Your answer would be: "Sir, I have done you no injustice. I have deprived you of nothing that is your due. I have even given to my friends that which was not theirs."

And so it is with original sin. In losing the gifts of God, man lost nothing that was due to his nature. He was reduced to a state in which God might possibly have created him, with the difference that the loss of the gifts weakened his intellect and will, but did not make his nature intrinsically corrupt. Imagine a line of soldiers; notice one of these in particular. He resembles all the others in dress, appearance, and action, but yesterday he was an officer, thanks to a political preferment rather than to meritorious advancement. For an act of misdemeanor he was degraded, and the badge of his office was taken from him. He was reduced to the state in which you see him now. Original sin, then, is not to be in the state we are in, but to have fallen into that state.

Secondly, this sin of Adam was not merely the sin of an individual; it was the sin of all humanity, for Adam was the head of all humanity. If he had been faithful, we would have enjoyed all of his gifts, for he acted in our name. Since he was unfaithful, we suffer his loss, for he acted in our name. This is not an injustice. All human beings are bound up with one another. In 1917, for example, President Wilson proclaimed war without any explicit declaration on the part of any of us. He was our political head, and he acted in our name. Adam was our head, and he acted in our name. When he declared war against God, we declared war in like manner, without any explicit declaration on our part, because of our oneness with him. And just as in the physical order the infected blood of a parent may pass on to a child, so too the stain of the first man has passed on to the whole human race and stained every one but our "tainted nature's solitary boast"—the Blessed Mother of our Lord and Savior Jesus Christ.

Finally, original sin alone can explain the almost contradictory character of human nature that makes man aspire to higher things and at the same time succumb to baser. The only reason we ever seek the nobler things of God is that we once possessed them; we seek because once we found.

The Moral Universe

IF GOD IS POWER, love, and justice, then why did He create this kind of world? If He is powerful, why does He permit evil? If He is love, why does He tolerate hate? If He is justice, why does He allow unrighteousness? These questions, I suppose, have been asked by everyone whose eyes have ever seen, whose minds have ever known the terrible contrast between the sin of the world and the goodness of God.

In order to answer correctly the question why God made this kind of world, it is important, first of all, to remember that this is not the only kind of world that God could have made. He might have created ten thousand other kinds of worlds, in which there never would have been struggle, pain, or sacrifice. But this is the best possible kind that God could have made for the purpose He has in mind. An artist is to be judged not so much by the masterpiece he produces, as by the purpose he had in mind in creating the masterpiece. An architect is not to be judged a poor architect because he designs a birdhouse instead of a cathedral, for his intention may have been only to construct a haven for the winged creature of God instead of a dwelling for God Himself. In like manner, God must not be judged only by this particular kind of world He created, but also by the intention and will He had in making it.

This brings us to the other question: What purpose did God have in mind in making this kind of world? The answer is very simply that God intended to construct a moral universe. He willed from all eternity to build a stage on which characters would emerge. He might, of course, have made a world without morality, without virtue, without character—a world in which each and every one of us would sprout virtues as an acorn sprouts an oak, or a world in which each of us would become saints with the same inexorable necessity that the chariot of the sun mounts the morning sky or the rain falls to embrace the earth. God might have made us all like so many sticks and stones, in which he would be guided by the same necessity by which fire is hot and ice is cold. God might have done this, but He did not.

And He did not because He willed a moral universe in order that, by the right use of the gift of freedom, characters might emerge. What does God care for things, piled into the infinity of space, even though they be diamonds, for if all the orbits of heaven were so many jewels glittering like the sun, what would their external but necessarily undisturbed balance mean to Him in comparison with a single character, which could weave the skeins of an apparently wrecked and ruined life into the beautiful tapestry of saintliness and holiness? The choice before God in creating the world lay between creating a purely mechanical universe, peopled by mere automata, or creating a world of pure spiritual beings, for whom the choice of good and evil was, at any rate, a possibility.

Suppose, now, it be granted that God chose to make a moral universe, or one in which characters would emerge. What condition would have to be fulfilled in order to make morality possible? If God chose to make a moral universe, then He had to make man free; that is, endow him with the power to say yes and no and to be captain and master of his own fate and destiny. Morality implies responsibility and duty, but these can exist only on condition of freedom. Stones have no morals because they are not free. We do not praise iron because it becomes heated by fire, nor do we condemn ice because it is melted by heat. Praise and blame can be bestowed only on those who are masters of their own will.

It is only those who have the possibility of saying no who can have so much charm in their hearts when they say yes. Take this quality of freedom away from man, and it is no more possible to be virtuous than it is for the blade of grass that we tread beneath our feet. Take freedom away from life, and there would be no more reason to honor the fortitude of the martyrs who offered their bodies as incense in testimony of their faith, than to honor the flames that kindled their faggots. Take away liberty, and where would be the concern in how children will mold their lives and write their eternal destiny in the invisible ink of their free choice? Take away freedom that gives life the interest of an everlasting plot, and with how little care would we watch the curtain rise, and with what feeble regret would we watch the drop screen fall?

Is it any impeachment of God that He chose not to reign over an empire of chemicals? If, therefore, God has deliberately chosen a kind of empire not to be ruled by force but by freedom, and if we find His subjects able to act against His will, as stars and atoms cannot, does this not prove that He has possibly given to them the chance of breaking allegiance in order that there may be meaning and glory in that allegiance when they freely choose to give it?

Conscience, the Interior Sinai

CONSCIENCE IS AN INTERIOR GOVERNMENT, exercising the same functions as all human government: namely, legislative, executive, and judicial. It has its congress, its president, and its supreme court: it makes its laws, it witnesses our actions in relation to the laws, and finally it judges us.

First of all, conscience legislates. One needs only to live to know that there is in each of us an interior Sinai, from which is promulgated, amid the thunder and lightning of daily life, a law telling us to do good and avoid evil. That interior voice fills us with a sense of responsibility, reminding us, not that we *must* do certain things, but that we *ought* to do certain things, for the difference between a machine and a person is the difference between *must* and *ought*. Without even being consulted, conscience plays its legislative role, pronouncing some actions to be in themselves evil and unjust, and others in themselves moral and good. Hence, when citizens fail to see a relationship existing between a human law and the law of their own conscience, they feel that they are free to disobey, and their justifying cry is, "My conscience tells me it is wrong."

Secondly, conscience not only is legislative, in the sense that it lays down a law, but it is also executive, in the sense that it witnesses the application of the law to actions. An imperfect but helpful analogy is to be found in our own government. Congress passes a law, then the president witnesses and approves it, thus applying the law to the lives of citizens. In like manner, conscience executes laws in the sense that it witnesses the fidelity of our actions to the law. Aided by memory, it tells us the value of our actions, tells us if we were total masters of ourselves, the extent to which passion, environment, force, and fury influence us; whether our consequences were foreseen or unforeseen; shows us, as in a mirror, the footsteps of all our actions; points its finger at the vestiges of our decisions; comes to us as a true witness and says: "I was there; I saw you do it. You had such and such an intention." In the administration of human justice the law can call together only those witnesses who have known me externally, but conscience as a witness summons not only those who saw me, but summons also *me who knows myself.* And whether I like it or not, I cannot lie to what it witnesses against me.

Finally, conscience not only lays down laws, not only witnesses my obedience or disobedience to them, but it also judges me accordingly. The breast of every person bears a silent court of justice. Conscience is the judge, sitting in judgment, handing down decisions with such authority as to admit of no appeal, for no one can appeal a judgment that one brings against oneself. That is why there gather about the bar of conscience all the feelings and emotions associated with right and wrong—joy and sorrow, peace and remorse, self-approval and fear, praise and blame.

If I do wrong it fills me with a sense of guilt from which there is no escape, for if the inmost sanctuary of my being is assaulted by the stern voice of this judge, I am driven out of myself by myself. Whence, then, can I fly but to myself with the sickening sense of guilt, remorse, and disgrace, which is the very hall of the soul? If, on the contrary, conscience approves my action, then there settles upon me, like the quiet of an evening dew, the joy that is a stranger to the passing pleasures of sense. The world may call me guilty, its courts may judge me criminal, its irons may weight down my flesh and bones like deep-sea anchors, but my soul builds a paradise within, against the raging opposition without, and floods it with an interior peace that the world cannot give and that the insults of the world cannot take from me.

Yearnings of the Pre-Christian World

ONE OF THE GREATEST EPIC POETS who ever lived was Homer, whom Plato called the educator of the Greeks. Homer wrote two great works, one called the *Iliad* and the other the *Odyssey*. The *Iliad* ends with the story of a defeated king, and the *Odyssey* with the story of a sorrowful woman. The first poem ends with a beautiful tribute paid to Hector as one of the greatest of Trojan heroes. In the other poem, the *Odyssey*, which is concerned with Odysseus traveling about the world, there is the story of his wife, who was courted by many suitors. She said that when she finished weaving a particular garment, she would then decide on a suitor. The suitors did not know that each night Penelope undid the stitches that she put in during the daytime and thus remained faithful to Odysseus until he returned.

Great classical scholars such as Christopher Hollis have wondered why Homer threw into the current of literature the story of a king who was made great in defeat and a woman glorious in sadness and tragedy. Greek philosophy was concerned with answering this question. As Chesterton put it, "The role of Hector anticipates all the defeats through which our race and religion were to pass." It was impossible for all the Greek philosophers to understand how there would be victory in defeat, how there could be nobility in suffering. There was really no answer given to this problem until the day of Calvary, when a defeated man hanging on a Cross ultimately became the conqueror, and a Mater Dolorosa at the foot of the Cross became the Queen of Christendom.

More than five hundred years before the Christian era lived the great dramatist Aeschylus, who wrote *Prometheus Bound*. Prometheus is pictured as bound to a rock because he had stolen fire from Olympus and given it to mankind. An eagle comes and devours his entrails—a symbol of modern man, whose heart is being devoured, not by an eagle, but by anxiety and fear, neuroses and psychoses. For these thousands of years mankind had been yearning for some kind of deliverance; that aspiration found its answer in the speech of Hermes to Prometheus, "Look not for any end, moreover, to his curse, until some God appears to accept upon his head, the pangs of thy own sins vicarious."

In the second dialogue of Alcibiades one reads that as Alcibiades was about to go into the temple, he came to Socrates, the wise man, and said, "What shall I ask of the gods?" And Socrates said, "Wait! Wait for a wise man who is to come, who will tell us how we are to conduct ourselves before God and man." Alcibiades said, "I am ready to do all He desires. When will He come?"

Socrates said, "I know not when, but I know that He also desires your good."

But Greek literature was not alone in picturing man craving for another wisdom than that of earth, and another relief from inner misery than that given by man alone.

The Eastern people had it, too. The ancient Hindus sacrificed a lamb to Ekiam as they prayed, "When will the Savior come? When will the Redeemer appear?" Their avatars were not incarnations, but rather a descent of *deities* to the realm of man, such as Krishna, a deity who visited humanity, Bhagavad-Gita, who became a brother to all men, and Brahma, who was often pictured as one who would repair the faults of Kaliga, the ancient serpent.

Confucius in his *Morals* continued this universal craving for a Savior when he wrote, "The Holy One must come from heaven who will know all things and have power over heaven and earth."

One may ask if Buddha pointed to Christ? Buddha, the founder of Buddhism, lived from c. 563 to c. 483 B.C. On dying he said, "I am not the first Buddha who came upon earth, nor shall I be the last. I will die, but Buddha will live, for Buddha is Truth. The Kingdom of truth will increase for about five hundred years. . . . In due time another Buddha will arise, and he will reveal to you the self-same eternal truth that I have taught." His disciple Ananda asked, "How shall we know him?" Buddha answered, "The Buddha who will come after me will be known as Maitreya, which means, 'He whose name is Love.' "

Roman civilization struck the same chord, for all humanity is one. Because they felt that philosophy based on self-sufficiency was not sufficient, the Romans craved for some inner purification; this prompted them to develop mystery religions. These cults led to many excesses, but their *subjective dispositions* were right inasmuch as they saw man must have mystery as well as philosophy.

Cicero, the great orator, quotes a sibyl as saying, "A king will come who must be recognized to be saved." Then Cicero asks, "Of what man and of what time did the sibyl speak?" In Latin, his question was:

In quem hominem?

Was that question answered by another Roman?

Ecce Homo!—"Behold the Man."

Suetonius, in his life of Augustus, continued the traditional aspiration: "Nature has been in labor to bring forth a personage who would be King of the Romans." The Senate was disturbed by this general expectation and passed a law forbidding anyone to let live a male child *that year*. The order was not executed because many of the senators' wives were with child. But it did show how much the ancient air was filled with a hushed expectancy that some great king was coming to the world.

Tacitus confirmed this in his *History:* "Mankind is generally persuaded that the ancient prophecies of the east will prevail, and it will not be long until Judea would bring forth one who would rule the universe."

Horace in his "Sixteenth Epode" has the Golden World on the Far Eastern seas, bidding his readers emigrate there to escape the hopeless horror of reality. Vergil's *Eclogue* answers, "No, the golden age is here," in the year 31 B.C. as he wrote the "Fourth Eclogue" to honor Augustus. This poem has through the centuries been looked upon as messianic, and recent studies at Oxford favor that judgment. . . . *Jam nova progenies caelo demittitur alto:* "Already a new generation is being sent down from high heaven."

Vergil lived in a world that gave no great dignity to women. Yet in this poem, after describing "promise of a Jove to be" and the child as yet unborn, Vergil starts the last four lines by speaking to the child as already born. *Incipe, parve puer, risu cognoscere matrem:* "Begin, little child, to recognize your mother with a smile."

And now as these expectations multiply, the greatest of them all is the Hebrew. The Hebrew civilization was destroyed by the King of Babylon in 586 B.C. He had taken back with him into Babylon one who was called the wisest and the handsomest of the Jews, Daniel. The King had a dream one night that neither he nor any of his aides could interpret. In the dream he saw a great and tremendous colossus. The head was of gold, the breast and arms were of silver, the belly and thighs were of brass, and the feet were part iron and part clay. And the great stones hewn from the mountains without hands, rolled down from the mountains, struck it in the feet of clay, and ground it into dust.

Since his own sages could not tell the meaning, Daniel was summoned by the King to interpret it: "These are the kingdoms that will divide the world until the coming of the expected One of the world." "The empire of gold," he said, "is you. You will fall and be devoured by the empire of silver; the empire of silver will, in its turn, be conquered by the empire of brass; and the empire of brass will go down before the empire of iron and clay."

In 538 B.C., the Medes and Persians came to this great city of Babylon, which was sixteen miles square, with sixteen gates of solid bronze giving entrance to it. Cyrus turned aside the waters of the Euphrates, which ran through the center of the city, and went into it under the walls in the dry bed of the river. That night Belshazaar was slain, and the empire of gold was taken over by the empire of silver.

Then there arises a new power—the empire of brass. Trained in their games, knowing where to hazard and when to abandon, the Greeks now arose to swallow up the Persians, as the Persians had swallowed the Chaldeans. Greece could not bear the thought of being subdued by Asia. Every Greek prepared to defend his liberty, and the only dispute among them was who should do more for the public. Then arose the great Alexander of the Greeks; brave as Darius III was, he could not stop either the genius or the arms of the great Greek, who carried his conquests into every land of the Persians and at thirty-three years of age was destined to show the vanity of all earthly glory. Sighing for new worlds to conquer, he little suspected that, at that age, the one world left to conquer and the only one worth conquering was the next. He died without time to settle his affairs and left his ambition to a simpleton brother. It was the first great war between Europe and Asia.

The beasts of paganism were devouring one another. The last great empire that God prepared now was ready to appear on the stage of the world's history. It was the mightiest of all! Rome, the empire of iron, looked to Greece and Carthage as its prey. Rome's screaming eagles went to war. Dragging the ponderous battering rams like chains, shaking the earth like marching mountains, her unbridled horses darting like hawks, the Romans moved on, while there came from ten thousand times ten thousand throats the cry of hate: *Delenda est Carthago!* "Carthage must be destroyed!" Rome under Scipio went to battle, and Carthage fell finally in 146 B.C. as nothing has fallen since Satan fell from heaven.

Rome became supreme. With her arms of iron, she crushed the agonizing kingdoms of the world, one after another. The world was at peace. There was nothing more to conquer. The Temple of Janus, which was kept open to pray for success in war, and which was closed only twice in seven hundred years, was now closed again. Perhaps its doors were clogged with the dead bodies of its citizens. In any case the world was at peace, and it was prophesied the King of Men would be born when the world no longer bore arms or went to battle.

Caesar Augustus, now that the world was at peace, resolved to take a census of the greatest empire the world had ever known. In the great hall of his palace by the Tiber, he, the master bookkeeper of the world, was casting up the accounts of the nations of the earth. Before him stretched on a frame was a chart labeled laconically: *Orbis terrarum—Imperium Romanum:* "The circle of the earth—the Roman Empire." A careful and thrifty man was Augustus, the Caesar of the earth. No one should escape the census, for Rome was the mistress of all. From the western ocean to the Persian plains, from the frozen north to the edge of the southern desert, the list went out from his hand to every sweating governor and satrap and tetrarch and king. The world was to be brought to unity. The human race had only one capital: Rome; one master: Caesar; one language: Latin. Morally the world was one in its sin and corruption; materially it was one, for it had reached the highest peak of organization and unity. There were no longer Medes or Persians, no longer Scythians or barbarians, no longer Greeks or Babylonians. There were only Romans; there were only men. Nations were not awaiting a king, but rather mankind was awaiting a king.

Little did the bookkeeper of the Tiber know that he was aiding in the fulfillment of the Jewish prophet Micah that the "Expected of the Nations" would be born in Bethlehem. The census notice was finally posted in the little village of Nazareth that a carpenter might read it—he who belonged to the defunct royalty of the family of David, whose city was Bethlehem. He and his espoused wife Mary journeyed to Bethlehem.

"But there was no room at the inn"; the inn is the gathering place of public opinion; so often public opinion locks its doors to the King. Out to the stables they go. There rings out over the softness of the evening breeze a cry, a gentle cry, the cry of a newborn baby. The sea could not hear the cry, for the sea was filled with its own voice. The great ones of the earth could not hear the cry, for they could not understand how God could be greater than a man.

Wise men came from the East, perhaps Persia. They saw the Babe—a Babe whose tiny hands were not quite long enough to touch the huge heads of the cattle, and yet hands that were steering the reins that keep the sun, moon, and stars in their orbits. Shepherds came, and they saw baby lips that did not speak, and yet lips that might have articulated the secret of every living person that hour. They saw a baby brow under which were a mind and an intelligence compared with which the combined intelligences of Europe and America amount to naught.

The Babe could not walk because those baby feet could not bear the weight of Divine Omnipotence. Eternity is in time; Omnipotence in bonds; God in the form of man. The yearnings of Buddha, of Confucius, of Aeschylus, of Vergil, of Socrates, of Plato—all were now realized in a Child in the stable.

The Eternal Galilean

THE GREAT CHARACTERISTIC OF OUR AGE is not its love of religion, but its love of talking about religion. Even those who would smite God from the heavens make a religion out of this irreligion, and a faith out of their doubt. On all sides—from a thousand pens, a hundred microphones, scores of university rostrums—we have heard it repeated, until our very head reels, that the "acids of modernity" have eaten away the old faith and the old morality, and that modern man must have a new religion to suit the new spirit of the age.

This new religion, we are told, must be absolutely different from anything that ever existed before. It must be just as fresh and modern as the brilliant age in which we live, with its new hopes, new visions, and new dreams. When we inquire diligently into the characteristics of this new religion, we are told it must be social, it must be political, it must be worldly.

By social they mean it must dedicate itself, not to the illusory pursuit of the spirit, but to the practical needs of the body. . . .

Next, we are told that the new religion must be political, and by that is meant that it should cease talking about the Kingdom of God and begin talking about the republics of earth. . . .

The final characteristic of the new cult will be its worldliness. . . .

Now let us ask the new prophets: How old is their new religion? Is it really a new thing, or is it merely an old error with a new label? Let us go back two thousand years to the Eternal Galilean and learn not only that the new religion is just an old temptation, but also that resistance to it is the pledge and promise of Life Everlasting.

Divinity Is Always Where You Least Expect to Find It

WHEN GOD CAME TO EARTH there was no room in the inn, but there was room in the stable. What lesson is hidden behind the inn and the stable? What is an inn, but the gathering place of public opinion, the focal point of the world's moods, the residence of the worldly, the rallying place of the fashionable and of those who count in the management of the world's affairs? What is a stable, but the place of outcasts, the refuge of beasts, and the shelter of the valueless, and therefore the symbol of those who in the eyes of public opinion do not count and hence may be ignored as of no great value or moment? Anyone in the world would have expected to have found Divinity in an inn, but no one would have expected to have found It in a stable. *Divinity, therefore, is always where you least expect to find It.*

If in those days the stars of the heavens by some magic touch had folded themselves together as silver words and announced the birth of the Expected of the Nations, where would the world have gone in search of Him? The world would have searched for the Babe in some palace by the Tiber or in some gilded house of Athens or in some inn of a great city where gathered the rich, the mighty, and the powerful ones of earth. They would not have been the least surprised to have found the newborn King of Kings stretched out on a cradle of gold and surrounded by kings and philosophers paying to him their tribute and obeisance.

But they would have been surprised to have discovered him in a manger laid on coarse straw and warmed by the breath of oxen, as if in atonement for the coldness of the hearts of men. No one would have expected that the One whose fingers could stop the turning of Arcturus would be smaller than the head of an ox; that He who could hurl the ball of fire into the heavens would one day be warmed by the breath of beasts; or that He who could make a canopy of stars would be shielded from a stormy sky by the roof of a stable; or that He who made the earth as His future home would be homeless at home. No one would have expected to find Divinity in such a condition; but that is because *Divinity is always where you least expect to find It.*

Shepherds and Wise Men

THE SHEPHERDS WERE THE SIMPLE SOULS who knew nothing of the politics of the world, nothing of its art, nothing of its literature. Not one of them could recite a single line of Vergil, though there was hardly an educated person in the Roman Empire who was ignorant of his poetry. Into their fields and simple lives, there never came a rumor of the scandals of Herod's voluptuous court, nor even a word about the learned Gamaliel, who sat in the temple counting out the seventy weeks of years. The great broad world of public opinion ignored them as of no account in the progress of men and nations.

And yet these simple shepherds, whose early kings were shepherds, *did know* two very important things: the God above their heads and the sheep about their feet. But that was enough for simple souls to know, and on that night when the heavens were so bright that they burst to reveal their radiant minstrelsies, an angel announced that He for whom they yearned with breathless expectancy was now born among common people in a common stable, in the common little town of Bethlehem. And gathering one of the things they knew, a little lamb, they brought it and laid it at the feet of the only other thing they knew—the God of the heavens who came to earth as the Lamb slain from the beginning of the world. At last the shepherds had found their Shepherd.

The other class who found him were wise men—not kings but teachers of kings, not mere dilettantes in knowledge, but searchers of the heavens and discoverers of the stars. In both science and religion they held first rank in their nations, the kings consulting them before they went to war, and the peasants before they tilled their land. One night a new star appeared in the heavens. Thousands of others besides the Wise Men saw its brilliant light, but these thousands were not wise with the wisdom of the Wise Men; they were wise only in their conceit. They saw only a star, but these first scientists of the Christian age saw a star and envisaged a God. To the proud man the star is only a star; but to the wise man the star is a handiwork of God—a telltale and a revelation of something beyond.

And so they followed the light of the star, but instead of leading them over the mountains beyond the sun and the shining chandeliers of the Pleiades to the hidden battlements of heaven, it rather led them along the sandy courses of earth to the end of the trail of the golden star, where the Wise Men, bent on the voyage of discovery, made the great discovery of God. These wise, learned, and mighty men, kneeling in pontifical robes upon a bedding of straw, before a Babe who could neither ask nor answer questions, offered their gifts and themselves as pledges of the obedience of the world. Their gifts were three: gold, frankincense and myrrh—gold, because He would rule as a king; frankincense, because he would live as a priest; and myrrh, because He would die like a man. At last the Wise Men had discovered Wisdom.

Nazareth

THIS IS THE DOUBLE LESSON OF NAZARETH contained in the only two simple facts we know about His hidden years: first, that He was subject in obedience to His parents; and secondly, that He was a poor village carpenter.

First, a word about power. Nazareth is not a trite story about the beauty of slavery and subjection, as some enemies of Christianity would have us believe. If Our Lord were merely a human child without any Divine prerogatives, then the carpenter shop might reveal a lesson that power was wrong. But obedience is only half the lesson of Nazareth. Our Lord was obedient; He was a servant; He was subject. But He was more than that! He was a Power who became obedient, a Master who became a servant, and a Lord who came not to be ministered unto but to minister.

His power in the human order reached back through forty-two generations to Abraham, and in the Divine order to the eternal generation in the bosom of the Eternal Father; His power at birth was saluted by the harping symphonies of angelic glorias; His power at twelve confounded the wise doctors of the temple as He unraveled to them the wisdom of a Son on the business of His Heavenly Father; His power at thirty made the unconscious waters blush into wine and the seething sea hush into calm; and His power at thirty-three reminded a Pontius Pilate about to execute his authority as governor and ruler that the real seat of his power was not in Rome but in the heavens above.

Yet He who had all this power and who said that to Him "all power is given in heaven and on earth," passed practically the whole of His life in a despised village and degraded valley, with no flash of outward pomp and circumstance, subject to a Virgin and a just man, whom He knew before they were made, and who after they were made were really his own children. What was all this but a lesson to the world that misunderstands power, either by glorifying it or by overthrowing it: namely, that no man has a right to command until he has learned to serve, and no man has a right to be a master until he has learned to be a servant, and no man has a right to power until he has learned to be obedient. . . .

Nazareth has yet another lesson to teach, and that is that no one is entitled to wealth until he has learned to be detached. In other words, Nazareth is not just a simple glorification of poverty, a fatalistic resignation to squalor, a calm indifference about hardship and hunger. Neither is it a condemnation of wealth. In Nazareth Our Lord was poor; He worked as a needy village carpenter for the mere necessities of life. But He was more than that! He was not just a poor man. He was a rich man who became poor, just as He was a powerful man who became obedient. His wealth was the treasures of Heaven that rust does not eat, moths consume, nor thieves break through and steal; His wealth was the wealth, not of a carpenter of Nazareth, but the wealth of a carpenter who made the universe with its canopy of glittering stars and its carpet of lilies that toil not, neither do they spin. His wealth was the mansions of His Father's house that he had seen, but the beauty of which the human eye hath never seen, nor the ear heard, nor the heart of man conceived. Yet, with all the wealth of God, He became poor; for He chose to be born in a shepherd's cave, work as a tradesman, preach as a vagabond, with nowhere to lay His Head, die on a poor man's cross, and be buried in a stranger's grave.

The world before had heard of wealthy men giving away their wealth to be philanthropists. The world had heard Buddha ask his disciples to renounce wealth, had seen Crates of Thebes give his gold to the poor, and heard the Stoics eulogize poverty at banquets; but the world before had never heard of poverty being not an ascetic rule, not a proud disguise for ostentation, not a philosophical ornament nor a mystic mood, but a step to higher perfection that is union with the Spirit of God. Others had said, "Sell all you have"; but only He added, "Then come follow Me."

His life and doctrine are not those of many of our social reformers who, seeing the abuses of wealth and the excesses of capitalism, provoke class conflict and demand the division of wealth even though it was honestly earned. The communists who harangue the rich find no support in the simple Nazarene. *No one has a right to despise the rich until like Our Blessed Lord he has proved he is free from the passion of wealth.* That is why He could be as hard on the selfish rich and say to them that it was easier for a camel to pass through the eye of a needle than for a rich man to enter the Kingdom of Heaven. The poverty of Nazareth was not a condemnation of wealth; neither was it a glorification of wealth; neither was it a canonization of poverty as such. It was the preachment of the beautiful doctrine of detachment, by which men free themselves from the passion of wealth for the glory of God and the salvation of souls—even though the wealth is only their own will and a few fishing boats and tangled nets.

The Temptations

Our Lord was about to preach a divine religion. Satan tempted Him to preach a religion that was not Divine, but a religion that the modern world calls new: The three temptations of Satan against Christ are the three temptations of the world against the Church today, namely, to make religion social, political, and worldly.

Satan first tempted Our Lord to make religion social: to

make it center about the materialities of life, such as bread for starving bodies like His own. Pointing from the top of the mountain to the stones whose shapes resembled little loaves of bread, he said: "Command that these stones be made bread." It was Satan's challenge to God to make religion center around the materialities of life. But the answer of Our Blessed Lord was immediate: "Not in bread alone doth man live, but in every word that proceedeth from the mouth of God." By that response, Our Lord declared that religion is not social, in the sense that its primary function is to give food to the body, but rather divine, in the sense that it must give food to the soul. Men must have bread! There is no disputing that point. Our Lord taught us to ask the Father to "give us this day our daily bread"; He even went so far, when men were in dire need of it in the desert places, to multiply bread even to excess. But beyond that, he told the thousands at Capernaum, He would not go. "You seek me . . . because you did eat of the loaves and were filled. Labor not for the meat that perisheth, but for that which endureth unto life everlasting."

Religion is not purely social. If salvation were only economic relief, if religion were only to give bread to hungry stomachs, then dogs would be invited to its banquet. No! Man has a higher principle than that of the beasts, and a higher life than that of the body. We come into this world not just to sit and rest, to work and play, to eat and drink. Hence, a religion that would make the securing of bread its chief object in life and would seek no divine food, will starve with hunger in the midst of plenty. There must come dark hours when God must be trusted, even in hunger. There must even come moments in starvation when bread must be refused, if it means the sacrificing of a principle that endangers the soul. . . .

Satan next tempted Our Lord to make religion political by exchanging the Kingdom of God for the kingdoms of earth. "And the devil . . . showed all the kingdoms of the world in a moment of time. And he said to Him: To thee will I give all this power, and the glory of them; for to me they are delivered, and to whom I will, I give them. If thou therefore wilt adore before me, all shall be thine. And Jesus answering said to him: It is written: Thou shalt adore the Lord thy God, and him only shalt thou serve."

By this answer Our Lord declared to all future ages that religion is not politics, that patriotism is not the highest virtue, that nationalism is not the highest worship, that the State is not the highest good. Devotion to the State there must be; loyalties to the kingdom of earth there must be; tribute to Caesar there must be. Man is social, and living in society he must govern and be governed; he must be a patriot not only by supporting the just policies of those who rule, but even to the extent of laying down his life in just warfare for the common good. These things are self-evident. But Satan would have Christ adore the kingdoms of earth, convert the pulpit into a platform, and the Gospel into a national anthem. Our Lord would have us know that earthly kingdoms are but scaffoldings to the Kingdom of Heaven, that patriotism toward country is but the nursery to the adoration of God, and that it profits us nothing if we gain the whole world and lose our immortal soul. Politics and religion are related something like the body and the soul. Both have their rights and their duties, but one is superior to the other.

The primary concern of religion is not the rehabilitation of the kingdoms of earth or the support of economic policies, for Our Lord came not to restore the politics of the world but to make a new Kingdom that needs neither armies nor navies, soldiers nor monies, slaves nor judges, but only renewed and living souls. He did not say religion must not be concerned with social injustice or indifference to political graft. Our Lord loved His own country so deeply and warmly that, as the first Christian patriot, He wept over it. *But he also loved the Kingdom of Heaven so much more that He was willing to be put to death by the very country that He loved.* While time endures, Satan will always tempt religion to be wholly political, but until the end of time the due order must be preserved: "Render therefore to Caesar the things that are Caesar's; and to God the things that are God's."

Satan's last assault was an effort to make religion worldly. The Gospel tells us Satan "brought Him to Jerusalem, and set Him on a pinnacle of the temple, and he said to Him: If thou be the Son of God, cast thyself from hence. For it is written, that he hath given his angels charge over thee, that they keep thee. And that in their hands they shall bear thee up, lest perhaps thou gash thy foot against a stone. And Jesus answering said to him: It is said: *Thou shalt not tempt the Lord thy God.*"

What a lesson is hidden in that answer for those who would make religion worldly, by emptying it of all responsibility and by making God merely a passive spectator of our falls and our suicides. The plea to cast Himself down from the pinnacle was not a sign of trust in God, but disbelief in God. It was an appeal, not to a natural appetite, but to a perverted pride that assumes that God is indifferent to our actions and disinterested in our decisions. The answer of Our Lord was a reminder that religion centers about responsible persons, and not about falling bodies; that man is endowed with free will and is therefore responsible for each of his actions down even to the least; that the universe in which he lives is moral and therefore one in which we mount by making our dead selves stepping stones to higher things. That worldly religion, which denies responsibility, sin, and judgment, would reduce us all to mere stones falling from the giddy heights of stony pinnacles; it would make us merely material bodies obeying the law of gravitation that pulls us to the earth, instead of spiritual beings that, like fire, mount up beyond the stars to the Light of the World. Real religion does not say: "Cast thyself down," but "Lift thyself up"; for we are destined not to be stones of earth, but immortal children of God. Heaven and not the world is our final destiny. And so, instead of casting Himself down like a cheap and vulgar magician, Our Lord casts Satan down, and then goes out to another mountaintop to give from its heights the Beatitudes of God, which lead to beatitude with God in the everlasting glory of heaven.

The Sermon on the Mount

THE OFT-REPEATED DEMAND that the modern world wants a religion based upon the Sermon on the Mount is founded upon a false dogma that only those words of Our Lord that please the modern world shall be accepted as a basis for religion, while all others that do not please it shall be rejected. And, as a matter of fact, the Sermon on the Mount contains a fearful and wonderful complexity of dogmas such as the first shall be last, and the last first, and that those who sow in tears shall reap in joy, and that the way to save your life is to lose it. There is probably more of dogma in the Sermon on the Mount than in any other sermon ever preached by Our Lord, such as the dogma of the existence of God, the Providence of God, the existence of the soul, the existence of heaven and hell, the beauty of purity and, above all, the dogma that is opposed to everything the modern world holds dear, namely, those who are really God's children will always be hated, reviled, and persecuted by the world.

The Beatitudes

THE MODERN WORLD talks of the Beatitudes as if they were just a kind of lecture and a very dull lecture at that, forgetful that the Beatitudes contain more dogma, more mortification, more hardships, more unmodernities than anything else in the Gospel. The Sermon on the Mount is just the prelude to the drama of Calvary.

Contrast the Beatitudes with what we might call the beatitudes of the world; the one is the antithesis of the other. The world says: "Blessed are the rich"; Christ says: "Blessed are the poor in spirit." The world says: "Blessed are the mighty"; Our Lord says: "Blessed are the meek." The world says: "Laugh and the world laughs with you"; Christ says: "Blessed are they that mourn." The world says: "Be for yourself and your country right or wrong"; Christ says: "Blessed are they that hunger and thirst after justice." The world says: "Sow your wild oats, you are young only once; blessed is the sex appeal"; Christ says: "Blessed are the clean of heart." The world says: "In time of peace prepare for war"; Christ says: "Blessed are the peacemakers." The world says: "Blessed are those who never suffer persecution"; Christ says: "Blessed are they that suffer persecution." The world says: "Blessed is popularity"; Christ says: "Blessed are ye when they shall revile you and persecute you and speak all that is evil against you for My sake."

In so many words the Sermon on the Mount placed an irreconcilable opposition between the world and Christ. He upset every maxim of the world as He upset the tables of the moneychangers in the temple, and said openly that He prayed not for the world: "If the world hate you, know ye that it hath hated Me before you. If you had been of the world, the world would love its own: but because you are not of the world, but I have chosen you out of the world, therefore the world hateth you."

Every standard the world ever held He upset with a ruthless abandon. He was the iconoclast of the world, smashing to fragments its false idols. He talked in the language of the paradox, for only the paradox could express that opposition between Himself and the world. The lofty, He said, shall be brought low; the first shall be last; the overlooked shall be preferred; the scorned shall be reverenced; the needy shall possess all things; the reviled shall bless; the persecuted shall suffer patiently; the blasphemed shall entreat; the weak shall be strong, the strong shall be weak; the fool shall be wise, and the wise shall be foolish. He wrote the law of Christianity by the example of His own life, and that law is: The death of all things in their first stage is the necessary condition of infinite progress. Nothing is quickened unless it die.

BLESSED ARE THE MEEK

OUR LORD both *preached* and *practiced* meekness.

He preached it in those memorable words that continue the Beatitudes: "You have heard that it hath been said: An eye for an eye and a tooth for a tooth. But I say to you not to resist evil; but if one strike thee on thy right cheek, turn to him also the other: and if a man will contend with thee in judgment, and take away thy coat, let go thy cloak also unto him. And whosoever shall force thee one mile, go with him another two. . . . You have heard that it hath been said: Thou shalt love thy neighbor and hate thy enemy. But I say to you: Love your enemies: do good to them that hate you: and pray for them that persecute and calumniate you that you may be the children of your Father who is in heaven, who maketh His sun to rise upon the good and bad, and raineth upon the just and the unjust. For if you love them that love you, what reward shall you have? do not even the tax collectors do this? And if you salute your breathren only, what do you more than others? do not also the pagans this? Be you therefore perfect, as also your heavenly Father is perfect."

But He not only preached meekness, He also *practiced* it. When his own people picked up stones to throw at Him, He threw none back in return; when His fellow townsmen brought Him to the brow of the hill to cast Him over the precipice, He walked through the midst of them unharmed; when the soldier struck Him with a mailed fist, He answered meekly: "If I have spoken evil, give testimony of the evil: but if well, why strikest thou me."

When they swore to kill Him, He did not use His power to strike dead even a single enemy; and now on the Cross, meekness reaches its peak, when to those who pierce the hands that feed the world, and to those who pierce the feet that shepherd souls, He pleads: "Father, forgive them, for they know not what they do."

BLESSED ARE THE MERCIFUL

A PERSON IS MERCIFUL when he or she feels the sorrow and misery of another as if it were one's own. Disliking misery and unhappiness, the merciful person seeks to dispel the misery of a neighbor just as much as one would if the misery were one's own. That is why, whenever mercy is confronted not only with pain, but also with sin and wrongdoing, it becomes forgiveness that not merely pardons, but even rebuilds into justice, repentance, and love.

Mercy is one of the dominant notes in the preaching of

Our Lord. His parables were parables of mercy. Take for example the hundred sheep, the ten pieces of money, and the two sons. Of the hundred sheep, one was lost; of the ten pieces of money, one was lost; of the two sons, one led a life of dissipation.

It is interesting to note that the lost sheep is the one that was sought, and the shepherd, finding it, places it upon his shoulders and brings it into the house rejoicing. But there is no record in the gospels of any such attention being paid to the ninety-nine sheep who were not lost.

When the woman lost a piece of money and found it, she called in her neighbors to rejoice. But there is no record that she ever called in her neighbors to rejoice in the possession of the other nine that were never lost.

One son went into a foreign country and wasted his substance living riotously. And when he came back he was given the fatted calf. But the brother who stayed at home was not so rewarded. All these illustrations Our Lord followed with the simple truth: "There shall be more joy in heaven upon one sinner that doth penance than upon ninety-nine just who need not penance."

One day Peter went to Him to inquire just what limitation should be placed upon mercy. And so he asked Our Lord a question about mercy and gave what he thought was rather an extravagant limit: "How often shall my brother offend against me, and I forgive him? till seven times?" And Our Lord answered, "Not till seven times, but till seventy times seven times." And that does not mean four hundred and ninety—that means infinity.

BLESSED ARE THE CLEAN OF HEART

THIS, OF COURSE, IS NOT THE BEATITUDE of the world. The world is living today in what might be described as an era of carnality, which glorifies sex, hates restraint, identifies purity with coldness, innocence with ignorance, and turns men and women into Buddhas with their eyes closed, hands folded across their breasts, intently looking inward, thinking only of self.

It is just precisely against such a glorification of sex and such egocentrism that is so characteristic of the flesh that Our Lord reacted in His third Beatitude: "Blessed are the clean of heart."

BLESSED ARE THE POOR IN SPIRIT

MODERN SOCIETY is what might be characterized as acquisitive, for its primary concern is to acquire, to own, to possess; its aristocracy is not one of blood or virtue, but of money; it judges worth not by righteousness but in terms of possessions.

Our Blessed Lord came into the world to destroy this acquisitiveness and this subservience of moral to economic ends by preaching the blessedness of the poor in spirit. It is worth noting immediately that the poor in spirit does not necessarily mean the indigent or those in straitened circumstances of life; poor in spirit means interior detachment and as such includes even some who are rich in the world's goods, for detachment can be practiced by the rich just as avarice can be practiced by the poor.

The poor in spirit are those who are so detached from wealth, from social position, and from earthly knowledge that, at the moment the Kingdom of God demands a sacrifice, they are prepared to surrender all.

The Beatitude means then: Blessed are those who are not possessed by their possessions; blessed are they who whether or not they are poor in *fact* are poor in their inmost spirit.

Our Lord not only preached poverty of spirit, He also lived it, and He lived it in such a way as to conquer the three kinds of pride—the pride of what one *has,* which is economic pride; the pride of what one *is,* which is social pride; and the pride of what one *knows,* which is intellectual pride.

BLESSED ARE THEY THAT HUNGER AND THIRST AFTER JUSTICE

NOT ONLY NEGATIVELY but positively did He preach the necessity of zeal for the justice of the Kingdom of God. His circumcision was a kind of impatience to run His course of justice that led to the garden and the cross; His teaching the doctors in the temple at twelve years of age was an impatience to teach men the sweetness of His Father's ways.

At the beginning of His public life we find Him driving merchants out of the temple, in fulfillment of the prophecy of apostleship: "The zeal of thy house hath eaten me up." Later on, He made use of a dinner invitation to save the soul of Magdalen and, on a hot day, made use of a common love of cold water to bring the Samaritan woman to a knowledge of everlasting fountains.

He came, He said, "not to destroy souls, but to save"; and, "seeing the multitude, he had compassion on them because they were distressed, and lying as sheep having no shepherd." Then he said to His disciples: "The harvest indeed is great, but the laborers are few. Pray ye therefore the Lord of the harvest, that he send forth laborers into his harvest." His whole mission in life was one of zeal, a hunger and thirst for the justice of God, which He perhaps best expressed in words of fire: "I am come to cast fire on the earth: and what will I but that it be kindled? And I have a baptism wherewith I am to be baptized. And how am I straitened until it be accomplished?" "And other sheep I have that are not of this fold: them also I must bring. And they shall hear my voice, and there shall be one fold and one shepherd."

And now at the end of His life, He yearns still more for justice, as He who called himself the Fountain of Living Waters, and He who was figuratively the Rock that gave forth water as Moses struck it in the desert now lets well from out His Sacred Heart the shepherd's call to all the souls of the world: "I thirst."

It was not a thirst for earthly waters, for the earth and its oceans were His. And when they offered Him vinegar and gall as a sedative for His sufferings, He refused it. It was therefore not a physical, but a spiritual thirst that troubled Him—the thirst for the beatitude of justice—an insatiable thirst for the souls of humans.

BLESSED ARE THE PEACEMAKERS

WHAT IS THE PEACE spoken of in this Beatitude? The most perfect definition of peace ever given was that of St. Augustine: "*Peace is the tranquillity of order.*" It is not tranquillity alone; rather it is the tranquillity of order in which there is no oppression from without, but rather a subordination of all things to the sovereign good that is God. Therefore the subjection of senses to reason, reason to faith, and the whole person to God as the eternal end and final perfection—that is the basis of peace.

It was just such a tranquillity of order that our Lord brought to earth as the angels sang at His birth: "Glory to God in the highest, and on earth peace to men of good will." He bade His disciples to have peace with one another. Into whatsoever house they entered, they were first to say: "Peace be to this house."

The very Beatitude we are considering is a blessing on such peacemakers, and His words over Jerusalem a reminder of His sorrow at those who loved not peace: "If thou also hadst known, and that in this thy day, the things that are to thy peace; but now they are hidden from thy eyes."

The night of His arrest in the garden, when Peter drew his sword and cut off the right ear of the servant of the high priest, Our Lord rebuked him, saying: "Put up again the sword into its place, for all that take the sword shall perish with the sword." Touching the ear of the wounded servant, He made it whole.

The next afternoon, He who came to preach peace was put to death in the first world war of man against his Redeemer; but before He died He pronounced the last and final words of peace: "It is finished."

BLESSED ARE THEY THAT MOURN

THE WORLD never regards mourning as blessing, but always as a curse. Laughter is the gold it is seeking, and sorrow is the enemy it flees.

It can no more understand the beatitude of mourning than it can understand the Cross. In fact, many modern people steel themselves even against the suffering of another by wearing the mask of indifference, quite unmindful that such a thickening of the spiritual skin, though it may sometimes protect them from sorrow, nevertheless shuts in their own morbidity until it festers and corrupts.

But it must not be thought that the beatitude of Our Lord is either a condemnation of laughter and joy or a glorifica-

tion of sorrow and tears. Our Lord did not believe in a philosophy of tragedy any more than we do. As a matter of
fact, He upbraided the Pharisees because they wore long
faces and looked sad when they fasted, and His Apostles
summed up His Life and Resurrection in the one word
rejoice.

The difference between the beatitude of the world,
"Laugh and the world laughs with you," and the beatitude
of Our Lord, "Blessed are they that mourn," is not that the
world brings laughter and Our Lord brings tears. It is not
even a choice of having or not having sadness; it is rather a
choice of where we shall put it: at the beginning or at the
end. In other words, which comes first, laughter or tears?

Shall we place our joys in time or in eternity? for we cannot have them in both. Shall we laugh on earth or laugh in
heaven? for we cannot laugh in both. Shall we mourn before we die or after we die? for we cannot do both. We cannot have our reward both in heaven and on earth.

That is why we believe one of the most tragic remarks of
Our Lord is what He will say to the worldly at the end of
time: "You have already had your reward."

BLESSED ARE THEY
THAT ARE PERSECUTED

THE EIGHTH BEATITUDE, in the language of St. Thomas
Aquinas, "is a confirmation and a declaration of all those
that precede. Because from the very fact that a man is confirmed in poverty of spirit, meekness, and the rest, it follows that no persecution will induce him to renounce them.
Hence the eighth beatitude corresponds in a way to all the
preceding seven."

The Way

IT WAS A SABBATH when He made His way across the town to the synagogue. His reputation had gone before Him, for it was generally known that He had worked a miracle at Cana and that He had gathered certain followers about Him at the Jordan and a few more at Capernaum. When every one assembled in the synagogue, the chazzan, or clerk, whose duty it was to keep the sacred books, drew aside the silk curtain of the painted ark that contained the manuscripts and handed Him the megillah, or roll, of the Prophet Isaiah.

Our Lord unrolled the scroll at the well-known sixty-first chapter that foretold the great day of mercy when one sent by God would fathom the depths of contrition, break the chains of the slavery of sin, and bring solace to a wounded world. In slow, clear tones that thrilled the hearts of every one in the synagogue that memorable Sabbath morning, He read:

> *The spirit of the Lord is upon me,*
> *because the Lord hath anointed me.*
> *He hath sent me to preach to the meek,*
> *to heal the contrite of heart,*
> *and to preach a release to the captives*
> *and deliverance to them that are shut up:*
> *To proclaim the acceptable year of the Lord*
> *And the day of vengeance of Our God.*

He stopped reading and restored the scroll to the chazzan. A moment of silence followed, which seemed like an Eternity. The silence was broken as the Eternal seemed to step out of His eternity and let ring out over that little group of

His townsmen the fulfillment of the prophecy of Isaiah: "This day is fulfilled this Scripture in your ears."

For the moment they did not catch the full import of His words. Then it dawned upon them that the most precious tradition and hope of their people were verified; that the Messiah for whom they had yearned these four thousand years was now standing before them; that He was the one to whom Isaiah had pointed seven hundred years before to proclaim the acceptable year of the Lord; that all that the kings, prophets, and judges of the past had written about the Nazarene who was to come, that all the heartfelt longing David sung on his lyre, were now fulfilled in their ears on this very day: for He was the one in whom all Scriptures were fulfilled; He was the Expected of the Nations; He was Emmanuel; He was the unique Way of Salvation; He was God with us.

The Truth

As soon as Jesus appeared, He was sought out by the throng, for some were saying, "He is a good man," and others said, "No, but He seduceth the people." At any rate the crowd felt they had a right to ask Him for His credentials. With a wonderful leap into the infinite and eternal, He declared to them that His doctrine is the very doctrine of God who sent Him and whose Eternal Son He is.

The evening came and found Him seated in the court of the women, which contained the thirteen chests into which the people cast their gifts. In this court, and therefore very close to Him, probably on either side of Him, were two gigantic candelabra, fifty cubits high and sumptuously gilded, on the summit of which were lit lamps that shed their soft light over the temple. Around these lamps the people in their joyful enthusiasm, and even the stateliest Pharisees, joined in festal dances, while to the sound of flutes, the Levites on the fifteen steps that led to the court, chanted the beautiful psalms that were known as the Songs of Degrees.

As Our Lord sat between those two great lights that illumined the kindly faces of friends and the sinister faces of enemies, they seemed to shine upon Him as on no one else, throwing a beautiful golden aureole about His majestic head. It was His constant plan to shape the illustrations of His discourses by those external incidents that would fix the words most indelibly on the minds of His hearers.

Just as before He had given the parable of the vineyard as He stood near a vineyard, and the parable of the fisherman as He talked to fishermen at the lake, so now did He declare His mission to the world as He stood in the light of those candles. In the color of their imagery, in the flaming brilliance of their light, on the very threshold of the Holy of Holies, the Holy of Holies proclaimed that the light of God had come to the darkness of men:

"I am the Light of the world."

"He that followeth Me walketh not in darkness, but shall have the Light of life."

There was no mistaking His words. He did not say He was like a light; He did not say He was something like those candles now illumining the darkness; He did not say that He was the light of any particular people, but the very light that is identical with truth and that illumines every one coming into the world. To make such a statement He had to know all things. To their memory, in none of the great schools of Jerusalem had He ever learned, nor did He ever sit at the feet of their great Gamaliel. And so His auditors turned to one another saying: "How doth this man know, having never learned?" And when they asked Him: "Who art thou?", they were stunned with the declaration that He whose truth was the light of the world possessed it from all eternity. Jesus said to them: "The beginning who also speak to you. . . . If you continue in my work you shall be my disciples indeed. And you shall know the truth, and the truth shall make you free." His hearers, not grasping the great truth that He was the Light of the world, asked: "Art thou greater than our father Abraham who is dead?" The response of Our Lord was an affirmation of His eternity: "Abraham your father rejoiced to see my day: he saw it and was glad." They therefore said to Him: "Thou art not yet fifty years old, and hast Thou seen Abraham?" Jesus said to them: "Amen, amen, I say to you, before Abraham was made, I am."

The Life

IT WAS THE DAY AFTER He had fed five thousand who had followed Him into the desert, and from whom He hid lest they make Him king. They had sought long for Him, and when at last they had found Him, on the other side of the sea, their first question was: "Rabbi, whence camest thou hither?" But Our Lord ignored their question, for that did not concern them. What did concern them was a proper understanding of the miracle He had worked for them when He gave them bread and fish. He knew they were slow to understand. He had pointed out to them that the more He did for them the more they looked upon Him as a material benefactor and would not see the greater spiritual things that were beyond. They were bent only on earthly life and kingdoms of this world.

He would now make one last effort to bring them to an understanding of His mission: "Amen, amen, I say to you: you seek me not because you have seen miracles, but because you did eat of the loaves and were filled. Labor not for the meat which perisheth, but for that which endureth unto life everlasting which the son of man will give you, for Him hath God, the Father, sealed." They said to Him,

"Lord, give us always this bread." And Jesus answered: "I am the Bread of Life. He that cometh to Me shall not hunger, and he that believeth in Me shall not thirst." "I am the living bread that came down from heaven. If any man eateth this bread, he shall live forever, and the bread that I will give is My flesh, for the life of the world. As the living Father hath sent Me, and I live by the Father; so he that eateth Me, the same also shall live by Me."

The last words were clear and emphatic. As He had before said that He was the way and the light, so now He was saying that He was the life of the world. To believers and unbelievers alike it came as a shock. He was now identifying Himself with life as He had identified Himself with truth. Impossible or not, He had said it. The old murmurs broke out again, not this time from the vulgar-minded mob but from His own disciples who were scandalized at His saying that He came down from heaven and that His life was the life of the world.

Some of them murmured: "The saying is hard, and who can hear it?", and then left and walked with Him no more. They had understood Him aright, otherwise He would not have let them go.

The only ones who remained were those grouped around Peter, to whom Jesus said: "Will you also go away?"

Peter, the rock, answered: "Lord, to whom shall we go? Thou hast the words of eternal life, and we have believed and have known that Thou art the Christ, the Son of God."

Buddha, Confucius, Lao-tse, Socrates, Mohammed

GO BACK TO ANY OTHER MORAL TEACHER the world has ever known and find a similar message. Take any of them, Buddha, Confucius, Lao-tse, Socrates, Mohammed—it makes no difference which. Not one of them identified himself either with the Way of Salvation or with Truth or with Life. They all said, "I will point out the way," but our Lord said: "I am the Way." They all said: "I will tell you how to possess truth or how to discover Light," but our Lord said: "I am the Truth—I am the Light of the world." They all said, "I will help you attain undying life," but Our Lord said, "I am the Life."

Every reformer, every great thinker, every preacher of ethics in the history of the world pointed to an ideal outside himself. Our Lord did not. He pointed to Himself. Every founder of a world religion asked men to look to their systems, which was apart from their persons. Our Lord did not. He pointed to His person. Alcibiades, for example, asked Socrates what he should ask of the gods. Socrates told him "to wait for some greater teacher who would tell us how we were to conduct ourselves before God." Socrates did not say, "Look to me; I am the way." Rather, he said, "Look after me, and beyond me, and outside me." There was a distinction between the master and his system.

What is true of Socrates is equally true of Buddha. In the *Book of the Great Decease,* Ananda tries to obtain from Buddha, when his end was near, direction and consolation. Buddha did not say, "Believe in me," or "Live by me," but answered, "Be a lamp unto yourself and a refuge unto yourself." He was practically saying "I am not the light. I am not the truth." It was something outside him. Confucius, the great reformer of the Orient, repeatedly disclaimed any special excellence in himself. "How dare I," he said, "rank myself with the sage and the man of perfect virtue?" He was practically saying, "The life is not in me. These ideals are distinct from my historical existence." Even in the religion of Israel, the Hebrew prophets were moral teachers of their nation, who demanded without compromise obedience to the words spoken by them, but they claimed that their words demanded reverence, not because they were their words, but because they were the words of God. Hence the frequency of the expression among the writings of the Hebrew prophets: "Thus sayeth the Lord."

What is true of the past is true of the present. There is no reformer or preacher today who believes that he is the incarnation of the ideal. At best, most of them would say that they were signposts pointing to a heavenly Jerusalem, but in no case that they were the city itself.

It is in this that Christ differs from all of them. While Socrates was saying, "Wait for another," Christ was saying, "I am here. The Scriptures are fulfilled in your ears." While Buddha refused to be a lamp to guide the poor dying Ananda, Christ was saying, "I am the Light of the world." While Confucius refused to see in himself a personification of his ideal of sinlessness, Christ was saying that He was Life and Resurrection. While the prophets of Israel pointed beyond themselves, Christ proclaimed Himself as the Expected One of the Nations.

Priest

A PRIEST IS AN INTERMEDIARY or link between God and man. His mission is to do two things: to bring God to man by the infusion of divine life; and to bring man to God by redeeming man from sin. This Our Lord declared was the double purpose of His coming into this world: "I am come that they may have life, and may have it more abundantly"; and, "The Son of man is not come to be ministered unto, but to minister, and to give his life a redemption for many."

The first purpose of the priesthood of Christ is to bring God to man or divine life to human life. We have no right to say there is no higher life than ours, any more than the worm has a right to say there is no higher life than its life. The very fact that man is never satisfied with his mere earthly life is a proof of something beyond. Like a giant, imprisoned bird, his wings beat uneasily against the gilded cage of space and time. He has always sought to be more than he is; that is why he has ideals; that is why he has hopes; that is why the Roman emperors called themselves gods; that is why man, when he forgets the true God, adores himself as god.

But man can never acquire that higher life by his own power, any more than he can change a stone into a serpent. If he is to be possessed of a higher life, it must be given to him from above. If the animal is to live the higher life of man, it must surrender its lower existence and be reborn in man, who comes down to it to take it up as food. If man is to live the higher life of God, he must die to his lower life of the flesh and be reborn to the higher life of the Spirit who comes down to him with that divine life. This is the message our Lord gave the carnal-minded Nicodemus who, hearing it, said: "How can a man be born when he is old? Can he enter a second time into his mother's womb and be born again?" The Savior replied that He meant not the fleshly birth, but that spiritual regeneration of water through which man was reborn as a child of God. . . .

The second function of the priestly life of Christ consisted not only in linking the life of God to man, but also in reconciling man to God by redeeming him from sin. Many of the emasculated lives of Christ today picture Him merely as a moral reformer, a teacher of humanitarian ethics, or a sentimental lover of birds and beasts. Our Lord is primarily none of these things. He is first and foremost a Redeemer. In that, He breaks with all reformers and preachers who ever lived. Take any of them: Buddha, Plato, Confucius, Socrates, Lao-tse—why did they come into the world? Each and every one of them came into this world to live. But why did Our Lord come into this world? *He came into the world to die.* It was the supreme business that engaged Him from the day of His birth: "The Son of man," He said of Himself, "is come to seek and to save that which was lost."

King

DID HE EVER CALL HIMSELF A KING? Recall that terrible day we call Good Friday, to mask its heinousness and to declare our *felix culpa*. Our Lord is led before the Roman procurator Pontius Pilate in the name of Tiberius Caesar. To have some idea of Pilate's personality and his vision of the world worldly, make a mental picture of him in terms of one of our modern intelligentsia—a reader of Mencken, Bertrand Russell, and Shaw, with Swinburne and Wells on his bookshelves, one whose emotional life was dictated by Havelock Ellis and his mental life by Julian Huxley, who says there is no such thing as truth.

Standing between the pillars of His judgment seat, touched somewhat with the nobleness of the divine prisoner, Pilate asks with pitying wonder: "Art thou a king?" The very way he said it was meant to imply: Art thou, whom the world receives not, who are a poor, worn outcast, in this the hour of thy bitter need—"Art thou a king?"; art thou, pale, lonely, friendless, wasted man in poor peasant garments and tied hands—"Art thou a king?"; art thou who fled when the crowd attempted to make thee a worldly king, and who only last Sabbath entered the palmstrewn streets of this holy city amidst pompous splendor—"Art thou really a king?" There came from that beaten figure, rising to its full stature, expressing kingship in every gesture despite ropes and chains: "Thou sayest it." I am. My kingdom is not of this world. If my kingdom were of this world, my servants would certainly strive that I should not be delivered to the Jews, but now my kingdom is not from hence. "For this was I born, and for this came I into the world; that I should give testimony to the truth. Every one that is of the truth, heareth my voice."

As Pilate listened to this king of truth, he felt rising within the impulse for higher things. But the thought of an unworldly king was too much for him; and as the first pragmatist of Christian times, turning his back, he sneered the question of the twentieth century: "What is truth?" And with those momentous words the worldly rejected the unworldly, which is God. And so Christ became the only king in the whole history of the world who ever stumbled to his throne. The world was certain that no king could be a success who was such a failure. But such are the ways of God. Many times, during His public life, He said that those who loved Him would be hated by the world; that He would draw men to Himself by being lifted up on a cross in seeming defeat; that the greatest love man can show is to lay down his life for his sheep.

Now the solemn hour had struck. The King was hanging on a peg. For a crown He wore a wreath of thorns, for a scepter, an iron nail; for a throne, a cross; for royal purple, His own blood; for His army, those who shouted: "If he be the king of Israel, let him come down from the cross"; for His courtroom, the Hill of the Skull [Golgotha]; for His courtiers, thieves; and for His battle cry: "Father, forgive them, for they know not what they do."

When the king was enthroned, those who expected a worldly king, and not an unworldly God, saw an inscription above the cross painted on wood in huge red letters. It was written in three languages of which at least one was known by every single man in that multitude—in the official Latin, the current Greek, and the vernacular Hebrew—informing all that this Man whom the world rejected and who loves when hated—this Man dying between two common thieves in the sight of the world—was: "The King of the Jews."

Prophet

HE DID THE VERY THINGS any other prophet would have called foolish. He chose the very method the others labeled unsuccessful. His teaching possessed the three opposite characteristics of the world. He made his message not smart, but simple; not liberal, but transforming; not modern, but eternal.

In contrast with the message of modern prophets, the message of Our Blessed Lord was not smart and sophisticated, but plain and simple. There is nowhere an attempt to impress His auditors either with His omniscience or with their nescience. He is never complex. We find no trick of rhetoric, no appeal to the intelligentsia, no pomp of demonstration, no monotonous deserts of laws and precepts such as are found in Buddha or Mohammed.

On most occasions His sermons were given under the open sky, by the hillside, alongside the lake, or in the roadway. His words flowed as sweetly to single listeners as to enraptured crowds and could be caught up just as well by the learned inquirer in the lonely midnight as by the frail woman at the noonday well. His phrases are taken out of common life and common experience that make them plain to every age.

His lessons were drawn from the very incidents of life before Him at the moment. On one occasion, speaking to poor workingmen on a street corner, He made use of their patched clothing, their old bottles and new wine, to bring home to them the truth of His kingdom. On another, standing in the entrance to the temple, ablaze with lights, and its pinnacles flaming torches, He said to His disciples: "I am the light of the world." One day on a hillside near the Lake of Galilee, He saw on the opposite hill a man going out to sow his seed, and pointing His finger said: "Behold the sower went forth to sow"; and as His disciples watched the man they heard the parable of the sower and his seed. He sees the fishermen gathering in their nets and calls them to be fishers of men. He sees a man whose name means rock, and makes him the rock upon which He builds His Church.

He spoke of everyday joys and sorrows; of the salt on the table; of the village perched on the hill; of the candlestick on the window sill; of their sheep and their goats; their camels and the eyes of needles; their daily bickerings before the local judge, and their coarse language that He overheard on the street; the hot sun beating down on them; the lightning flash from east to west; the ditch over there between the fields; thorns and thistles; the sheep and wolves; the reeds shaken by the wind, and burning weeds; eggs and serpents; nets and fish; pearls and pieces of money; corn and oil; stewards and gardeners; kings and shepherds; the raven hovering over them; the daily wages hidden at home in moneybags; the cottage, near the lake, that had been built on sand and had fallen to ruins, and the one built on rocks that survived the flood; courtiers in soft clothing, brides in nuptial robes, and the stones on the hillsides with snakes and scorpions beneath them.

And who shall ever forget the day that He stood on the plain, when His eye was first caught by the flight of a bird overhead, and then by a lily at His feet, which He took in His hand with the remark that it grows though it labors not, neither does it spin. Suddenly He elevates the minds of His hearers from that flower to their national heroes and the flamboyant colors of their palaces: "Not even Solomon in all his glory was arrayed as one of these"; and then finally, by a third thought, shrivels it to nothing with a gesture of one who might fling it away: "And if the grass of the field, which is today, and tomorrow is cast into the oven, God doth so clothe, how much more you, O ye of little faith." It was like building a great tower by magic and then suddenly crumbling it into dust when it had made us look up into the sky. There was nothing smart or sophisticated about it; it was a thing so simple that no worldly minded person would ever think of it if he wished to impress us with his wisdom. Smart people say smart things to convince us of their smartness. It remained for a God to say simple things to convince us of His wisdom.

The second difference between the modern teacher and Our Lord is that the former believes that the message should be liberal, broad, and free from restraint and mortification. Our Blessed Lord said it should not be liberal. But in opposing a liberal doctrine He was not narrow; He was not revolutionary; He was not making an innovation. Rather He was renovating. His doctrine was transforming. He begins a recast of the race of Adam. Socrates reformed the mind, Moses the law, and others altered codes, systems, and religions; but Our Lord did not alter a part of man, but the whole man from top to bottom, the inner man that is the motive power of all His works and deeds. He therefore makes no compromises, or concessions. He has a real contempt of a broad-mindedness that is synonymous with indifference.

He tells us that if we do not believe, we shall be condemned, and that if we despise His ambassadors, we despise Him. Unprofitable servants are to be cast into utter darkness where there "shall be weeping and gnashing of teeth." Sodom and Gomorrah shall be more tolerated on the Day of Judgment than the city that rejects the Apostles. Capernaum, which was exalted to the heavens, shall be thrust into hell. Add to all this His attacks on the Pharisees, which suggest anything but a gentle, liberal, broad-minded enthusiast, too mild even to criticize his bitterest opponents: "Ye foolish . . . you blind guides . . . whited sepulchres . . . you serpents, generation of vipers, how will you flee from the judgment of hell?"

Finally, modern prophets, it was said, would rather be up-to-date than right, rather be wrong than behind the times. Our Blessed Lord upset this spirit by dwelling not on timely topics, but on eternal truths. He taught in such a manner as to disprove forever that His ideas were suited to His time and therefore unsuitable to any other. He never used a phrase that made His philosophy dependent on the social order in which He lived; He never made His morality dependent on the existence of the Roman Empire, or even the existence of the world: "Heaven and earth shall pass away, but my words shall not pass away." He did not get His argument against divorce from the Mosaic Law or the Roman Law or Palestinian custom. It was an ideal outside time; difficult in all times; impossible at no times.

• Because He did not adapt Himself to past times, nor to present time, nor to future times, He never fell into a platitude. Platitudes belong only to those who say we must have new morals to suit the new science. Platitudes are the heritage of time, but not of the eternal. For example, there are no platitudes about war, about its waste, about its hate, about its slaughter. What there is, running through His teaching, is a little phrase that is a mighty phrase, a phrase that separates time from eternity, a phrase that began a new system of education: "But I say unto you." In the Sermon on the Mount, He begins every example with the words, "Ye have heard it said . . ." and then He purifies the so-called timely, the platitudinous, with an eternal command: "But I say to you. . . ." It recurs like an antiphon in his preaching. "You have heard that it was said to them of old: Thou shalt not kill. . . . But I say to you, that . . . whosoever shall say, thou fool, shall be in danger of hell fire." "You have heard that it was said to them of old: Thou shalt not commit adultery. But I say to you, that whosoever shall look on a woman to lust after her, hath already committed adultery with her in his heart." "You have heard that it hath been said: An eye for an eye, and a tooth for a tooth. But I say to you not to resist evil: but if one strike thee on thy right cheek, turn to him also the other." It was better according to His logic that the face should suffer rather than the soul.

Enlarging the doctrine of charity, He gave a new law in

which hate is transformed into love: "You have heard that it hath been said: Thou shalt love thy neighbor, and hate thy enemy. But I say to you: Love your enemies: do good to them that hate you, and pray for them that persecute and calumniate you." There is only one way of driving enemies from the earth, and that is by loving them.

The Seven Last Words

THREE ELEMENTS conspire in the making of every great message: a pulpit, an audience, and a truth.

These three were present in the two most notable messages in the life of Our Blessed Savior, the first and the last that He delivered to mankind. The pulpit of His first message was the mountainside; His audience, unlettered Galileans; His truth, the Beatitudes. The last message He delivered had for its pulpit the Cross; for its audience, Scribes and Pharisees, who blasphemed; temple priests, who ridiculed; Roman soldiers, who gambled; timid disciples, who feared; Magdalen, who wept; John, who loved; and Mary, who grieved as only a mother can grieve. Magdalen, John, and Mary—penitence, priesthood, and innocence—the three types of souls to be found forever beneath the Cross of Christ. The sermon that audience heard from the pulpit of the Cross was the seven last words, the dying sayings of a Savior, who, by dying, slew death.

FATHER, FORGIVE THEM

"FATHER, FORGIVE THEM, for they know not what they do." Forgive whom? Forgive enemies? The soldier in the courtroom of Caiaphas who struck Him with a mailed fist; Pilate, the politician, who condemned a God to retain the friendship of Caesar; Herod, who robed Wisdom in the garment of a fool; the soldiers who swung the King of Kings on a tree between heaven and earth—forgive them? Forgive them, why? Because they know what they do? No, because they know not what they do. If they knew what they were doing and still went on doing it; if they knew what a terrible crime they were committing by sentencing Life to death; if they knew what a perversion of justice it was to choose Barabbas to Christ; if they knew what cruelty it was to take the feet that trod everlasting hills and pinion them to the limb of a tree; if they knew what they were doing and still went on doing it, unmindful of the fact that the very blood that they shed was capable of redeeming them, they would never be saved! Why, they would be damned if it were not for the fact that they were ignorant of the terrible thing they did when they crucified Christ! It was only the ignorance of their great sin that brought them within the pale of the hearing of that cry from the Cross. It is not wisdom that saves; it is ignorance!

THIS DAY . . . IN PARADISE

"THIS DAY thou shalt be with me in paradise."

Amidst the clamor of the raving crowd and the dismal universal hiss of sin, in all that delirium of man's revolt against God, no voice was lifted in praise and recognition except the voice of a man condemned. It was a cry of faith in Him whom every one else had forsaken, and it was only the testimony of a thief. If the son of the widow of Nain, who had been raised from the dead, had cried out a word of faith in the kingdom of one who was seemingly losing his kingdom; if Peter, who, at the Transfiguration on the Mount, had seen His face shine like the sun and His garments whiten like snow, had acknowledged Him; if the blind man of Jericho whose eyes were opened to the light of God's sunshine had been opened anew to proclaim His Divinity, we should not have been surprised. Why, if any of these had cried out, perhaps the timid disciples and friends would have rallied, perhaps the Scribes and Pharisees would have believed! But at that moment when death was upon Him, when defeat stared Him in the face, the only one outside the small group at the foot of the Cross to acknowledge Him as Lord of a Kingdom, as the Captain of Souls, was a thief at the right hand of Christ.

BEHOLD THY SON

"Behold thy son!"

It was the second Nativity! Mary had brought forth her first-born without labor, in the cave of Bethlehem; she now brings forth her "second-born," John, in the labors of the Cross. At this moment Mary is undergoing the pains of childbirth, not only for her second-born, who is John, but also for the millions who will be born to her in Christian ages as "Children of Mary." Now we can understand why Christ was called her first-born. It was not because she was to have other children by the blood of flesh, but because she was to have other children by the blood of her heart. Truly, indeed, the divine condemnation against Eve is now renewed against the new Eve, Mary, for she is bringing forth her children in sorrow.

WHY HAST THOU FORSAKEN ME?

"My God! My God! Why hast Thou forsaken Me?"

It is a cry in the mysterious language of Hebrew to express the tremendous mystery of a God "abandoned" by God. The Son calls His Father, God. What a contrast with a prayer he once taught: "Our Father, Who art in Heaven!" In some strange, mysterious way, His human nature seems separated from His heavenly Father, and yet not separated, for otherwise how could He cry, "My God, My God"? But just as the sun's light and heat can be withdrawn from us by the intervening clouds, though the sun remains in the sky, so there was a kind of withdrawal of His Father's face in the terrible moment in which He took on Himself the sins of the world. This pain and desolation He suffered for each of us, that we might know what a terrible thing it is for human nature to be without God, to be deprived of a divine remedy and consolation. It was the supreme act of atonement for three classes of people: those who abandon God, those who doubt the presence of God, and those who are indifferent to God.

I THIRST

"I thirst!"

He, the God-Man, who threw the stars in their orbits and spheres into space, who "swung the earth a trinket at His wrist," from Whose fingertips tumbled planets and worlds, who might have said, "The sea is mine and with it the streams in a thousand valleys and the cataracts in a thousand hills," now asks man—man, a piece of His own handiwork—to help Him. He asks man for a drink! Not a drink of earthly water, that is not what He meant, but a drink of love. "I thirst"—for love!

IT IS CONSUMMATED

"It is consummated."

The heavenly Father in His divine mercy willed to restore man to his pristine glory in order that the portrait might once more be true to the original. God willed to send to earth His Divine Son, according to whose image man was made, that the earth might see once more the manner of man God wanted us to be. In the accomplishment of this task, only Divine Omnipotence could use the elements of defeat as the elements of victory. In the divine economy of Redemption the same three things that cooperated in our Fall shared in our redemption. For the disobedient man Adam, there was the obedient man Christ; for the proud woman Eve, there was the humble Virgin Mary; for the tree of the garden, there was the tree of the Cross.

The Redemption was now completed. The work that His Father had given Him to do was accomplished. We were bought and paid for. We were won in a battle fought not with five stones, like those with which David slew Goliath, but with five wounds, hideous scars on hands and feet and side; in a battle fought not with armor glistening under a noonday sun, but with flesh hanging like purple rags under a darkened sky; in a battle where the cry was not "Crush and kill," but "Father, forgive"; in a battle fought not with spitting steel, but with dripping blood; in a battle in which he who slew the foe lost the day.

Now the battle was over. For the last three hours He had been about His Father's business. The artist had put the last touch on his masterpiece and with the joy of the strong He uttered the song of triumph: "It is finished."

INTO THY HANDS

"FATHER, INTO THY HANDS I commend My spirit."

Centuries whirled around into space, and the new Abel, Christ, is put to death by his jealous brethren of the race of Cain. The life that came out from the boundless deep now prepares to return home. His sixth utterance was a cry of retrospect: "I have finished the work." His seventh and last one is a word of prospect: "I commend My Spirit." The sixth word was man-ward; the seventh word was God-ward. The sixth word was a farewell to earth; the seventh His entrance into Heaven. Just as those great planets only after a long time complete their orbit and return again to their starting point, as if to salute Him who sent them on their way, so He who had come from heaven had finished His work and completed His orbit, now goes back to the Father to salute Him who sent Him out on the great work of the world's redemption: "Father, into Thy hands I commend My spirit."

Execution

TO THE ROMAN EXECUTIONERS it was just another Roman holiday. Under a festal sky they led the procession to the Hill of the Skull, where tradition marked the grave of Adam, and where the new Adam would now lay down His life to take it up again. When their job was finished, and the last nail driven into His throne as a word of forgiveness bore into their hearts, they rested and divided the garments—for the Man on the cross had no further use for them. This was the perquisite of the executioners, and it came to them by law. Four soldiers divided the spoils, leaving only the tunic or seamless robe. It would be a sin to cut it, for after that it would be of no use to any one; but one of them, an old gambler, took out his dice, threw them, and the tunic woven by His sinless Mother was awarded by luck to sinful men. Then in those terrible, simple words of the Gospel: "They sat and watched Him. . . ."

They talked about the latest cockfight in Jerusalem; about a wrestling match one of them had seen in Antioch; about the great chariot race that was to be run in Rome the coming ides of May; about the gambling gains of a soldier of their garrison; about the possibility of Rome some day stamping Jerusalem under her heels; about the new dancing girl in the court of Herod; about the thousand and one indifferent things such individuals would talk about—everything, in a word, except the one thing that mattered. And yet there within a stone's throw of them—why, they might even have thrown their dice at Him!—was being enacted the tremendous drama of the Redemption of mankind; and they *only sat and watched*. Here they were in the presence of the most stupendous fact in the history of the world, actors in the supreme event for which all creation groaned, and they saw nothing.

And the Three Hours slipped by—opportunities soon pass. The young and divine body, which suffered so much because it had so great a soul, was now turned into a funeral pyre of suffering where all the suffering of the world burned together. As the executioners watched passively, He commends His Soul to His heavenly Father, His friend at the right, to Paradise, His Mother to John; and they *only sat and watched*.

The Folly of the Cross

IF LOVE IS EQUIVALENT TO SACRIFICE, and all sacrifice from the world's point of view is foolishness, Christ on the Cross is the supreme folly. From the standpoint of the world He was the greatest failure in history; in the ledger or the world's estimate of things, He suffered the greatest defeat. First of all, He could not win and could not keep friends. Peter, His chief apostle, denied Him to a maidservant; John, who leaned on His breast, is silent when the Master is accused; Judas, whom he called to be one of the judges of the twelve tribes of Israel, sells Him for thirty pieces of silver. In His four trials, before the four judges, He failed to have a single witness to testify in His favor. He could not keep His friends, and is not that the test of one's success in life?

More than that, if He were God, why did He not try to win the favor of Pilate when he said, "Know you not that I have power to release you?" He could have won his freedom by ingratiating Himself with the Roman government, and He did not.

"Folly," cries the world.

If He is all powerful, why does He not strike dead those who scourge and mock Him?

"Folly," again cries the world.

If He could raise up children of Abraham from the stones, why could He not raise up friends at the moment of arrest?

"Folly," cries the world.

If He could have won His release from Herod with just a miracle, why did He not work one?

"Folly," cries the world.

If He could sustain the whole world in the palm of His hand, why did He permit Himself to fall beneath the weight of the cross?

"Folly," cries the world.

If the magic touch of His hands could restore sight to the blind and hearing to the deaf, why did He permit hard nails to pierce them?

"Folly," cries the world.

If He could have proven His divinity by coming down from the cross, "Let Him now come down from the cross and we will believe Him," why did He not step down as a king from His throne?

"Folly," cries the world.

As a demagogue He would have succeeded; as a God He was crucified. The cross is a folly and Christ a failure.

Hence it is that every lover of Christ and Him crucified must share His folly. The law is no different for the disciple than for the Master. The world calls everyone a fool who leaves his riches and his friends, his wine and his song, for the cloister or the convent, and exchanges his silks and satins for the hair shirt and the discipline. The world calls him a fool who does not strike back when he is struck and who does not malign when he is maligned; for is it not divine foolishness to say: "To him that striketh thee on the one cheek, offer also the other"? The world calls him a fool who follows the so-called old and "antiquated" laws of the Church on the sanctity of marriage and rejects the modern views that glorify license and lust. The world brands him as a fool who hangs himself on the cross of mortification when he might come down and shake dice with the soldiers even for the garments of a God.

Yes, but "the foolishness of God is wiser than men," and "the wisdom of this world is foolishness with God." It is only from the world's point of view that we are a fool as our Master was before the court of Herod. In the sublime words of St. Paul, "We are fools for Christ's sake." Common sense never drove any man mad; common sense is said to be sanity, and yet common sense never scaled mountains and much less has it ever cast them into the sea. Common sense is not violence and yet, "the kingdom of heaven suffereth violence, and the violent bear it away." Common sense never makes a man lose his life, and yet it is in losing our life that we shall save it. Life sometimes can be saved by stepping within an inch of death in jumping a precipice, but common sense never makes the leap. The soldier at times can cut his way out from his enemies, but he must have a carelessness about dying—and common sense has

not that carelessness. The kingdom of heaven can sometimes be gained only by plucking out an eye—but common
sense never plucked it out. "It is common sense that makes
a man die for the sake of dying"; it is love that makes a man
die for the sake of living—and so too, it is this love of Jesus
Christ and Him crucified that produces the wisdom of
heaven at the cost of the foolishness of earth; that makes
men throw down their lives to take them up again; that
makes men sell fields for the pearl of great price; that makes
creatures fling "the world a trinket at their wrist," laugh at
death, and say with a modern saint, "I need no resignation
to die but resignation to live."

Resurrection

THINK FOR A MOMENT on the conduct of the Apostles before
the Resurrection, and the way they acted when the Spirit
gave them the fullness of belief in the Risen Savior. What
new force so transformed the souls of the Apostles so as to
make the abject, the venerated; the ignorant, masters; the
egotists, the devoted; and the despairing, saints? What
power was it that laid hold of Peter who once said he knew
not the Man, and now before a learned audience of Par-
thians and Medes and Elamites, of Mesopotamians,
Phrygians and Egyptians and Romans, arises to startle their
hearts and thrill their souls with the message, "You have
killed the Author of life. Do penance and be baptized every
one of you in the name of Jesus Christ for the remission of
sins." What hand was it that laid hold of Saul, the bitter
enemy of Christians, converted him into a Paul and the
preacher who counted all things as naught save the glory of
the Risen Christ? What new spirit entered into that crude,
fish-smelling group of Galilean fishermen which compelled

them to go to the capital of the world, which brushed them aside with disdain, and there preach the seemingly grotesque creed that He who was executed as a common criminal by a Roman procurator was the Resurrection and the Life?

Some new dynamics, some new colossal power had to enter into such simple souls to disrupt a Jewish world and impress itself in twenty years on the entire shore of the Mediterranean from Caesarea to Troas. There is only one force in the world that explains how habitual doubters, such as Thomas, sensitive tax gatherers such as Matthew, dull men such as Philip, impetuous characters such as Peter, gentle dreamers such as John, and a few seafaring men reeling under the shock of a Crucifixion, could be transformed into men of fire, ready to suffer, dare, and if need be to die—and that is the force of love that showed itself in the Christ whom the builders rejected, and who now was made the head of the corner. Everywhere, they gave the secret of their success: they were witnesses of a Resurrection; He who was dead, liveth. And eleven of them met painful deaths in testimony of that belief—and men generally do not have their throats cut for an hallucination. There was only one conclusion their blood will let us draw and that is the lesson of Easter Day that they preached—*It was not Christ who died; it was Death.*

Easter

UNROLL THE SCROLLS of time and see how the lesson of that first Easter is repeated as each new Easter tells the story of the Great Captain, who found His way out of the grave and revealed that lasting victory must always mean defeat in the eyes of the world. At least a dozen times in her life of twenty centuries, the world, in the first flush of its momentary triumph, sealed the tomb of the Church, set her watch, and left her as a dead, breathless, and defeated thing, only to see her rising from the grave and walking in the victory of her new Easter morn.

In the first few centuries thousands upon thousands of Christians crimsoned the sands of the Coliseum with their blood in testimony of their faith. In the eyes of the world Caesar was victor, and the martyrs were defeated. And yet, in that very generation while pagan Rome with her brazen and golden trumpets proclaimed to the four corners of the earth her victory over the defeated Christ—"Where there is Caesar, there is power," there swept from out the Catacombs and deserted places, like their leader from the grave, the conquering army chanting its song of victory: "Wherever there is Christ, there is Life." Who today knows the names of Rome's executioners? But who does not know the names of Rome's martyrs? Who today recalls with pride the deeds of a Nero or a Diocletian, but who does not venerate the heroism and sanctity of an Agnes or a Cecelia? And so, on Easter Day, I sing not the song of the victors but of those who go down to defeat. . . .

Finally the Easter lesson comes to our own lives. It has been suggested it is better to go down to defeat in the eyes of the world by accepting the voice of conscience rather than to win the victory of a false public opinion; that it is better to go down to defeat in the sanctity of the marriage bond than to win the passing victory of divorce; that it is better to go down to defeat in the fruit of love than to win the passing victory of a barren union; that it is better to go down to defeat in the love of the Cross than to win the passing victory of a world that crucifies.

And now it is suggested in conclusion that it is better to go down to defeat in the eyes of the world by giving to God that which is wholly and totally ours. If we give God our energy, we give Him back His own gift; if we give Him our talents, our joys, and our possessions, we return to Him that which He placed in our hands not as owners but as mere trustees. There is only one thing in the world we can call our own. There is only one thing we can give to God that is ours as against His and that not even He will take away, and that is our own will with its power to choose the object of its love. Hence the most perfect gift we can give to God is the gift of our will. The giving of that gift to God is the greatest defeat that one can suffer in the eyes of the world, but it is the greatest victory we can win in the eyes of God. In surrendering it we seem to lose everything, yet defeat is the seed of victory as the diamond is the child of night—the giving of our will is the recovery of all our will ever sought—the Perfect Life, the Perfect Truth, and the Perfect Love, which is God! And so on Easter Day sing not the song of the victor but of those who go down to defeat.

What care we if the road of this life be steep, if the poverty of Bethlehem, the loneliness of Galilee, and the sorrow of the cross be ours? Fighting under the holy inspiration of One who has conquered the world, why should we shrink from letting the broad stroke of our challenge ring out on the shield of the world's hypocrisy? Why should we be afraid to draw the sword and let its first stroke be the slaying of our own selfishness? Marching under the leadership of the Captain of the Five Scars, fortified by His sacraments, strengthened by His infallible truth, divinized by His redemptive love, we need never fear the outcome of the battle of life; we need never doubt the issue of the only struggle that matters; we need never ask whether we will win or lose. *Why, we have already won—only the news has not yet leaked out!*

Reparation or Atonement

EVERY INFRACTION OR VIOLATION OF A LAW demands reparation or atonement. We need only go into the hospitals to see that every violation of a law of nature has its reckoning day; we need only go into our asylums to see there that nature itself takes revenge on excesses and squares her accounts with sin. A judge seems to be sitting there in judgment executing sentence upon those who would violate her commands.

In a still higher sphere parents who love their children demand reparation for their faults, and judges who love society impose sentences in atonement for crime; for a Justice that sees evil and does not punish it is not Justice. Since God is Infinite Love, He might pardon man and forget the injury, but pardon without compensation would eclipse the justice that is the nature of God. Without setting any limits to the mercy of God, I could understand His action better if His mercy were preceded by a satisfaction for sin, for one can never be merciful unless one is just. Mercy is the overflow of justice.

But assuming that man should give satisfaction, could he satisfy adequately for his son? No, because the satisfaction or reparation or atonement that man had to offer was only finite. At this point it may be asked: Why cannot man give an infinite recompense for his sin? If he can commit an infinite crime, why can he not make an infinite retribution? The answer is that while injury is in the one injured, honor or reparation is in the one honoring. If a citizen of the Soviet Union, a minister of finance of France, a senator of a South American republic, and the king of Great Britain come to call on the president of our country, they would not all render him equal honor. Honor would be in the one honoring, and he who held the highest office would render the greatest tribute. Now I have said that man owes honor and reparation to God; but since man is finite, it follows that the honor that he will render to God would also be finite. And there is the problem of the Incarnation.

Man, who is finite, owes an infinite debt. But how can a man who owes a million pay the debt with a cent? How can the human atone to the Divine? How can justice and mercy be reconciled? If satisfaction is ever to be made for the Fall of man, the finite and the infinite, the human and the divine, God and man must in some way be linked together. It would not do for God alone to come down and suffer as God alone, for then He would not have anything in common with man; the sin was not God's, but man's. It would not do for man alone to suffer or atone, for the merit of his sufferings would be only finite. If the satisfaction were to be complete, two conditions would have to be fulfilled: First, man would have to be man to act as man and to atone. Man would have to be God in order that his sufferings should have an infinite value. But in order that the finite and the infinite should not be acting as two distinct personalities, and in order that infinite merit should result from man's suffering, God and man in some way would have to become one, or in other words, there would have to be a God-man. If justice and mercy were to be reconciled, there would have to be an Incarnation, which means God assuming a human nature in such a way that He would be true God and true man. There would have to be a union of God and man, built upon somewhat the same lines as the union of spirit and matter in man. Man has a double nature, the nature of a body that is material, the nature of the soul that is spiritual, and yet he is only one person. The Incarnation of God would imply some such union of two natures in the unity of a Person, but quite naturally a far more perfect one.

Let me make this solution clear by an example. On the desk before me is a pencil. That pencil represents human nature; of itself the pencil cannot write. My hand now goes down to the pencil, takes it up, moves it across a paper, and immediately the pencil is endowed with a power that before it had not. If after I had written, you should ask me who wrote the lines, I would not say my fingers wrote them, nor would I say my pencil wrote them, but I would say, I wrote them. In other words, we attribute the actions of various natures to a person, and the one thing that characterizes the person is not action, not nature, not direction, but responsibility. That is why I do not say my stomach is hungry, but I am hungry; not my eyes see, but I see. Actions belong to a person.

Now let the pencil represent poor human nature, of itself unable to pay an infinite debt to God. Imagine now a divine person with a divine nature coming down to that human nature, taking it up and becoming united with it in a far more perfect way than my hand is united with the pencil. If such an act of condescension should ever happen, the action of the human nature and the action of the divine nature would not be attributed to either nature alone, as the action of the pencil would not be attributed to the nature of the pencil or to the nature of the hand alone; it would be attributed to the person. But if the Person were one of the Persons of the Blessed Trinity, namely, the Second Person, the Eternal Son of God, it would follow that every thought, every word, every sigh, every tear of the human nature of that Person would be the very thought, very word, very sigh, and very tear of God. Then justice and mercy could be reconciled. God would be just in demanding infinite satisfaction; God would be merciful in making that possible by coming down to earth and being found in the habit and the form of man.

What I have just imagined for you is what has actually taken place. Love tends to become like the one loved; in fact, it even wishes to become one with the one loved. God loved unworthy man. He willed to become one with him, and that was the Incarnation.

The Church

THE CHURCH IS CHRIST and Christ is the Church, and until this equation is understood, there can never be an understanding of how Christ prolongs His Incarnation beyond Galilee and His infallibility beyond the first years of the Christian era. The Incarnation is the union of the world with an individual human nature. The continuation of the Incarnation is the union of Christ with every individual human nature in the world. The personal union in the Incarnation is the prelude to the mystical union in the Church. In becoming Incarnate, the Word assumed a human body that became the instrument of His messages, His teachings, His miracles, and even His Redemption. Possessing a body, He could suffer as man; being God, His sufferings had an infinite value. But He "assumed" another body; this time not an individual, physical one, but a mystical one, a body made up of all baptized souls, and this mystic body that is the Church has as its head the historical Christ born in Bethlehem and crucified in Jerusalem. The union of the two, viz., the body, which is the baptized members and the head, the historical Christ, make up the Mystic Christ, or the Church. Just as all the citizens of this country under the leadership of our president constitute the American nation, so too the union of all baptized under Christ constitutes the Mystic Christ, or what St. Augustine called the "totus Christus" or the Church.

Is not this the sense of the words of Paul: "No man ever hated his own flesh: but nourisheth it, as also Christ does the Church, because we are members of His body, of His flesh, and of His bones." And did not this same fiery vessel of election, when he was yet Saul, have that lesson driven home to him the moment of his conversion? Saul hated the Christians, as few men ever hated them. Armed with letters, he set out for Damascus to bind those who were there and bring them to Jerusalem. Suddenly a light shines round about him, and he hears a voice saying, "Saul, Saul, why persecuteth thou Me?" The heat of the Eastern sun fires his lips to speak and nothingness dares ask the name of Omnipotence, "Who art thou?", and the voice answers, "I am Jesus Whom thou persecuteth." Saul is persecuting the

Church, and the voice says, "I am Jesus Whom thou per-secuteth." Christ and the Church—are they the same? Pre-cisely, we are other Christs as an individual fact, and the Church is the Mystic Body of Christ, as a social fact.

Religion Without Dogma

THE MODERN MAN must decide for himself whether he is going to have a religion with thought or a religion without it. He already knows that thoughtless policies lead to the ruin of society, and he may begin to suspect that thoughtless religion ends in confusion worse confounded.

The problem is simple. The modern man has two maps before him: one the map of sentimental religion, the other the map of dogmatic religion. The first is very simple. It has been constructed only in the last few years by a topographer who has just gone into the business of map making and is extremely adverse to explicit directions. He believes that each man should find his own way and not have his liberty taken away by dogmatic directions. The other map is much more complicated and full of dogmatic detail. It has been made by topographers who have been over every inch of the road for centuries and know each detour and each pit-fall. It has explicit directions and dogmas such as, "Do not take this road—it is swampy," or "Follow this road; al-though rough and rocky at first, it leads to a smooth road on a mountaintop."

The simple map is very easy to read, but those who are guided by it are generally lost in a swamp of mushy senti-mentalism. The other map takes a little more scrutiny, but it is simpler in the end, for it takes you up through the rocky road of the world's scorn to the everlasting hills where is seated the original Map Maker, the only One who ever has associated rest with learning: "Learn of Me . . . and you shall find rest for your souls."

Every new coherent doctrine and dogma add to the pabulum for thought; it is an extra bit of garden upon which we can intellectually browse; it is new food into which we can put our teeth and thence absorb nourishment; it is the discovery of a new intellectual planet that adds fullness and spaciousness to our mental world. And simply because it is solid and weighty, because it is dogmatic and not gaseous and foggy like a sentiment, it is intellectually invigorating, for it is with weights that the best drill is done, and not with feathers.

It is the very nature of a man to generate children of his brain in the shape of thoughts, and as he piles up thought on thought, truth on truth, doctrine on doctrine, conviction on conviction, and dogma on dogma, a very coherent and orderly fashion, so as to produce a system complex as a body and yet one and harmonious, the more and more human he becomes. When, however, in response to false cries for progress, he lops off dogmas, breaks with the memory of his forefathers, denies intellectual parentage, pleads for a religion without dogmas, substitutes mistiness for mystery, mistakes sentiment for sediment, he is sinking back slowly, surely, and inevitably into the senselessness of stones and into the irresponsible unconsciousness of weeds. Grass is broad-minded. Cabbages have heads—but no dogmas.

The Psychology of Conversion

EVERY CONVERSION starts with a crisis: with a moment or a situation involving some kind of suffering, physical, moral, or spiritual; with a dialectic, a tension, a pull, a duality, or a conflict. This crisis is accompanied, on the one hand, by a profound sense of one's own helplessness and, on the other hand, by an equally certain conviction that God alone can supply what the individual lacks. If there were *only* a sense of helplessness, there would be despair, pessimism, and eventual suicide. This is, indeed, the condition of the post-Christian pagan: he feels the total inadequacy of his own inner resources against the overwhelming odds of a cruel universe and thus falls into despair. He has one-half of the necessary condition for conversion—namely, a sense of crisis—but he fails to link up his powerlessness with the Divine Power, who sustains and nourishes the soul. But when this is done, paganism vanishes and gives place to what might be called creative despair: "despair" because one realizes his own spiritual disease; "creative" because he knows that only a Divine Physician outside himself can bring healing to his wings. This despair does not usually arise from a sense of one's stupidity or ignorance or mistakes, but because of one's inadequacy, one's sense of dependence, or even one's admission of guilt.

The soul becomes the battlefield of a civil war during a conversion. It is not enough that there be a conflict between consciousness and unconsciousness or self and environment, for such tensions can be simple psychological phenomena without profound significance for the soul. So long as the conflict is only psychological, so long as it is capable of being manipulated by the mind itself or by another human mind, there may result an integration or sublimation, or so-called peace of mind but there is no Deo-version, or peace of soul. The tension or conflict is never very acute when the dueling forces are contained within the mind itself; conversion is not autosuggestion, but a flash of lightning from without. There is a great tension only when the self is confronted with the nonself, when the within is challenged by the without, when the helplessness of the ego is confronted with the adequacy of the Divine.

Not until the tug of war begins, with the soul on one end

of the rope and God on the other, does true duality appear as the condition of conversion. This crisis in the soul is the miniature and cameo of the great historical crisis of the City of God and the city of man. There must be in the soul the conviction that one is in the grip of and swayed by a higher control than one's own will; that, opposing the ego, there is a Presence before whom one feels happy in doing good and before whom one shrinks away for having done evil. It is relatively unimportant whether this crisis, which results in a feeling of duality, be sudden or gradual. What matters is the struggle between the soul and God, with the all-powerful God never destroying human freedom. This is the greatest drama of existence.

The Theology of Conversion

NATURE *makes* human nature, but grace *remakes* human nature. Every person who has been born can also be regenerated, renewed, and revived if he establishes contact with new and divine sources of energy. Christianity puts a high value on human nature, but it does not trust its unaided powers too far. It says that man in his human nature is neither a saint nor a devil; he is neither intrinsically corrupt nor immaculately conceived. He needs divine assistance to perfect this nature. And it is available to him, no matter how wicked he has been in the past; even a man who stoned a martyr like Stephen, as Paul did, can still be saved, not of himself, but by the grace of God—as Paul was. And since the new energy and new power to rescue him come from God, it is beside the point for any man to plead, "I am not good enough." Of course not—no man is good enough. But hidden reserves of power are available to anyone who so desires. That was why our Savior said, "Ask, and it shall be given you; seek, and you shall find: knock, and it shall be opened to you" (Matt. 7:7).

Those who lack grace—that gift of God that is given so freely—have physical life but do not have spiritual life. This raises the question, "Why does not everyone accept grace?" The answer is to be found in the fact that man, alone in all nature, is free. The grass does not need to consult the moisture before it absorbs it to itself; the cow need not plead with the grass to come with it into the animal kingdom; but man is free, and God will break down no doors to force a higher destiny upon our wills. The Divine may only entreat and plead; He will show how much He loves us by dying to redeem us. But He will not use force, even to save us from our own shortsighted preference for a meaner share of life.

Some people in backward countries refuse vaccination; they fear to be saved by a mystery they do not comprehend. Some sick people do not want to see a doctor; they are afraid that he may advise an operation as a condition of recovering their health. In the spiritual realm, too, we can refuse to be healed. We cannot initiate our own salvation— for the first movement of regeneration comes from God— but we can prevent it by our refusal to cooperate. Grace and human freedom are related like the two wings of a bird; both are needed for flight. Grace is a gift, and any gift can be rejected. Love is never imposed—to impose it would be to destroy love.

Because the acceptance of grace is a free act, implying a choice, it follows that some men will always be unwilling to accept it, especially since it invariably demands a sacrifice. The rich young man in the Gospel went away sad because he had great possessions. St. Augustine, at one time in his life, said, "Dear Lord, I want to be good, but later on, not now." The great problem facing every human concerns not sublimation, but elevation. Is he willing to surrender the lower to find the ecstasies of the higher? Does he want God

enough to overcome the obstacles that keep Him away?
Does he love the sunlight enough to open the blinds his
own agnosticism has drawn down?

The acceptance of grace is not a passive thing; it demands
a surrender of something, even if it is only our pride. This
fact alone should give pause to those naturalists who tell us
that the supernatural is only a myth, for since when do
myths and fantasies call for such sacrifices or make demands that are so hard to meet? Myths ask only for credu-
lity—never for the plucking out of an eye or the cutting off
of an arm, as does the Gospel. Yet these sacrifices must be
made, this price paid, if we are to live full lives. No sculptor
can chisel, no artist can paint, unless he detaches himself
from noisy chatter in order to commune with the beautiful;
so we can gain intimacy with the Divine only if we respond
to God's invitation of grace with a willingness to give up
some tawdry treasure, to surrender the field in order to buy
the pearl of great price.

Then life can really begin, for, without the supernatural
gift, every man is undeveloped still. Feed a man until he is
fed up; surround him with the materials to satisfy his every
passion; give him license to do whatever he pleases; castle
him; cage him; satiate him; cuddle him; amuse him! And
invariably, time and time again, he will still be seeking for
that which he has not, grasping for something already
beyond his reach, hungering for the unworldly in the heart
of the world. Without this great reality of God, man knows
himself to be only half real and adequately describes himself as "I am not." Thus does he dimly perceive the great
need of Him Who defines Himself as, "Amen, amen I say to
you, before Abraham was made, I am (John 8:58).

The refusal of God's supernatural gift is the most tragic
mistake a man can make. Its acceptance is called conversion. Contrary to the common belief, a conversion is not
caused by the emotions; emotions reflect only a mental
state, and this change concerns the soul. Conversion, again,
has nothing to do with sublimation; that process, too, is re-

stricted to the order of nature. Conversion looks upward, not inward; it is an experience in no way related to the upsurge of unconsciousness into the consciousness of a man. Conversion, first and foremost, and above all else, is due to divine grace, a gift of God that illumines our intellect to perceive truths that we never perceived before and strengthens our will to follow those truths, even though they demand sacrifices in the natural order. Conversion is due to the invasion of a new power, to the inner penetration of spirit and spirit, to the influence of the changeless upon the fluid character of man.

In his new awareness of the presence of a Divine Power, the individual turns over his *whole* personality, not to his "higher self," but to the higher new self, which is God. Those who have responded to that gift of grace begin to feel the presence of God in a new way. Their religion ceases to be "moralistic" in the sense that means that a man merely submits himself to a code, to laws, and feels the necessity of obeying them as a duty. Religion also rises above the pietistic level on which there is a loving remembrance of Our Lord, a kind of sentimental fellow traveling, through hymns and sermons, with One who lived 1900 years ago. For although some people have found a considerable emotional fulfillment on this pietistic plane, it is not Christianity and does not become so until one enters the third stage, the mystical. Here at last—where Christ actually dwells in our hearts, and where there is an awareness rooted in love, and where the soul feels the tremendous impact of God working on itself—here is found the joy that surpasses all understanding.

The Effects of Conversion

THERE ARE, first, *a recentering of life and a revolution of all its values.* This fresh, intellectual readjustment of thought to make room for God is one proof that conversion is not an emotional matter, for the emotions do not normally control the judgments. Before conversion, life is a confused and unintelligible blur like the figures on a flattened Japanese lantern; afterward, it resembles that same lantern opened to its full height, with a candle inside to reveal the unity of pattern and design. Faith not only puts the candle into the lantern of life—it also lights it. A highly educated person before conversion may have had a vast knowledge of history, literature, science, anthropology, and philosophy, but these branches of his knowledge were divided into watertight compartments with no live correlation of one to the others; they were only isolated tidbits of information, a vast hors d'oeuvre of detail. After conversion the same facts are gathered into a unity, ordered in a hierarchy of knowledge that reveals an overwhelming evidence of Providence in history and also confers a new unity on one's personal life. What was before information has now become wisdom. . . .

A second perceptible result of conversion is a *definite change in behavior and conduct of life.* Not only does conversion change one's values; it also reverses the tendencies and energies of life, directing them to another end. If the convert before conversion were already leading a good moral life, there is now less emphasis on keeping a law and more emphasis on maintaining a relationship of love. If the convert has been a sinner, his spiritual life frees him from habits and excesses that before weighed down the soul. He no longer need resort to alcohol or sleeping tablets. He often finds that these practices were not so much appetites as attempts to flee responsibility or to ensure, by plunging into unconsciousness, that he could avoid the necessity of choice. Before conversion, it was behavior that to a large extent determined belief; after conversion, it is belief that determines behavior. There is no longer a tendency to find scapegoats to blame for the faults of self, but rather a consciousness that the reformation of the world must begin with the reformation of self. There is still a fear of God, but it is not the servile fear a subject has for a dictator, but a filial fear, such as a living son has for a good father whom he would never wish to hurt. From such a love one does not ever need to run away, and the previous acts of dissipation, which were disguised forms of flight, are now renounced. . . .

But even this does not end the list of the convert's new benefits. He also receives *certitude*. Philosophy gives a proof for the existence of God; the science of apologetics gives the motives for believing in Christ, the Son of God; but all the incontrovertible proofs they offer fall short of the certitude that actually comes to a convert through the gift of faith. Imagine a young man whose father has been lost for years. A friend, returned from a trip, assures him that he has certain evidence that his father really exists on another continent. But the young man is not fully satisfied with the evidence, however convincing it is; until he is restored to his father's actual presence, he will not have peace. So it is with conversion; before, one knows *about* God; afterward, one *knows* God. The first knowledge the mind has is notional and abstract; the second is real, concrete, and it becomes bound up with all one's sentiments, emotions, passions, and habits. Before conversion, the truths seemed true but far off; they did not touch one personally. After conversion, they become so personalized that the mind knows that it is through with the search for a place to live; it can now settle down to the making of a home. The convert's certitude is so great that his mind does not feel that *an* answer has been given, but *the* answer—the absolute, final solution, which one would die for rather than surrender. . . .

As a result, all the doubts and despair of the intellectual vanish—and here the Church differs from all other world religions. In other religions, doubts increase with the development of reason, but in the Church faith intensifies as reason develops. This is because our reason and our faith in Christ and his Mystical Body both derive from the same God of Light, whereas reason and belief in a pagan teacher often have different sources. Reason is from God, but a belief in pagan teaching comes merely from the external environment or through propaganda. It is historically true that an age of great faith in Christ is always an age of profound reason; the *Summa* of the thirteenth-century Thomas Aquinas is an example. This relation is a logical one: just as reason is the perfection of the senses, so faith is the perfection of reason. A man neither sees nor walks as well when he is drunk as when he is sober; his senses lack the perfecting power of reason. In the same way, a mind reasoning without faith does not function as well as reason with faith. . . .

The full tale of the benefits from conversion is not ended. We must speak of another christening gift— *peace of soul*. There is a world of difference between peace of mind and peace of soul. Peace of mind is the result of bringing *some* ordering principle to bear on discordant human experiences; this may be achieved by tolerance, or by a gritting of one's teeth in the face of pain, by killing conscience, or denying guilt, or by finding new loves to assuage old griefs. Each of these is an integration, but on a very low level. This kind of peace our Lord calls false, and He likens it to living under the dominion of Satan: "When a strong man armed keepeth his court, those things are in peace which he possesseth" (Luke 11:21). It is the peace of those who have convinced themselves they are animals; the peace of the stone-deaf whom no word of truth can pierce; the peace of the blind who guard themselves against every ray of heavenly light. It is the false peace of the slothful servant who had the same talent at the end as at the beginning because he ignored the judgment that would demand an account of his stewardship. It is the false peace of the man who built his house on the shifting road, so that it vanished with the floods and the storms. With such false peace of mind, Satan tempts his victims; he makes it seem refined to the refined, sensual to the sensual, and coarse to the coarse. . . .

A final effect of complete conversion is less pleasant: one becomes the target of opposition and hate. A man can join any other movement, group, or cult without provoking hostile comment from his neighbors and friends; he can even found some esoteric sun cult of his own and be tolerated as a citizen exercising his legitimate freedom and satisfying his own religious needs. But as soon as anyone joins the Church, hatred, opposition appear. This is because his friends intuitively know that he no longer shares the spirit of the world, that he is now governed by Spirit, is lifted into a truly supernatural order, is united with Divinity in a special way, which is a challenge and reproach to those who would make the best of two worlds.

The Effect of Conduct on Belief

IT IS NOT THE CREED that keeps most people away from Christ and his Mystical Body; it is the Commandments. The intellectual factors of belief are generally known, as is the important factor of divine illumination; but here we wish to concentrate upon three neglected factors influencing a person's assent to divine truth:

1. Good will.
2. Living up to the truth already known.
3. Habits of living.

Why is it, that when a strong intellectual argument for the Faith is given to person A and person B, A will accept and B will not? Since the cause is the same, the effect ought to be the same—but it is not. There must be some other factor present that makes one person embrace, the other reject, the truth—something in the mind it touches. A light striking a wall appears different from a light striking a window. Similarly, this *x* factor, which makes for the rejection of divine truth in one case and its embrace in the other, is the will. As St. Thomas put it in his finely chiseled way: "Divine things are known in different ways by men according to the diversity of their attitudes. Those who have good will perceive divine things according to truth; those who have not good will perceive them in a confused way that makes them doubt and feel that they are mistaken."

What a person will intellectually accept depends to a great extent on what a person *is* or what a person wants to be. The will, instead of admitting a truth presented to the mind, can ward it off and bar it out. God's pursuit of a mind is bound to fail unless the mind is also in pursuit of goodness. The message of the angels on Christmas night told us that only men with good will would become God's friends. This good-will factor is so important that it seems probable there is no such thing as intellectual atheism. Reason is on God's side, not the Devil's; and to deny His absolute is to affirm a competing absolute. But if there is no intellectual atheism, there is a frequent atheism of the will, a deliberate rejection of God. That is why the Psalmist places atheism not in the mind but in the heart: "The fool has said in his *heart:* there is no God." This primary requirement of good will holds not only for those who are looking for Divine Truth but also for those who found it and who still make little progress spiritually. God's grace is never wanting to those who long to cooperate with it. The will to be wealthy makes people rich; the will to be Christ's makes people Christians.

The second important prerequisite for coming to God in

the domain of the will is living up to the demands of divine truth as we presently see it. A sculptor could have an idea for a statue in his or her head for years, but the idea would gradually fade and disappear if he or she did not finally work it out in stone; so a person could have a particular Christian truth in his or her head for a lifetime, but unless it is put into practice, he or she might never be given another, larger truth. Many of us know a great deal about God, but few of us realize that knowledge in our lives. Those who do become all they ought to *be*. They know the truth in their hearts—a different thing from knowing it as a blackboard demonstration. There is no longer a partition in them separating intellectual truth from action. Some professors and knowledgeable people know the proofs of the existence of God and the dogmas of the Church, yet never become people of God. The reason is that they have never acted on that knowledge. Since they never dynamized the degree of truth they knew, they were given no more; the knowledge they refused to fertilize by action remained sterile. The corn that is kept in the cribs too long will rot. To such unproductive souls, the Savior orders: "Take ye away therefore the talent" (Matthew 25:28).

But the simple soul, living up to the moral implications of the knowledge he possesses, is given new knowledge, and finally his wisdom surpasses that of the intellectuals. Our Blessed Lord went so far as to thank his Heavenly Father that he hid his talents from the intelligentsia of his day and revealed them to the little ones, who would live by them. A simple girl like Catherine of Alexandria confounded the learned professors with the wisdom given her by God, because she had won to a practical understanding of divine truth. When we climb a hill, a new vista is opened, which was hidden from the valley below. If, then, we rest passively on that hill, no new perspective will ever be revealed; but if we act on the knowledge received, walk to the end of the vista, then we shall discover that still new horizons open to the eyes and mind. . . .

The final factor affecting assent to the truth is our habit patterns. These are the *result* of our failure to act upon the moral truths we already recognize (the second obstacle to belief just described). Customs have won through, now, to a hegemony of their own. They are so strong they can defy the weakened will. They stand as armed and angry guards at the gates to the intelligence and will let past no truth that threatens them. When the Christian truth comes to any mind, it is known according to the manner of the knower; and some knowers have a vast army of acts and habit patterns, prejudices and desires ready to war upon the divine purpose of life. What the mind receives is received against a background that already forms a pattern of its own—and one it will reluctantly disarrange or change. In the face of divine truth, the habit patterns with their inferior motives arise to contest the high motive driving the mind toward the true. Then one may say: "I fear to believe because I will be ridiculed," or "Because my family will not like it," or "Because I will have to break with my companions and will make enemies."

A struggle ensues between the intellectual comprehension of the truth and the habit patterns of inferior motives inherited from the pre-Christian way of life. When a man stands off from religion and admires the truth from afar, he is full of praise of it and says: "If I ever became religious, I would certainly join the Church." But the real crisis begins when the truth is seen as personal—when admiration gives way to obligation, and when the Word becomes flesh. The Divine Word, when He became flesh, suffered crises such as suffering, hunger, thirst, contempt, the Cross—all as experienced facts; something of the same kind faces the mind that sees the truth, and it shrinks back. Many souls fear to make truth personal, intimate, or incarnate, because they know it may involve a Golgotha.

Habits

A HABIT BEGINS WITH AN ACT of will, which is more or less deliberate and conscious and under our command. The choice of a vocation, such as developing the *habitus* of being a doctor or lawyer or a musician, begins with a decision. The habit of smoking begins with a deliberate choice of a first cigarette; the habit of drinking begins with an act of the will, usually, "Yes, I'll have one." The habit of prayer began with an initial act of humility, by bending the knee to the Omnipotence of God. I know a young man who, while still in the seminary, made an act of will to make an hour a day of meditation in the presence of Our Lord in the Blessed Sacrament, and to this day he has never missed a holy hour.

The mere fact that we have done anything once not only creates a *facility* in doing it again, but also prompts a desire to repeat the action because of the pleasure it gave. An automobile runs better after it is broken in; a key turns more readily in a lock after it has been used for some time; paper, folded once, more readily folds again; water always takes the line of least resistance and chooses the path over which it has flowed before.

Physiologically, currents of blood flow through the sensory-nerve routes and, like the routes of rivers, make permanent paths and channels. Repeated acts are like beaten tracks in the forest; ease attends the repetition, until finally the act becomes automatic. Consciousness now retires, very much like a designing engineer when a machine is delivered. As Thomas Aquinas said, "The habit engenders necessity, . . . especially in unexpected circumstances."

A habit is a kind of automatic pilot. When the automatic

pilot takes over, the aviator is able to do other things, such as checking instruments or eating, while the machine follows its course. Habits puts us on a beam, and we are able to follow a course without great effort. A habit simplifies movements in doing things. When one learns to play an organ or a piano, it will be noticed how often, as one presses keys, the head moves downward toward the keys. This is done because the player is consciously thinking and willing a movement, and the impulse affects the whole body. After a while, the movement is limited solely to the fingers, and the playing becomes more accurate, while the body is at rest. Perhaps the only musician who never gets over the habit of moving the body is the trumpet player; he seems to make up for the feebleness of the instrument by the grotesqueness of his gestures. A surgeon, in like manner, develops more accuracy as he gives less attention to every single detail.

If we never learned habits, think of how difficult it would be to dress. We would probably have the same trouble as a man has taking off his trousers in an upper berth; that is one action when a man seems to lose all resemblance to the image and likeness of God. If there were no habits, we might spend all day dressing. . . . A child who is just learning to wash the hands is very clumsy with the soap, and would be that way all during life if it were not for the ability to develop skill through habit.

Habits make actions more accurate and lessen fatigue because they diminish attention and therefore aid in economizing energy. Each of them calls up its appropriate successor without any alternative suggesting itself. Anyone who has learned a language will recall how much energy was spent by the mind in thinking out the tenses and genders and numbers and pronunciation of each word; but after the habit of language has been cultivated, the flow of words and the proper grammar are free from effort. All that is needed, for example, to start a chain reaction of words is the stimulus of the language spoken by another person.

Thanks to habits, we not only do the right things with little attention, but sometimes it is also possible to become absent-minded. . . . The habit of contradicting other people can even make us unconscious of being discourteous in human relationships. Think of how much fatigue is saved in knowing which way a door swings. Nobody knows which sock he puts on first or which shoe he puts on first unless he is consciously superstitious. A man can think even while he is shaving, thanks to the economy of energy that comes from a habit.

And one of the reasons it is possible to have distractions in prayer is that the words become automatic. One also wonders why women are able to talk while they knit. Is it possible because the habit of knitting involves so little concentration?

Sex and Love

WE ARE NOW LIVING in what might be called the era of carnality. The Victorian pretended sex did not exist; our age says that it is the only thing that exists. This one organic reaction has been so insanely magnified, boomed, popularized, vulgarized, and propagandized that it is no longer kept in its own place, like enjoying a meal or laughing at a joke. Undoubtedly, sex has its particular part to play in life, but it is beautiful only when it is part of the whole, that is, part of that human nature given to us by Almighty God, which is not only biological, but also intellectual, moral, and religious. Its isolation from the whole nature of humans and its consequent exaggeration have resulted in a wild orgy of frenzied filth, which has destroyed the sense of chivalry in men and the sense of delicacy in women. The Church has been dealing with marriage for twenty centuries, and yet nowhere in her marriage ceremony does she speak of sex—but she does speak of love. There is an important difference between the two.

Sex is like a lightning flash between two drifting clouds, a momentary brilliance followed by the dread rumblings of thunder. Love is less like a spark than a light, which goes out from the great white throne of God, permeating, infusing, and indwelling in hearts and attuning them to the vibrations of the great heart of God. Sex is a mutual conflict in which two hearts fall satiated and cry out at the goal, "Enough!" But love has no such word as *enough,* but only the word *always.* Sex takes life and ends in mutual slaughter; love, craving to give life, discovers itself in the other and thus becomes immortal.

Sex is a wild boar wallowing among the lilies and yet always thirsty, for in vain do hands think to snare the music who break the lute; love is as the flight of a bird suffering the loss of earth to purchase those higher and more rarefied levels where the spirit moves with the glorious liberty of the children of God. Sex belongs to the animal; love belongs to God. Hence if any of the depersonalized and unsouled men and women of our day would recover the happiness of their married life, they must seek it not in sex, which is selfishness, but in love, which reached its highest peak and its sublimest expression in the sacrifice of the Cross where a God-man gave His life that we might live it in abundance.

Liking and Loving

IT IS NOT EASY to like certain people, but it is possible to love them. The difference is this: Liking is instinctive, emotional, organic, physiological, a sensible reaction over which sometimes we have as little control as over the grumbling of a stomach. . . .

When Herbert Hoover was president, the young son of a congressman was invited to dinner. The president ordered a menu boys like, such as chicken, ice cream, and cake. The cook, on his own, added spinach. The boy later on told his companions that he had eaten dinner with the president, and he recounted the menu. His friends would not believe him because a president does not have to eat what nobody likes, and nobody likes spinach. It took a letter from the president to convince the other boys that he did sit at the president's table—even though spinach was served.

But loving is in the will, not in the glands; it is in that part of our being that is subject to moral command and is not a bodily reaction, like a wink. Hence, though we do not like certain medicines, we can put ourselves under the dictate of the will and take them. Liking is reciprocal, but love is not necessarily reciprocal. The friends we say we like, like us. But a mother can love a wayward son even though he does not return the affection. God can love us even when we spurn His graces.

The divine command was not "like thy neighbor" but "love thy neighbor," because it is hard to like certain kinds of people, such as those who step on our toes or make funny noises when they drink soup. But they can be loved, at the beginning, sometimes only by a good deed done to them. That is why the urgency to love thy neighbor is followed by the command: "Do good." At first it may be very difficult when our feelings are contrary to the command, such as telling a six-year-old boy: "Now, go out and kiss your Aunt S——." But doing good deeds that love demands makes the heart warmer. When there is no spontaneous love, love begins only as a duty. But as we learn to write by writing, to cook by cooking, to be courteous by practicing kindliness, so we learn to love by loving. The "I ought" after a while passes to "I love."

This becomes clearer as we grasp the mystery behind

"love thy neighbor as thyself." First of all, the neighbor is not the one next door or the one who borrows sugar. The neighbor is the one in need, or maybe even an enemy. But how can he or she be loved as I love myself? Well, how do I love myself? Do I love myself always or at certain moments? Do I love myself when I do something embarrassing or when I steal or when I hurt my neighbor's reputation? On the other hand, do I not love myself when I visit the sick, send money to lepers, or find a job for the father of a family?

When analyzed, it becomes clear that I love myself when I do what is good, and I hate myself when I do what is wrong. There will be certain things in my neighbor that I love, and other things that I will not love, and they are the same things that were loved and hated in me.

Applying it in a general way, I will love the sinner but hate the sin; love the thief but hate the thievery; love the communists but hate communism. The Church, therefore, will always accept the heretic back into the treasury of her souls, but never the heresy into the treasury of her wisdom.

It is easy to like and love those who love us. But when it comes to loving those who are not very likable, it takes the love of God to give the inspiration. Socialism is the love of neighbor without the love of God; it is the organization of society on a technical, scientific basis rather than on charity. Love is not love unless it is directed to a person. Every human being ought to be loved in the unique mystery of his or her concrete personality. And when we come across many persons whom we do not "like," then we have to do what God does with us, who are not very lovable. He puts His love in love and thus finds us very lovable.

Those Who Love

ONE CAN NEVER LOVE in a hurry. Those who are particularly committed to loving service are the clergy and the doctors. To hurry the distressed and the disturbed, either through the confessional or the parlor or the clinic, is to make oneself a merchant dealing with things, rather than a dedicated servant of the poor, the sick, and the disturbed.

Love requires three terms, not only the lover and the beloved, but also that mysterious bond uniting both, which is love. Such human love reflects the divine love where there is an endless cycle of love in the Godhead. Every human person has within himself or herself a rhythm or a tempo to which the one who serves must tune in. To love means to be considerate of others; it may never be a carnal aggressiveness that seeks to devour the prey and be glutted; rather, it means listening to others, putting oneself in their frame of mind, rather than critically analyzing what they have to say. The speeding up of confessions, the rushing through a consultation, or imposing one's own mind on others in counseling, are failures to love. To love anyone means to give one's talent, to give one's time, to give one's money; in a word, to become identified with the soul in crisis.

A tendency in human nature, particularly among the strong, is to despise weakness. Boswell, in his life of Johnson, often remarks how unimaginative he was toward the sufferings of frailer constitutions. Sometimes unbroken health incapacitates one for sympathy with others and weakens the power of insight into other minds; it makes one anxious to dispatch the burdens of others, as if they were wholly of their own making.

Love is patient, tolerant, benevolent. It extends to those beyond our own set, and is exercised not only to the good, but also even toward the dull and the foolish who stumble. But to be patient with them requires that kind of love that sees in every single person an immortal soul, more precious to the Lord than the universe itself. No doctor and no members of the clergy can do anything for a person whom he or she dislikes. Medicine and theology prosper only in love.

Though we cannot love the weaknesses of others, yet we can love the weak and bear their infirmities, not breaking the bruised reed, nor quenching the burning flax. Infants are not cast out of doors because they cry and are troublesome.

Though Our Blessed Lord limited His public life to three years, one never finds Him impatient. Two of His greatest converts were made when He was tired. On His way to work one miracle, despite an interruption, He stopped to work another. Several times it is recorded of Him that He had no time to eat, indicating that He never hurried souls through their problems in order to fit His life into a routine. The one thing that He asked to be done in a hurry was the betrayal by Judas, as if to indicate that that kind of speed and impatience belongs to the work of evil.

The parable of the lost sheep is the story of long, patient searching; when the sheep is found, it is put upon the finder's back; it is not returned to the sheepfold by dogs nipping at its heels. The attitude of the one who finds the sheep is described as rejoicing. As the Good Shepherd found all His care centered upon the lost sheep, so He now finds all His joy flowing from it. Not only the lost sheep, but also even the Cross rested upon His shoulders as a lesson to us that not only the wanderers but even the burden of the world's guilt are to be assumed by those who love.

Purity

PURITY *is reverence for mystery*. Mystery, like a sacrament, is made up of two elements; one is visible, and the other is invisible; one is material, and the other ethereal.

A handshake is a mystery or a sacrament; there is something visible about it, namely the clasping of hands; there is something invisible and spiritual too, namely, the communication of friendship. A word is mystery. There is something material about it, namely, the auditory stimuli or the sound. The horse hears a joke as much as you do, but the horse does not give a horselaugh, and you do. Why? Because the horse does not have the capacity and the power to understand the invisible spiritual element, namely, the meaning of words. A kiss is a mystery. There is something visible or material, such as the touching of lips; the invisible, spiritual element is the communication of affection. When the spiritual element is wanting, it becomes an insult.

Purity is a reverence for mystery. What mystery? The mystery of sex. Sex has two elements. One is material—everyone is male or female. The other is spiritual, namely, the power of creativeness that has been given to man and woman. Almighty God has prolonged His great creative power to man and woman. It is this urge for creativeness that drives man and woman to marry and then stirs them to bring forth the mutual incarnation of their love or the raw material for the kingdom of heaven.

So sacred has been this consciousness of the power of creativity, that all people, Jewish, Christian, and pagan, have always surrounded marriage with religious, sacred, liturgical rites in order to indicate that there is the communication of a great God-given power.

Purity is reverence for the mystery of creation. Why is it that no one is ever scandalized at seeing people eat in public? There are some who do not mind eating near the front window of a restaurant on a fashionable street. In warm weather, people in Paris eat outside. But why is it that we are scandalized by seeing people make love in public? Is a manifestation of affection wrong? Certainly not! Why then are we shocked? We are shocked because there is something so personal, so intimate, so sacred and mysterious about love that we do not want to see it vulgarized, profaned, and made common.

Obscenity is the turning of mystery into a jest. It is the making of something holy, unholy, and something personal, vulgar. Vulgar comes from the Latin word *vulgus,* meaning "crowd." Purity is the sacristan of love, a tribute to mystery, the giving of the primacy to the spiritual over the carnal. Impurity is the using of a person as a means to satisfy one's ego. But purity never allows a material sign to be robbed of its spiritual content. If a person is pure, he or she keeps the vital urges controlled until the divinely appointed time when both God and society sanction their use.

Joy

JOY HAS MUCH MORE TO DO with the affections than with reason. To the man with a family, his wife and children call out and sustain his delights much more than his intellect could ever stimulate. Standing before a cradle a father seems face to face with the attributes of the everlasting Being who has infused His tenderness and love into the babe. The power of rejoicing is always a fair test of a man's moral condition. No man can be happy on the outside who is already unhappy on the inside. If a sense of guilt weighs down the soul, no amount of pleasure on the outside can compensate for the loss of joy on the inside. As sorrow is attendant on sin, so joy is the companion of holiness.

Joy can be felt in both prosperity and adversity. In prosperity it consists not in the goods we enjoy but in those we hope for; not in the pleasures we experience but in the promise of those we believe without our seeing. Riches may abound, but those for which we hope are the kind that moths do not eat, rust consume, nor thieves break through and steal. Even in adversity there can be joy in the assurance that the Divine Master Himself died through the Cross as the condition of His Resurrection.

If joy be uncommon today it is because there are timid souls who have not the courage to forget themselves and to make sacrifices for their neighbor, or else because the narrower sympathies make the brighter things of the world to come appear as vanities. As the pull from the belief in God and the salvation of the soul fade from life, so also joy vanishes and one returns to the despair of the heathens. The old Greeks and Romans always saw a shadow across their path and a skeleton at their feet. It was no surprise that one day a Roman who had nothing to live for, nothing to hope for, entered his bath and opened a vein and so bled quietly and painlessly to death. A famous Greek poet once said of life that it was better not to be born, and the next best thing was to quit life as soon as possible. All this is at the other extreme from St. Paul, who said: "Rejoice in the Lord always and again I say, rejoice."

Ecstasy

ECSTASY MEANS TO BE "carried out of oneself" and, broadly speaking, the very fact of loving carries the lovers out of themselves by leading them to center their thoughts, beyond themselves, on the beloved. Adolescent boys and girls are often surprised to find that their elders know they have fallen in love; they give themselves away by their dreamy inattention, by staring into space, and by indifference to such things as mealtimes. Love has "carried them away". . . .

Great love . . . makes the lover indifferent to physical hardships and sordid surroundings. The hovel of a husband and wife who love each other is a far more joyous place than the rich apartment of the couple who have lost their love. Love of God begets an even greater indifference to our environment: a saint such as St. Vincent de Paul was so carried away by his love for God's poor that he forgot to feed himself. As Edna St. Vincent Millay wrote of the Christian life: "If you pitch your tent each evening nearer the town of your true desire, and glimpse its gates less far, then you lay you down on nettles, you lay you down with vipers, and you scarcely notice where you are."

But there is one great difference between human love and the love of God, although both of them "carry us away." In human love, the ecstasy comes at the beginning. But when it is a matter of loving God, the ecstasy is attained only after one has passed through much suffering and agony of soul. In bodily enjoyments, we encounter first the feast and then the fast, and maybe the headache, as well. But the spirit encounters first the fast, and perhaps the headache, only as a necessary prelude to the feast. The ecstatic pleasures enjoyed by a young husband and wife at the commencement of their marriage are, in a sense, a "bait" inducing them to fulfill their mission of parenthood. The honeymoon is a kind of divine credit extended to those who, later on, will have to pay the costs of rearing a family. But no great ecstasy, either of the spirit or of the flesh, is given us as a permanent possession without our having to pay for it. Every ecstasy carries a price tag with it.

"First fervor is false fervor" in marriage as in religion. The earliest ecstasy is not the true, lasting love we seek to find and hold. That may come to us—but only after many purging trials, fidelities under stress, perseverance through discouragement, and a steady pursuit of our divine destiny past all the allurements of this earth. The deep, ecstatic love of some Christian fathers and mothers is a beautiful thing to see: but they have won it after passing through their calvaries. Theirs is the true ecstasy, which belongs less to youth than to old age.

The first ecstasy of love is a thrill, but a somewhat selfish thrill: in it, the lover seeks to get from the beloved all that can be given. In both the second ecstasy, the lovers try to receive from God all that both of them can give. If love is identified with the early ecstasy alone, it will seek its prolongation in another person's presence; if it is identified with a unifying, enduring, and eternal love, it will seek the deepening of its mystery in the Divine, who put all loves into our hearts.

Too many husbands and wives expect their partners in marriage to give what only God can give: eternal ecstasy. Yet if any person could do that, that person would be God. We are right to want the ecstasy of love; but if we expect to enjoy it through the flesh, which is merely on pilgrimage to God, we prepare ourselves for disappointment. The first ecstasy of love is not an illusion; but it is only a kind of travel folder, a foretaste, a preview, urging body and soul to start the journey toward eternal joys. If the first ecstasy passes, this change is not an invitation to love another person, but to love in another way—and the other way is the Christ Way, the way of Him Who said: "I am the Way."

Modern Woman

MODERN WOMAN HAS BEEN MADE EQUAL with man, but she has not been made happy. She has been "emancipated," like a pendulum removed from a clock and now no longer free to swing, or like a flower that has been emancipated from its roots. She has been cheapened in her search for mathematical equality in two ways: by becoming a victim of man and a victim of the machine. She became a victim of man by becoming only the instrument of his pleasure and ministering to his needs in a sterile exchange of egotisms. She became a victim of the machine by subordinating the creative principle of life to the production of nonliving things, which is the essence of communism.

This is not a condemnation of a professional woman, because the important question is not whether a woman finds favor in the eyes of a man, but whether she can satisfy the basic instincts of womanhood. The problem of a woman is whether certain God-given qualities, which are specifically hers, are given adequate and full expression. These qualities are principally devotion, sacrifice, and love. They need not necessarily be expressed in a family, nor even in a convent. They can find an outlet in the social world, in the care of the sick, the poor, the ignorant; in the seven corporal works of mercy. It is sometimes said that the professional woman is hard. This may, in a few instances, be true, but if so, it is not because she is in a profession, but because she has alienated her profession from contact with human beings in a way to satisfy the deeper cravings of her heart. It may very well be that the revolt against morality and the exaltation of sensuous pleasure as the purpose of life are due to the loss of the spiritual fulfillment of existence. Having been frustrated and disillusioned, such souls first become bored, then cynical, and finally, suicidal.

The solution lies in a return to the Christian concept, wherein stress is placed not on equality, but on equity. Equality is law. It is mathematical, abstract, universal, indifferent to conditions, circumstances, and differences. Equity is love, mercy, understanding, and sympathy. It allows the consideration of details, appeals, and even departures from fixed roles that the law has not yet embraced. In particular, it is the application of law to an individual person. Equity places its reliance on moral principles and is guided by an understanding of the motives of individual families that fall outside the scope of the rigors of law.

Equity, therefore, rather than equality should be the basis of all the feminine claims. Equity is the perfection of equality, not its substitute. It has the advantage of recognizing the specific difference between man and woman, which equality does not have. Man and woman are equal inasmuch as they have the same rights and liberties, the same final goal of life, and the same redemption by the blood of our Savior; but they are different in function. It is because man and woman are unequal that they complement each other.

When man loves woman, it follows that the nobler the woman, the nobler the love, and the higher the demands made by a woman, the worthier a man must be. That is why woman is the measure of the level of our civilization. It is for our age to decide whether woman shall claim equality in sex and the right to work with men, or whether she will claim equity and give to the world that which no man can give. In today's paganistic society, when women want only to be equal with men, they have lost respect. In Christian days, when men were strongest, woman was most respected. The choice before women in this day of the collapse of justice is whether to equate themselves with men in

rigid exactness or to rally to equity, mercy, and love, giving
to a lawless world something that equality can never give.

The World's First Love

EVERY PERSON carries within his or her heart a blueprint of
the one he or she loves. What seems to be love at first sight
is actually the fulfillment of desire, the realization of a
dream. Plato, sensing this, said that all knowledge is a rec-
ollection from a previous existence. This is not true, as he
states it, but it *is* true if one understands it to mean that we
already have an ideal in us, one that is made by our thinking, our habits, our experiences, and our desires. Otherwise, how would we know immediately, on seeing persons
or things, that we loved them? Before meeting certain people we already have a pattern and mould of what we like
and what we do not like. Certain persons fit into that pattern; others do not.

When we hear music for the first time, we either like it or
dislike it. We judge it by the music we already have heard
in our own hearts. Jittery minds, which cannot long repose
in one object of thought or in continuity of an ideal, love
music that is distracting, excited, and jittery. Calm minds
like calm music; the heart has its own secret melody and,
one day, when the score is played, the heart answers: "This
is it." So it is with love.

A tiny architect works inside the human heart drawing
sketches of the ideal love from the people who are seen,
from the books that are read, from the hopes and day-
dreams, in the fond hope that the eye may one day see the
ideal and the hand touch it. Life becomes satisfying the
moment the dream is seen walking and the person appears
as the incarnation of all that one loved. The liking is instan-
taneous—because, actually, it was there waiting for a long

time. Some go through life without ever meeting *what they call* their ideal. This could be very disappointing, if the ideal never really existed. But the absolute ideal of every heart does exist, and it is God. All human love is an initiation into the eternal. Some find the ideal in substance without passing through the shadow.

God, too, has within himself blueprints of everything in the universe. As the architect has in mind a plan of the house before the house is built, so God has in his mind an archetypal idea of every flower, bird, tree, springtime, and melody. There never was a brush touched to canvas or a chisel to marble without some great preexisting idea. So, too, every atom and every rose are a realization and concretion of an idea existing in the mind of God from all eternity. All creatures below man correspond to the pattern God has in his mind. A tree is truly a tree because it corresponds to God's idea of a tree. A rose is a rose because it is God's idea of a rose wrapped up in chemicals and tints and life.

But it is not so with persons. God has to have two pictures of us: one is what we *are,* and the other is what we *ought to be.* He has the *model,* and He has the reality: the blueprint and the edifice, the score of the music and the way we play it. God has to have these two pictures because in each and every one of us there is some disproportion and want of conformity between the original plan and the way we have worked it out. The image is blurred; the print is faded. For one thing, our personality is not complete in time; we need a renewed body. Then, too, our sins diminish our personality; our evil acts daub the canvas the Master Hand designed. Like unhatched eggs, some of us refuse to be warmed by the divine love that is so necessary for incubation to a higher level. We are in constant need of repairs; our free acts do not coincide with the law of our being; we fall short of all God wants us to be. St. Paul tells us that we were predestined, before the foundations of the world were laid, to become the children of God. But some of us will not fulfill that hope.

There is, actually, only one person in all humanity of whom God has one picture, and in whom there is a perfect conformity between what He wanted her to be and what she is, and that is His own Mother. Most of us are a minus sign, in the sense that we do not fulfill the high hopes the Heavenly Father has for us. But Mary is the equal sign. The ideal that God had of her, that she *is*, and in the flesh. The model and the copy are perfect; she is all that was foreseen, planned, and dreamed. The melody of her life is played, just as it was written. Mary was thought, conceived, and planned as the equal sign between ideal and history, thought and reality, hope and realization.

That is why, through the centuries, Christian liturgy has applied to her the words of the Book of Proverbs. Because she is what God wanted us all to be, she speaks of herself as the eternal blueprint in the mind of God, the one whom God loved before she was a creature. She is even pictured as being with Him not only at creation, but also before creation. She existed in the divine mind as an eternal thought before there were any mothers. She is the mother of mothers—she is the world's first love.

Supernatural Love

AFTER INSTITUTING the Holy Eucharist, the night before He died, Our Lord revealed the secrets of His heart by giving what he called a *new commandment*. "A new commandment I give unto you: That you love one another, as I have loved you, that you also love one another." (John 13:34)

Why was this precept of *charity* (for that is the proper term to describe supernatural love)—why was this precept new? Because the explicit command to love everyone, regardless of race or class or color, even though they be enemies, had never been affirmed before. From that time on, the one mark by which His followers would be known would be their supernatural love for all. "By this shall all men know that you are my disciples, if you have love one for another (John 13:35)."

On the last day when He will come to render to every man according to his works, it will be by charity to God and to fellowman that salvation will be decided. Until the consummation of time, Christ will move through the world hidden under the guise of the needy, the poor, and the oppressed.

"Then shall the king say to them that shall be on his right hand: Come, ye blessed of my Father, possess you the kingdom prepared for you from the foundation of the world. For I was hungry, and you gave me to eat; I was thirsty, and you gave me to drink; I was a stranger, and you took me in; naked, and you covered me: sick, and you visited me: I was in prison, and you came to me.

"Then shall the just answer him, saying: Lord, when did we see thee hungry, and fed thee; thirsty, and gave thee drink? And when did we see thee a stranger and took thee in? Or naked, and covered thee? Or when did we see thee sick or in prison, and came to thee? And the king answering shall say to them: Amen I say to you, as long as you did it to one of these my least brethren, you did it to me.

"Then he shall say to them also that shall be on his left hand: Depart from me, you cursed, into everlasting fire, which was prepared for the devil and his angels. For I was hungry, and you gave me not to eat: I was thirsty, and you gave me not to drink. I was a stranger, and you took me not in: naked and you covered me not: sick and in prison, and you did not visit me.

"Then they also shall answer him, saying: Lord, when did we see thee hungry or thirsty or a stranger or naked, or sick or in prison and did not minister to thee?

"Then he shall answer them, saying: Amen I say to you, as long as you did it not to one of these my least brethren, neither did you do it to me. And these shall go into everlasting punishment: but the just, into life everlasting" (Matthew 25:34–46).

One of the tests of our love of God is our love of neighbor, for it is certain that we will never love our neighbor perfectly unless we love God perfectly.

It is so easy to love those of our circle, but to love those who are "below" us or opposed to us or "ignorant," or apparently not "worth our time," requires true spiritual insight.

"For if you love them that love you, what reward shall you have? Do not even the publicans this? And if you salute your brethren only, what do you more? Do not also the heathens thus? Be you therefore perfect, as also your heavenly Father is perfect" (Matthew 5:46–48).

God's attitude toward us is regulated by our attitude toward our neighbor. That is why if we need something badly, the best way to *pray* for it is to give something away. If we have sinned and need forgiveness, then let us forgive our enemies. God will never be outdone by our love.

"For with what judgment you judge, you shall be judged: and with what measure you mete, it shall be measured to you again" (Matthew 7:2).

"Give, and it shall be given to you: good measure and pressed down and shaken together and running over shall they give into your bosom. For with the same measure that you shall mete withal, it shall be measured to you again" (Luke 6:38).

Brotherhood

It should be evident that the sharing of economic wealth will not make us brothers, but becoming brothers will make us share our economic wealth. The early Christians were not one because they pooled their wealth; they pooled their wealth because they were Christians.

The rich young man went to Our Lord asking: "What shall *I* do?" The Socialist asks: "What will *society* do?" It is man who makes society and not society that makes man. That is why all the economic schemes from Marx's communism to the latest form of democratic collectivism will never unite men until they have first learned to burn, purge, and cut away their own selfishness.

The "one world" will not come at the end of an ascending line of progress, but as the Resurrection from a tomb of a thousand crucified egotisms.

The reason Christianity lives and Socialist theories perish is that Socialism makes no provision for getting rid of selfishness, but Our Lord did: "Sell all whatever thou hast and give to the poor" (Luke 18:22).

The only place in the world where communism works is in a convent, for there the basis of having everything in common is that no one wants anything. Communism has not worked in Moscow, but it does work in a monastery.

All that economic and political revolutions do is to shift booty and loot from one party's pocket to another. For that reason, none of them is really revolutionary; they all leave greed in the heart of man.

The true inspiration for fellowship is not law but love. Law is negative: "thou shalt *not*." Love is positive: "*Love* God and *love* neighbor." Law is concerned with the minimum: "Speed limit, 55 miles." Love is concerned with the maximum: "Be ye perfect as your heavenly Father is perfect."

Law is for moderation; love is generous: "And if a man will contend with thee in judgment and take away thy coat, let go thy cloak also unto him. And whosoever will force thee one mile, go with him another two" (Matthew 5:40–41).

Natural generosity is limited by circumstances and relations within our own circle and, outside of these, is often vindictive. Love ignores all limits, by forgiveness.

"Lord, how often shall my brother offend against me, and I forgive him? Till seven times? . . . I say not to thee, till seven times; but till seventy times seven times" (Matthew 18:21–22). By moving from a little metaphor to a big one, Our Lord implies that precision in forgiveness is impossible. Leave it to love, and it is not likely to err on the lower side.

The love of which we speak is not natural, but supernatural. By faith and good works under God's grace, nourished by prayer and the Sacraments, we are led into intimate union with Christ—but this love we have toward Him must redound to all His creatures.

Friendship of Christians with Jews

OUR CHRISTIAN FAITH is like a grafted branch that grows from the roots of the olive tree of Israel. Shall Christians delay the day of the fellowship of all men in God by hatred of a people from whom salvation came as from a root?

"For if the first fruit be holy, so is the lump also; and if the root be holy, so are the branches. And if some of the branches be broken and thou, being a wild olive, art ingrafted in them and art made partaker of the root and of the fatness of the olive tree: Boast not against the branches. But if thou boast, thou bearest not the root, but the root thee. . . . Be not high-minded, but fear. For if God hath not spared the natural branches, *fear* lest perhaps he also spare not thee. . . ." (Romans 11:16–18; 20–21)

What would Christianity be without Jesus who came to the world from Israel?

What would the Church be without the background of Abraham, Moses, Isaac, John the Baptist, and the prophets who announced the Messiah?

Did not Our Lord Himself say: "Do not think that I am come to destroy the law or the prophets. I am not come to destroy, but to fulfil. For amen I say unto you, till heaven and earth pass, one jot or one tittle shall not pass of the law, till all be fulfilled" (Matthew 5:17–18).

Did not Philip cry out to Nathaniel when they saw Jesus: "We have found him of whom Moses, in the law, and the prophets did write, Jesus the son of Joseph of Nazareth" (John 1:45).

The promise of a Savior was made to the Jews, not to the Gentiles.

A Christian may attempt to justify his anti-Semitism on the ground that the Jews are hated by the world. Shall the Christian forget that if he were a real Christian, he, too, would be hated by the world: "I have chosen you out of the world, therefore the world hateth you" (John 15:19).

An anti-Semite seeks to justify his hatred on the ground that the Jews are our enemies. Even if they were, is not a Christian supposed to love his enemies? "Love your enemies: do good to them that hate you: and pray for them that persecute and calumniate you: That you may be the children of your Father who is in heaven, who maketh his sun to rise upon the good and bad and raineth upon the just and the unjust" (Matthew 5:44–45).

Few people on the face of the earth suffered as much in recent years as the Jews. Shall Christians despise them who through suffering have become more like our Master than they themselves become through their hate and criticism?

Our Blessed Lord in the story of the Good Samaritan told the Jew to love his neighbor—who, in that particular instance, was a despised alien and half-breed. The Jew today is *my* neighbor. I may not hate him whom Christ ordered me to love.

How does the Christian ever expect the Jew to accept the

Christian code unless he, the Christian, acts like a Christian? Hating the Jew will do more harm to the Christian soul than it will ever do to the Jew.

If a Christian loves the land that was sanctified by the feet of the Savior, he ought also to love the people from whom came His Christ, the Savior of the world. . . .

Anti-Semitism is anti-Christianity.

Friendship of Jews with Christians

A JEW KNOWS that anti-Semitism is not due to Christianity because he knows that his people were persecuted before the advent of Christianity.

A Jew will never say that a child in a Catholic School or Protestant Sunday School is taught "to hate the Jews because they crucified Christ." The fact is each child is taught to beat his own breast and to accuse himself because *his sins* were the cause of that Crucifixion.

The primary meaning of the crucifix to every Christian is: *I* sold the Lord; *I* betrayed Him; *I* crucified Him. "Now when you sin thus against the brethren and wound their weak conscience, you sin against Christ" (I Corinthians 8:12).

No Christian hates the Jew because of the Crucifixion related in the Gospels—any more than the British hate the Americans because of the Declaration of Independence.

A Jew knows it is just as unreasonable to say the Christian is made to hate the Jew whenever the Christian speaks of Calvary, as it is to say that Americans are told to hate the English whenever Americans sing "The Star-Spangled Banner."

A Jew knows that a good Christian is taught to love his neighbor and to love his enemies. Whenever therefore he falls from that ideal and hates his fellowman, it is not because he is Christian, but because *he is not.*

A Jew knows that today all religions are persecuted. No race or faith has a monopoly on persecution. Protestants have been persecuted in Germany, and Catholics, like the Jews, have been persecuted in every age.

No one has a right to talk on the subject of persecution unless he condemns it wherever he finds it, and irrespective of who is persecuted, whether it be a Jew, a Protestant, or a Catholic. Persecution is not essentially anti-Semitic, it is not essentially anti-Christian. It is anithuman.

Oversensitiveness is a great barrier to friendly relations. Not every Jew is a saint, and not every Christian is Christlike. If then a Christian deplores that a particular Jew publishes filthy books disruptive of morality, the Jews must not accuse the Christian of being anti-Semitic; and because a Jew deplores the social or political injustice of a particular Christian, the Christians must not retort that the Jew is anti-Christian or a Communist.

Christianity cannot be anti-Semitic because it honors such Jews as Abraham, Isaac, Jacob, Moses, David. Were not the twelve Apostles Jews? Was not the first Pope a Jew? Does not the Church use the Old Testament as much as the synagogue does? Have not its scholars defended the authenticity of the Old Testament?

The Jew and the Christian begin to hate each other at that moment when both look for *external* causes of their misery, the Jew putting all the blame on the Christian story of the Crucifixion, and the Christian putting all the blame on the Jews.

The Jew and the Christian begin to love one another when both look for the *internal* causes of their misery; that is, their sins and their forgetfulness of the moral law of God.

There is no Jew in the world who loves God and hates Christians, and there is no Christian in the world who truly loves God-made man and hates Jews. Anti-Christianity and anti-Semitism are the yardsticks of our mutual failure to be religious.

Someday we hope to see a parade with the Jews carrying banners protesting against the persecution of Christians, and Christians carrying banners protesting against the persecution of the Jews.

Charity and Philanthropy

THE FIRST TENDENCY in modern charity, if we are correctly observing contemporary movement, is toward greater organization, even to the extent of making it one of the big business concerns of the country. The breadbasket stage, the penny-in-a-tin-cup stage, the handout stage have given way to the bureau and the scientific-giving stage. Statistics are replacing sympathy, and social workers are replacing emotions. The complexities of modern life, the crisscrossing of economic and personal factors, demand a discipline in giving and a skill in investigation that can be attained only by the organized effort of those specially trained in such work and thoroughly conversant with such conditions. Whether or not this tendency is a desirable one is at present not the point at issue. It is the facts we are seeking, and to elaborate further the obviousness of the tendency toward organization would be only painting the lily.

The second tendency in modern charity is toward a deification of society at the expense of the individual. The philosophical principle behind this tendency is not that of the common good, which claims that individuals shall effectively cooperate for the well-being of society, but rather the principle that individuals should be submerged for the sake of the collectivity. In a text well known to social workers, one finds such a philosophy in these words, "Human nature itself is now regarded as a product of social inter-course"—which statement implies that society creates human nature, rather than that human nature creates soci-ety. Of the same mind, another sociologist carries glorifica-tion of society to the detriment of the individual to such a height that he makes "the service of God consist in the ser-vice of men," and consequently denies any such thing as an individual sin. The only sin is the social sin: "disloyalty to society."

The final tendency in modern philanthropy is toward absoluteness—not in the sense that it seeks to rid the world of poverty, crime, and disease, but in the sense that the al-leviation or partial elimination of these ills constitutes its full and final purpose. Giving bread means filling empty stomachs—it means nothing more, and it can mean nothing more. Improving home conditions means better sunlight, better food, warmer temperature—and nothing more. There is no other purposiveness behind social work than the tan-gible, and no other finality than the eradication from society of the *d's*—dependents, defectives, and delinquents. Any vision beyond that which can be embraced in a budget or compiled statistically or touched by hands is regarded as a form of idealism to which the philanthropists feel a positive antipathy. It is assumed throughout the whole process of alleviating the ills of mankind that mankind has no other destiny than the present, and that the fruits of helpfulness and philanthropy, if they extend beyond a stomach, a play-ground, or a clinic, never go any further than a formula gleaned from those experiences.

If our finger has been properly kept on the pulse of mod-ern philanthropy, it would seem to indicate a triple condi-tion or tendency: (1) a tendency toward organization as regards its *form;* (2) a tendency toward the hypersocial at the expense of the individual as regards its *method;* (3) a tendency toward the absolute as regards its *purpose.*

Now, what interpretation does the traditional philosophy of charity bring to these tendencies? Does it disapprove of them, does it approve of them, or does it inject a new spirit into them and consequently transform them? Catholic thought is essentially a transforming thought, elevating the baser things to higher planes in the hierarchy of values, thanks to its power of divine alchemy.

The true philosophy of charity would not condemn these modern tendencies and ask for their destruction. Rather, it would ask that they be elevated to conform to these three principles:

(1) Charity must not only be organized, but must also be organic. (2) Charity must deal not only with society but also with individual souls. (3) Charity must not be absolute, but sacramental, *i.e.*, not only of the earth earthly but of the heavens heavenly.

The assumption behind organized charity is that charity work becomes organized when individuals come together and unite themselves for the purpose of remedying the social ills of mankind, as people might come together and form a club. It is further assumed that charity work develops horizontally, that is, it begins with people and ends with people, proceeding from the organization through the social worker and finally out to the needy. There is thought to be no difference in kind, but only one of degree, between the will of the person, which calls the organization into being, and the poor disorganized persons who receive the fruits of the organization.

This conception of charity is not the Christlike one. For us, the source of charity is not the will of men, but the will of God. The origin of charity lies not in effective human groupings but in divine life, and hence its development or unfolding is not horizontal, like the history of a human institution, which begins with men and ends with men, but vertical, beginning with God at its summit and ending with man at its term. According to our philosophy, charity begins within the bosom of the triune God, for charity is the definition of God. From out that infinite source, charity comes in a never-ending procession, reaching down to our own days, because charity is naturally expansive and enthusiastic. God by a free act willed that others should share His love, and so Omnipotence moved and said to nothingness, "Be"; Eternity moved and said to Time, "Begin"; Light moved and said to Darkness, "Be light"—and lo! living, palpitating things were seen moving among Eden's fourfold rivers. That life rebelled against its God, but charity could not keep the secret of its love, and the telling of the promise of better things was Revelation. God was emptying Himself. He revealed his power in His Creation, His plans in His Revelation, and now last of all, He reveals Himself, and the tiny baby hands that clutched at straws and were not quite long enough to touch the huge heads of the cattle, were the hands of Charity Incarnate—Jesus Christ.

But charity has not exhausted itself. Palestine as a place and three and thirty years as a time were not enough to reveal the richness of that charity. How could they be, since eternity itself is not long enough! And so, He plans to assume another body—not just the physical body that He took from Mary, with which He obeyed her for thirty years, taught for three years, and redeemed for three hours, but a mystical body, made up of all the individual human natures scattered throughout the world—men, women, and children who would be united to Him not by the singing of hymns, by the reading of books, nor merely by following His example, but who would be vitally and organically one with Him by being reborn and regenerated and incorporated into His divine life in such a manner that they would be one with Him, part of Him, sharing His truth, His life, His blood, His love. And that body is His Church. And just as the historical Jesus Christ was true God and true man— divine and human in the unity of His Divine Person—so too the Church is human in the elements that make it up, divine in its life, and both are one in the unity of Christ. And in this sense, Christ is the Church and the Church is Christ, and hence the voice of one is the voice of the other, and the life of one is the life of the other. The Church then is the mystical body enshrining the charity of Jesus Christ brought to this world in the Incarnation.

Charity, then, is not horizontal, extending from kind-hearted persons to needy persons, but vertical, extending from the infinite source of charity, God himself, down to the members of the mystical body, through the Incarnation. Charity, then, is not organized, nor is charity work accomplished through organizations. An organization is an assembly of persons for the better securing of a particular object, but there is no intrinsic connection between the controlling head of an organization and its members. Charity is organic, in the sense that it belongs to an organism in which there is a vital connection between the cells or members that make it up, and a vital connection as well between the Head and the body, as in the human organism. Charity may embrace a grouping of people, records, statistics, committees, graphs, and budgets. It may be these, but something more: it is organic—organic because alive with the life of a body; organic because the flesh and blood of its members are the living members of the body of Christ. Looked at from this point of view, the first charity bureau was in Bethlehem, its first case was the case we are still working on—the salvation of humanity through the infinite life of Jesus Christ.

Some very practical conclusions follow from the organic nature of charity. First, the poor, the sick, the unemployed, the orphan, are fellow members with us in the body of Christ. As St. Paul puts it: "As in one body we have many members but all the members have not the same office; so we, being many, are one body in Christ, and every one members of one another."

Our relations to them are not external, like that of a gardener to his garden, but internal, like the organs of the body. If I burn my finger, my whole body hurts because my finger is inseparable from my whole organism; so too, if there are certain members of Christ's society who are thirsty, hungry, or in need—it is *we,* the whole body, who are thirsty, hungry, and needy, for we are members one of another in the body of Christ. Their needs, their wants are not theirs but *ours,* and no charity can call itself Christian unless it realizes this. The eye cannot be indifferent to the ear, and when it sees a blow directed to the ear, say: "It is not going to strike me. I shall, then, take no pains to avoid it." It does interest the eye, for the eye and ear are parts of the same body, and so the sufferings of the poor, weak members of the mystical body are our sufferings, and the sufferings of the body are the sufferings of Christ.

A second conclusion touches on the strictness of our obligation to the poor. There is a charity-sentiment, divine in its inspiration, that we should love all those who are near and dear to us. According to this charity-sentiment, man is in the center of several circumferences. In the first circle is the individual; in the second, the person's family; in the third, one's friends; and in the fourth, one's nation. The charity-sentiment toward each of these varies in ratio with their distance. As the circumferences widen, affection becomes less, as the heat of the sun becomes less with distance from the source.

But in addition to the charity-sentiment, there is the charity-duty, which is based not only upon natural affection one for another but also upon the divine affection of Christ for the members of His body. In the charity-sentiment, it is space or proximity that makes the neighbor; in the charity-duty, it is not proximity but the love for the increase of the body of Christ that makes the neighbor. In the charity-duty, not the closest to us but the farthest away are our neighbors. Such is the meaning of Paul: "In the charity of Christ, there is neither Greek nor barbarian, Jew nor free"; and the words of Our Divine Lord: "He who loves father or mother, brother or sister, more than Me is not worthy of Me." Who is my neighbor in organic charity? Our Lord answered that question in the parable: It was not the one who was of the same family, the same class, or the same social stratum as those who passed down the road; not the Levite for the Levite, not the priest for the priest, the Samaritan for the Samaritan. The neighbor was one who was not a neighbor—one on the fringe of affection, that is, a traveler besieged by robbers. And yet even those in the dim borderland of acquaintance—the chance passer-by on the road, the one whom we have never seen before—all possess a quality that identifies them even with another traveler Who one day sat tired at Jacob's well: "For what you have done to the least of these My brethren, you have done unto *Me*."

The very day that parable was told, organized charity was founded in the words Our Lord put into the mouth of the first social-service worker: "Take care of him and whatsoever thou shalt spend over and above, I, at my return, will repay thee." But it was already *organic*, for how could there be mercy unless there was first justice, and how could there be justice unless justice itself had come into the world to set it right with its God?

The second tendency in modern philanthropic work is that of merging the individual into society and regarding society as the unique field of its labors. I believe that there lies behind this tendency a wrong theory of society, inspired for the most part by the school of Levy-Bruhl and Durkheim, namely, that society is *sui juris* above individuals and independent of them. Their argument runs as follows: A composition is different from the elements that enter into it—for example, water is different from the two atoms of hydrogen and one atom of oxygen. But society is a composition of individuals. Therefore it differs entirely from the individuals who compose it.

This theory of society does not always come to the surface, but it is implied in a thousand and one modern attitudes toward social problems. The sterilization of the unfit, for example, is one form of the philosophy that maintains society's right to mutilate the integrity of human life. Eugenics, too, implies that society has a better right to choose the bride than the bridegroom has; birth-control propagandists and Malthus-minded groups maintain that ushering more children into the world than a society can assimilate is a form of bootlegging and is therefore unethical.

It is our contention that society is not a new being but only a new *mode of being.* Society is made up of like elements, not unlike ones, as the previous example would lead us to believe. Adding drops of water to drops of milk does not make water, but milk and water. So, too, adding individual to individual does not constitute a thing separate, distinct from the individuals, but only a new modality of the individuals' existences.

Society does not destroy individuals, nor can it exist apart from individuals. It has no unitary consciousness, it being only the resultant of the functional coordination of individuals in an organic whole. And this doctrine of common sense finds further verification in Revelation. The Church or the incarnate charity of Jesus Christ, it has been said, is an organism, a body made up of many members. Now we hasten to add that just as the life of a human organism does not destroy the individual cell life of its million of cells, so neither does the mystical body of Christ destroy the individuality of the members. We all share the individual life of Christ, and yet there is no absorption, no merging of offices; there still remains a diversity of ministries but the same spirit. There is unity, but there is also multiplicity.

If society in the natural order or the mystical body in the supernatural does not absorb, submerge, or swallow up the individual, it follows that the talk about "social processes," "social prevision," "humanitarianism," is beside the point. The problems of social work may be stated in the abstract, but *practically* the solution must touch an individual and an individual who has certain inviolable rights.

Juvenile delinquency, for example, is ultimately the problem of the young delinquent; crime is a problem of the criminal; tuberculosis, a problem of the tubercular; poverty, a problem of the poor man or poor woman; flood relief, a problem neither of the flood nor of relief but of a victim.

And so we might go on, always keeping in the back of our heads the sound principle that there is no such thing as humanity; there are only Peters and Pauls, Marys and Anns. And according to Christian doctrine, each of these has an individual soul. Hence social service is dealing not with *something* but *somebody*. Over and over again the Church insists that the least of the individuals, such as the poor human earthenware that is thrown into our gutters and those with focusless eyes who bat their heads against padded cells, is infinitely worth saving because he was infinitely worth redeeming. And any form of philanthropy that forgets the doctrine of the common good for the false principle that society is a new entity for which individuals must be sacrificed, sooner or later will be advocating elimination of the unfit; the murder of defective infants—and then we shall have once more a paganism in which mothers will throw their children from Tarpeian Rocks, and in which new Herods will arise to practice birth control as he did—even with the sword.

No abstract veneration of society, I care not how idealistic it is, can put a proper worth upon the individual. It is only the Gospel notion of charity, which preaches the individuality of the members of the body of Christ, that can give them dignity. A question naturally proposes itself to our minds: Charity came in with the Incarnation? Will it pass out with the dechristianization of society? What will be the motive force behind helping the poor and the needy fifty years from now if Christ's inspiration passes out of charity? Will love of humanity keep it alive? Hardly, for a self-centered humanity will be just as cold and as chilling as a self-centered individual. As Mr. Chesterton reminds us: "Few people are fired with a direct individual affection for the five people sitting on the other side of a railway-carriage; let us say a wealthy matron, given to snorting and sneering, a morning-suited stockbroker, a larger and vacant farmer, a pale and weary youth with a limp cigarette, and a young woman perpetually powdering her nose. All these are sacred beings of equal value in the sight of God with the souls of Hildebrand and Shakespeare; but a man needs to be a little of a mystic to think so." There may be much in humanity that is worth loving, even from human motives, but there is little to love from human motives in the wrecks that come to charities. If there is to be love for them, it must be inspired by Someone who first loved someone who was not worth loving—I mean Christ loving us—and unless the social worker sees Christ in the needy, he or she will not long love the needy.

The true philosophy of charity cannot accept without correctives the modern tendency to regard as the absolute end of charity the alleviation of the ills that afflict mankind, nor can it regard as an ideal a society that is free from disease, hospitals, and prisons—not because such an ideal is wrong, but because it is incomplete.

It is a tenet of the Catholic philosophy of charity that the lessening of the ills of mankind and the diminution of the traces of disease are not ends in themselves, but rather means to an end. In other words, philanthropy is not absolute in its end but sacramental. In the strict sense of the term, there are seven sacraments—material things used as means of spiritual sanctification. In the broad sense of the term, everything in the world is a sacrament, for everything in the world can be made a means of leading us on to Christ and hastening the reign of Christ.

This world is not a closed, mechanistic, completed achievement; it is rather a scaffolding up which souls climb to the kingdom of heaven, and when the last soul shall have climbed up through it, then the scaffolding shall be torn down and burned with fervent fire, not because it is base, but simply because it has done its work. If this is true of the universe in its entirety, it is true of the smaller things in it—bread, money, hospital beds, ministrations of the social worker—for all these are little sacraments, tiny means of spiritual sanctification and nurseries of the Father's eternal mansions. It is only the proximate end of charity that looks to the diminution of social ills. (Social ills must be remedied in order that the life of the soul and the spirit may be free to move on to God.) It is a very unidealistic social service that ends in filling empty stomachs and empty stockings; (it is a Christian social service that fills these things as a prelude to filling empty hearts.) One form of charity is the apostolate of truth, and that bureau that has not made its budget show an increase in spiritual harvest for Christ, which has not sacramentalized its work, has fallen just as short of the ideal and end of charity, as a certain social worker did who sent his budget to the Lord and it read: "I fast twice in the week; I give tithes of all I possess"; etc.

Charity is not absolute; it is sacramental. It is not opaque; it is transparent. The needy members with which we deal are not just needy members: Case No. 365 is not Case No. 365. It is Christ. Even the just social worker will be surprised on the Judgment Day when he learns from Christ: "When you did it to the least of these . . . you did it unto Me."

It is this sacramental, transparent character of charity that lends dignity and worth to its duller and harder side. It is love of society that enables some people to get out from their individual self-centeredness and selfishness. . . . But if there is no Christ beyond society, if there is nothing but society, then where can society find something that will make it forget its self-centeredness and selfishness? We must anchor outside the ship in which we are sailing, and the cosmos is too small for even man to do that. If there is any unhappiness in any modern social worker, it must come from his or her greatness because there is the infinite in man that with all his cunning he cannot quite bring under the finite.

Charity, in brief, centers about two realities—human natures, who dispense or receive benefices; and things, like gold and silver, clothing, and food. Charity embraces in its scope both what we are and what we have.

Since charity involves these two great visibilities of the

world, flesh and things, it is fitting that both of them should have figured in the supreme act of charity, which was the Redemption of mankind. And actually both of them did hold a prominent place. First, Christ assumed a human nature—and that was the Incarnation; secondly, He spiritualized material things—and these were the sacraments.

But the Incarnate did not exhaust Himself in the Incarnation. The Incarnational process continues. Charity workers are therefore to do with these great realities what He did. First of all, we are to offer our individual human natures to Him, that He may continue the work of His Incarnation—human natures with which He might visit the sick, instruct the ignorant, counsel the doubtful, open blind eyes to the light of His sunlight, unstop deaf ears to the music of the human voice. Secondly, we are to make use of things, our possessions, our talents, as kinds of sacraments, each one of which has pronounced over it the consecrating words: "This is offered on account of you, O Lord!" in order that the whole universe may become sacramentalized for His honor and glory.

This is the philosophy of Catholic charity, and since the day charity became organic with us, it has never been quite right to say that God is in His Heaven and all's right with the world; for Christ has left the heavens to set it right, and is found amongst us, even as we talk.

Why People Don't Pray

"PRAYING DOES NO GOOD." This statement has an element of truth in certain cases: not theological truth, but psychological. When it is said by those who are unwilling to curb their promiscuous habits or to tame their carnality, then the statement, "It does no good to pray," is true—but only of themselves. Their prayers are ineffective, not because God refuses to hear them, but because they refuse to fulfill the first condition of prayer, namely, a longing to revise their natures in accordance with God's laws. To have any effectiveness, a prayer for help must express an honest desire to be changed, and that desire must be without reservation or conditions on our part.

If we pray to be delivered from alcoholism, and yet refuse to stop drinking, that fact is an acknowledgment that we did not really pray. In like manner, those who pray to be delivered from sexual perversions and excesses—and that very day deliberately court or seek such pleasures—have destroyed the efficacy of the prayer by a reservation. All prayer implies an act of the will, a desire for growth, a willingness to sacrifice on our own part; for prayer is not passive, but is a very active collaboration between the soul and God. If the will is inoperative, our prayers are merely a list of the things we would like God to give us, without ever asking us to pay the price they cost in effort and a willingness to change. Prayer is dynamic, but only when we cooperate with God through surrender. The person who decides to pray for release from the slavery of carnal pleasures must be prepared, in every part of the being, to utilize the strength that God will give and to work unreservedly for a complete freedom from the sin. In dealing with others it is possible to have one's cake and eat it, but with God that is impossible.

Sometimes—even when the will is operative—a prayer seems worthless because we approach God with a divided will. We want Him, but we want something else incompatible with Him. We are demanding that the laws of the universe be lifted so that He will give us the reward of perfect trust in Him, while we continue to place half our trust in other things. In such a case, we keep one hand behind our back; we hold on to something that would compensate us if God should fail. We prepare a substitute satisfaction to fall back on if He does not come through—such as a comfortable bank account, when one is praying for guidance from

Divine Providence. Human friendships are often broken for want of a complete and total confidence; and Divine Friendship does not bestow all of its gifts, either, when complete trust in Him is wanting. Faith precedes the answered prayer.

It is not difficult to understand why many people do not pray, at all. Just as working persons can become so interested in what they are doing as not to hear the noonday whistle, so the egotists can become so self-infatuated as to be unconscious of anything outside of themselves. The suggestion that there is a reality beyond them, a power and an energy that can transform and elevate them, strikes them as absurd. Just as there are tone-deaf people who are dead to music and color-blind people who are dead to art, so the egotists are Deity-blind, that is, dead to the vision of God. They say they cannot pray, and they are right, *they* cannot. Their self-centeredness has paralyzed them. There is also some truth in their statement that they "do not need prayer," because they do not want to be any better than they are—their purpose is to remain unchanged, and this stultification can be accomplished by themselves alone. Animals do not need prayer, either, for none of them has a capacity for self-transcendence, which man has.

A man is the only creature in the world who can *become* more than he is, if he freely wills to grow. The persons who boast that they are their own creator need never acknowledge dependence on God; those who affirm that they have never done anything wrong have no need of a Savior. Before such egotists can pray, their selfishness must be corrected. Many refuse to correct it—not because they fear what they will become if they do, but because they cannot face the surrenders they would have to make before they could be elevated to a higher level of peace and joy.

There must always be a relationship between the gift and the recipient—there is no point in giving anyone a treasure he cannot use. A parent would not give a child with no talent for music a Stradivarius violin. Neither will God give to egocentrics those gifts and powers and energies that they never propose to put to work in the transformation of their lives and souls.

Some object that, inasmuch as God's will will always be done, it can make no difference whether we pray; this is like saying: "My friend will either get better or worse; what good will it do to send for a doctor and give him medicine?" In the physical order medical power takes into account the physical factors within a sick body; in the spiritual order God's will makes allowance for our desire to do better. It is true that in answering a prayer, God will not do what he did not will, merely because we asked Him; but He will do that which without our prayer He would not do.

God will not make the sun shine through a dirty window—but the sun will shine through the window if it is clean. God will not do what we can very well do for ourselves; He will not make a harvest grow without our planting the seed. It is a conditional universe in which man lives—to bring about an effect we wish, we must proceed along the road to it through its cause. If a child studies, it will know; if you strike a match, it will ignite. In the spiritual order we have the words of our Lord: "Ask, and the gift will come; seek, and you shall find; knock, and the door shall be opened to you" (Matthew 7:7). But there must be the preparation for God's help through the asking and the seeking and the knocking. Millions of favors are hanging from heaven on silken cords—prayer is the sword that will cut them.

Prayer of Petition

THE ESSENCE of prayer is not the effort to make God give us something—as this is not the basis of sound human friendships—but there is a legitimate prayer of petition. God has two kinds of gifts: first, there are those he sends us whether we pray for them or not; and the second kind are those that are given on condition that we pray. The first gifts resemble those things that a child receives in a family—food, clothing, shelter, care, and watchfulness. These gifts come to every child, whether the child asks for them or not. But there are other gifts, which are conditioned upon the desire of the child. A parent may be eager to have a child go to college, but if the child refuses to study or becomes a delinquent, the gift that the parent intended can never be bestowed. It is not because the parent has retracted the gift, but rather because the child has made the gift impossible. Of the first kind of gifts our Blessed Lord spoke when he said: "His rain falls on the just and equally on the unjust." (Matthew 5:45) He spoke of the second kind of gifts when he said: "Ask, and the gift will come."

Prayer, then, is not just the informing of God of our needs, for He already knows them. "You have a Father in heaven who knows that you need them all." (Matthew 6:32) Rather, the purpose of prayer is to give him the opportunity to bestow the gifts He will give us when we are ready to accept them. It is not the eye that makes the light of the sun surround us; it is not the lung that makes the air envelop us. The light of the sun is there if we do not close our eyes to it, and the air is there for our lungs if we do not hold our breath. God's blessings are there—if we do not rebel against His will to give.

God does not show Himself equally to all creatures. This does not mean that He has favorites, that He decides to help some and to abandon others, but the difference occurs because it is impossible for Him to manifest Himself to certain hearts under the conditions they set up. The sunlight plays no favorites, but its reflection is very different on a lake and on a swamp.

A person's prayer often keeps step with one's moral life. The closer our behavior corresponds with the divine will, the easier it is to pray; the more our conduct is out of joint with Divinity, the harder it is to pray. Just as it is hard to look in the face of someone whom we have grievously wronged, so it is hard to lift our minds and hearts to God if we are in rebellion against Him. This is not because God is unwilling to hear sinners. He does hear them, and He has a special predilection for them, for as He said: "I have come to call sinners, not the just" (Mark 2:17). "There will be more rejoicing over one sinner who repents, than over ninety-nine souls that are justified and have no need of repentance" (Luke 15:7). But *these* sinners were the ones who corresponded with His will and abandoned their rebellion against it. Where the sinner has no desire to be lifted from evil habits, then the essential condition for prayer is wanting.

Everyone knows enough about God to pray to Him, even those who say they doubt His existence. If they were lost in the woods, they would have no assurance whatever of anyone nearby who might help them find their way—but they would shout, nevertheless, in the hope that someone would hear. In like manner, the skeptic finds, in catastrophe and in crisis, that though he thought himself incapable of prayer, he nonetheless prays. But those who use prayer only as a last resort do not know God very well—they hold Him at arm's length most of the time, refusing Him the intimacy of every day. The little knowledge of God that such people possess does not become fruitful or functional because they never act upon that knowledge: the Lord ordered that the unproductive talent be taken away. Unless a musician acts upon knowledge that he already has of music, he will not grow either in knowledge or in love of it. In this sense, our conduct, behavior, and moral life become the determinants of our relations with God. When our behavior is Godless, licentious, selfish, egotistic, and cruel, then prayer is an extraneous thing—a mere attempt at magic, an attempt to make God serve our wishes in contradiction to the moral laws He has laid down.

The man who thinks only of himself says only prayers of petition; he who thinks of his neighbor says prayers of intercession; he who thinks only of loving and serving God says prayers of abandonment to God's will, and this is the prayer of the saints. The price of this prayer is too high for most people, for it demands the displacement of our ego. Many souls want God to do *their* will; they bring their completed plans and ask Him to rubber-stamp them without a change. The petition of the Our Father is changed by them to read: "*My* will be done on earth." It is very difficult for the Eternal to give himself to those who are interested only in the temporal. The soul who lives on the ego-level or the I-level and refuses to be brought to the Divine-level is like an egg that is kept forever in a place too cool for incubation, so that it is never called upon to live a life outside the shell of its own incomplete development. Every I is still an embryo of what a person is meant to be.

Meditation

A HIGHER FORM of prayer than petition . . . is meditation. Meditation is a little like a daydream or a reverie, but with two important differences: in meditation we do not think about the world or ourselves, but about God. And instead of using the imagination to build idle castles in Spain, we use the will to make resolutions that will draw us nearer to one of the Father's mansions. Meditation is a more advanced spiritual act than "saying prayers"; it may be likened to the attitude of a child who breaks into the presence of a mother saying: "I'll not say a word if you will just let me stay here and watch you." Or, as a soldier once told the Curé of Ars: "I just stand here before the tabernacle; He looks at me and I look at Him."

Meditation allows one to suspend the conscious fight

against external diversions by an internal realization of the presence of God. It shuts out the world to let in the Spirit. It surrenders our own will to the impetus of the Divine Will. It turns the searchlight of Divine Truth on the way we think, act, and speak, penetrating beneath the layers of our self-deceit and egotism. It summons us before the bar of divine justice, so that we may see ourselves as we really are, and not as we like to think we are. It silences the ego with its clamorous demands, in order that it may hear the wishes of the Divine Heart. It uses our faculties, not to speculate on matters remote from God, but to stir up the will to conform more perfectly with His will. It cultivates a truly scientific attitude toward God as Truth, freeing us from our prepossessions and our biases so that we may eliminate all wishful thinking from our minds. It eliminates from our lives the things that would hinder union with God and strengthens our desire that all the good things we do shall be done for His honor and glory. It takes our eyes off the flux and change of life and reminds us of our *being,* the creatureliness, the dependence of all things on God for creation, moment-to-moment existence, and salvation. Meditation is not a petition, a way of using God, or asking things from Him, but rather a surrender, a plea to God that He use us.

Meditation has two stages—withdrawal from worldly consideration and concentration on the Nature of God and His Incarnate Son, Jesus Christ. Meditation uses three powers of the soul: the memory, the intellect, and the will. By memory we recall His goodness and our blessings; with the intellect we recall what is known of His life, truth, and love; by the will we strive to love Him above all else. When we study, we know about God; when we meditate, we know God's presence in ourselves, and we capture the very heart of our existence. So long as the ego or the I stands aloof from God, we are unhappy. But when our personality becomes lost in God's, so that His Mind is our mind, His desires are our desires, His loves are our loves—then the I realizes itself in self-forgetfulness. In the words of St. Paul:

"And yet I am alive; or rather, not I; it is Christ that lives in Me" (Galatians 2:20).

For meditation in the ear of the soul is more important than the tongue; St. Paul tells us that faith comes from listening. Most people commit the same mistake with God that they do with their friends: they do all the talking. Our Lord warned against those who "use many phrases, like the heathens, who think to make themselves heard by their eloquence" (Matthew 6:7). One can be impolite to God, too, by absorbing all the conversation, and by changing the words of Scripture from "Speak Lord, Thy servant hears" to "Listen Lord, Thy servant speaks." God has things to tell us that will enlighten us—we must wait for Him to speak. No one would rush into a physician's office, rattle off all the symptoms, and then dash away without waiting for a diagnosis; no one would tune in the radio and immediately leave the room. It is every bit as stupid to ring God's doorbell and then run away. The Lord hears us more readily than we suspect; it is our listening to Him that needs to be improved. When people complain that their prayers are not heard by God, what often has happened is that they did not wait to hear His answer.

Prayer, then, is not a monologue, but a dialogue. It is not a one-way street, but a boulevard. The child hears a word before he ever speaks it—his tongue is trained through the ear; so our soul, too, is trained through its ear. As Isaiah the Prophet said: "He wakeneth in the morning, in the morning he wakeneth my ear, that I may hear him as a master." St. Paul tells us that the Spirit will tell us for which things we ought to pray; as the Spirit brooded once over the formless waters, so now it brings spiritual expression to the voiceless void of our hearts. If our tongues are crude in their petitions, it is because our ears have been dull in their hearing of the faith. One of the important details of the Sacrament of Baptism is the opening of the ear: the priest touches it and says, as Our Lord did to the deaf man, "Eph-pheta; be thou opened." The words imply that once a soul is brought into the state of grace, the ears that were closed are open to the world of God. There is a more sublime philosophy than we suspect in our saying that we learned our prayers from our parents' *lips*. Prayer is arduous when it is only a monologue, but it is a joy when our self-absorption gives way to the act of humbly listening.

The Practical Effects of Meditation

BESIDES THE JOY it brings in itself, meditation has practical effects on our spiritual lives.

First, it cures us of the habit of self-deception. Man is the only creature on earth capable of self-reflection; this possibility exists because he has a rational soul. Since the soul is also spiritual, it has a longing for the infinite; we sometimes seek to slake our infinite thirst in the waters of the world—which have a glamor for us that is lacking in the things of God—and when this effort temporarily provides us with pleasure, we deceive ourselves. Meditation enables us to hold the mirror up to our souls, to perceive the fatal disease of self-love in the blinding light of the radiant Christ.

Because talk is a principal cause of self-deception, our friends dupe us with their flattery, and much of our inward conversation with ourselves is likely to be pitched on a note of self-justification. The silence that meditation demands is the best cure for this; in silence the workmen of the soul clear away its rubbish, as trash collectors clean our cities in the quiet night. Anyone awake at night sees his sins more clearly than in daylight; this is because the soul is now beyond the distraction of all noise. Sleeplessness is thus more of a burden to those with a sense of guilt than to the innocent, who, like the Psalmist, can raise their right thoughts to God in prayer.

Meditation provides an artificial quiet by shutting out the

sins of day. It replaces the criticism of others, which is probably our mental habit, by a self-criticism that will make us less critical of others. The one who will see the most faults in his neighbor is the one who has never looked inside his own soul. Unjustified criticism of others is self-flattery—for by finding others worse than ourselves, we become comparatively virtuous; but in meditation, by finding ourselves worse than others, we discover that most of our neighbors are better than ourselves. The poorer a man is, the greater the fortune of which he dreams; so, the humbler we are in our meditation, the higher the ideal to which we aspire. As there is no egotist who is not also a self-deceiver, so no one accustomed to meditate has any illusions as to his own grandeur. The clearer we see our souls in relation to God, the less egocentric we become.

There is a definite correlation between knowing God and knowing oneself: God cannot be known unless we know ourselves as we really are. The less a man thinks of himself, the more he thinks of God. God's greatness does not depend objectively on our littleness; but it becomes a subjective reality to us only if we are humble. As we make ourselves "gods," we perceive God less and less. The consciousness of our need for help in being good is the condition of knowing Goodness itself.

Meditation also improves our behavior. It is often stated that it makes no difference what we believe, that all depends on how we act; but this is meaningless, for we act upon our beliefs. Hitler acted on the theory of Nazism and produced a war; Stalin acted on the ideology of Marx and Lenin and begot slavery. If our thoughts are bad, our actions will also be bad. The problem of impure actions is basically the problem of impure thoughts; the way to keep a man from robbing a bank is to distract him from thinking about robbing a bank. Political, social, and economic injustices are, first, psychic evils—they originate in the mind. They become social evils because of the intensity of the thought that begot them.

Nothing ever happens in the world that does not first happen inside a mind. Hygiene is no cure for immorality, but if the wellsprings of thought were kept clean, there would be no need to care for the effects of evil thinking on the body. When one meditates and fills his mind for an hour a day with thoughts and resolutions bearing on the love of God and neighbor above all things, there is a gradual seepage of love down to the level of what is called the subconscious, and finally these good thoughts emerge, of themselves, in the form of effortless good actions.

Everyone has verified in his own life a thousand times the ideomotor character of thought. Watching a football game, the spectator sees a player running with the ball; if there is a beautiful opening around right end, he may twist and turn his own body more than the runner does, to try to take advantage of the chance. The idea is so strong that it influences his bodily movements—as ideas often do. Thoughts of fear produce goose pimples and sometimes make the blood rush to the hands and feet. God has made us so that, when we are afraid, we should either fight or run.

Our thoughts make our desires, and our desires are the sculptors of our days. The dominant desire is the predominant destiny. Desires are formed in our thoughts and meditations; and since action follows the lead of desires, the soul, as it becomes flooded with divine promptings, becomes less and less a prey to the suggestions of the world. This increases happiness, external wants are never completely satisfied, and their elimination thus makes for less anxiety. If a man meditates consistently on God, a complete revolution takes place in his behavior.

If in a morning meditation he remembers how God became a humble Servant of man, he will not lord it over others during the day. If there were a meditation of His Redemption of all men, he would cease to be a snob. Since Our Lord took the world's sins upon Himself, the man who has dwelt on this truth will seek to take up the burdens of his neighbor, even though they were not of his making—for the sins the Lord bore were not of His making, either. If the meditation stressed the merciful Savior Who forgave those who crucified Him, so a man will forgive those who injure him, that he may be worthy of forgiveness. These thoughts do not come from ourselves—for we are incapable of them—nor from the world—for they are unworldly thoughts. They come from God alone.

Meditation effects far more profound changes in us than resolutions to "do better"; we cannot keep evil thoughts out of our minds unless we put good ones in their place. Super-nature, too, abhors a vacuum. In meditation one does not *drive* sin out of one's life; one *crowds* it out with the love of God and neighbor. Our lives do not then depend on the principle of avoiding sin, which is a tiresome job, but on living constantly in the climate of Divine Love. Meditation, in a word, prevents defeat where defeat is final: in the mind. In that silence where God is, false desires steal away. If we meditate before we go to bed, our last thought at night will be our first thought in the morning. There will be none of that dark brown feeling with which some persons face a meaningless day; and in its place will be the job of beginning another morning of work in Christ's name.

As a third largesse, meditation gives us contact with new sources of power and energy. "Come to me, all you that labor and are burdened; I will give you rest" (Matthew 11:28). No one has sufficient knowledge and power to carry him through all the difficulties and trials of living. We think we have sufficient wisdom when we give advice to others; but we learn we do not have it when we have to live on our own intellectual fat. The more an orchestra plays, the more it has to be tuned up; the farther an airplane flies, the more it needs to be serviced. When our spiritual batteries run down, we cannot charge them by ourselves; and the more active the life is, the greater the need to vitalize its acts by meditation.

But each meditation must be personalized—brought from

the realm of thought and reduced to a lesson we ourselves are able to apply. No man is better because he knows the five proofs for the existence of God; but he becomes better when that knowledge is permitted to transform his will. Purity of heart is therefore the condition of prayer; we cannot be intimate with God so long as we cling to unlawful attachments. The needed purity must be fourfold: purity of conscience, so that we will never offend God; purity of heart, so that we keep all our affections for God; purity of mind, so that we preserve a continual consciousness of God; and purity of action, so that we keep our intentions selfless and abandon our self-will.

Once our helplessness is rendered up to the power of God, life changes, and we become less and less the victims of our moods. Instead of letting the world determine our state of mind, we determine the state of soul with which the world is to be faced. The earth carries its own atmosphere with it as it revolves about the sun; so the soul can carry the atmosphere of God with it, in disregard of turbulent events in the world outside. There is a moment in every good meditation when the God-life enters our life, and another moment when our life enters the God-life. These events transform us utterly. Sick, nervous, fearful persons are made well by this communion of creature with Creator, this letting of God into the soul.

The Christ-Centered Life

A CHRIST-CENTERED LIFE does not mean a life in which one sings hymns, reads Scripture, and edifies one's neighbors by hanging texts on the walls. One does not become a Christian by doing a good deed a day, not by go-getting for religion, nor by engaging in economic and political reform movements, even though these things are done from the noblest of human motives. A Christian is one who, believing that Christ is the Son of God, has that Christ life in his or her soul.

The difference between a truly Christian life and a good human life is like the difference between a rose and a crystal—a difference in levels of living. "He who refuses to believe in the Son will never see life." (John 3:36.) *Omne vivum ex vivo.* Life must always come from life—it cannot emerge from the inanimate. Human life must come from human parents, and Divine Life must be fathered by the Divine. The possibility of supernatural life was brought to fallen man through the Incarnation, when we were redeemed. For justice to be done, the Redeemer of man had to be both God and man: He had to be a man, for otherwise He could not have acted in our name as representing us; He had also to be God, for otherwise He could not have paid the infinite debt owed to God by human sin. God did not forcibly take this human nature from mankind; He accepted it as the free gift of a woman, Mary, whose free answer to the angel messenger was: "Be it done unto me according to Thy Word."

Once in possession of His human nature, He offered it as a sacrifice for all the guilt due from human sin. Just as a kind father may pay the debts of a wayward offspring, so the heavenly Father had sent His Divine Son to pay our moral debts and so restore us into the loving relationship with the Father which we had broken in the Fall. Though Our Lord's human nature was sinless, it was, in the strong language of St. Paul, "made sin." Assuming our bankruptcy, He began the work of mankind's spiritual rehabilitation.

To understand how this could be, we may consider the analogy of a chalice; suppose that a chalice that has been used daily in the Holy Sacrifice of the Mass is stolen and beaten into a beer mug and delivered over to profane uses. Before it can be used again on the altar, it must be put into the fire and have its debased form burned away. Then it must be re-formed into the shape of a chalice. Finally, when it has been blessed and consecrated, it can be restored to the service of God.

That chalice is like our human nature: it was once well ordered, with its sense subjected to reason, its reason to faith, its body to soul, and the whole personality oriented to God. Then by a free act, human nature turned away from God to self-love. To undo this cosmic damage the Son of God took a sinless human nature from Mary and onto its purity grafted all the sins of the world, so that it was as if He Himself were guilty of them. It was this guilt and sin, frustration and fear that Our Lord felt as His own and that produced His bloody sweat in the Garden. To save us all, He plunged that human nature into the fires of Calvary so that all the evil shape of sin might be burned and destroyed. Beaten and hammered, made to suffer the greatest ignominy that sin could inflict—the Crucifixion of the Son of God—Our Lord rose again on the third day with a perfected human nature. Mankind is now restored to its supernatural destiny—but only if it keeps in contact with our Redeemer, uses His glorified humanity as the die or the pattern upon which we are to be cast.

This involves what is known as incorporation; for we do not become one with Christ by reading about Him or by thinking about Him or by admiring His Sermon on the Mount or by studying biographies of His times. Union with Him is a vital process, a participation in Him: "What is born by natural birth is a thing of nature; what is born by spiritual birth is a thing of the spirit." (John 3:6) The spiritual life is the gift of the living spirit of Christ, Who prolongs Himself in His Mystical Body and diffuses His life through its seven life-giving channels.

This new life starts with a birth: "A man cannot see the kingdom of God without being born anew." (John 3:3) For the economy of salvation is such that God descended to us in order that we might ascend to Him. He has presented us with an opportunity to become something higher than we are in nature—to become participants in His own Divine Life. He became the new head of the human race, as Adam was the old head; as we were descended from Adam by physical birth, so we can become incorporated to Christ by a spiritual birth. One of the effects of this incorporation—which St. Paul mentions—is that our bodies become the Temples of God; on this fact, St. Paul bases his appeal for purity, because the Temple of God should never be profaned.

The aim of Christian living is to make our own, to the fullest possible degree, the objective salvation that was given us by Christ. He brought salvation to us objectively, in all fullness and perfection; but the individual's free cooperation is still necessary for its fuller application and final perfection in his own soul. It is as if each of us had a fortune placed to our account in the bank; if we did not write checks on it, it would not help us very much to have it there. Subjective salvation is our free acceptance of the chance to become something we are not by nature— adopted sons of God. This is the beginning of a constant assimilation of His grace and vital strength; it brings forth fruit in the Christian's daily life and an ever-increasing vital fellowship with Him, through which the mystical body of Christ grows and develops.

Man is distinguished from the animals by the possession of a rational soul that gives him his special human dignity. It is fitting that the principal effects of the infusion of Divine energy should be manifested in the two main faculties of the soul—the intellect and the will. Once the Divine Power penetrates the intellect, it becomes Faith; once it infuses the will, it becomes Hope and Charity. Thus are born the three great supernatural virtues, by which we can believe in God and know Him and love Him.

It is the intellect that first feels the impact of the Christian life. Sanctifying Grace perfects the reason by the infusion of a new light. Just as the sun illumines our senses and the light of reason enlightens our human nature, so the light of

Faith illumines our ways in relationship to God. Faith is as necessary for complete human living as light is for sight: we have the same eyes at night as during the day, but we are not able to see at night because we lack the light of the sun. Two individuals with the same intellectual gifts see differently if one has faith and the other lacks it: gazing on a divine reality, such as Our Lord in the Holy Eucharist, one sees Emanuel, or God with us, and the other sees only bread. It is because one of them has a light that the other lacks.

This new light is to our reason what the telescope is to the eye. The telescope does not destroy the eye, nor does it create new worlds, but it enables the eye to see realities that, although they were there before, the naked eye could never reach. To a person who does not "believe in" telescopes, it would seem that the astronomer is merely imagining the things he says he sees—that in describing distant stars and planets he is the victim of a superstition. It is not uncommon for those who lack the gift of Faith to attribute all belief in the supernatural world to imagination or to fantasy.

Faith is also like a microscope in that it enables us to perceive a deeper meaning in truths that we already know; it gives a new dimension of depth to our natural knowledge. Knowledge without Faith is often made up of bits of information, jumbled in a heap, like steel filings in a random pile; Faith, like a magnet, marshals them in order. Faith takes out uncorrelated facts and relates them to a single unity. Thanks to its illumination, the intellect now has a new solid frame for judging and estimating all the various segments of reality. The world is now seen from the Divine point of view, and through the Christ-mind.

The Hound of Heaven

FRANCIS THOMPSON, the author of the poem "The Hound of Heaven," had been, on various occasions, a medical student, a bootblack, a newsboy, a vendor of matches, a dope fiend, a nocturnal denizen of the wharves, a vagrant amidst the rubbish and garbage of Covent Garden, and a poet, all before he was thirty. But within three years after his death, fifty thousand copies of "The Hound of Heaven" were sold, apart from anthologies, and less than thirty years after its publication, it was being studied at Tokyo University.

The world is full of literature that describes the story of man in pursuit of God; this poem narrates the drama of God in pursuit of man. Herein lies the difference between all Eastern religions and the Christian tradition. In all the Oriental religions, the direction is from man to God. Man goes to God through submission to His absolute will or through contemplation of Divine truth or through asceticism and successive births. In our modern religion, man goes to God through a kind of bootstrap religion, lifting himself up to Divinity by means of his own self-confidence. None of these forms of religion makes the supreme demand, not only because in them there is no sense of sin or guilt, but also because, if man seeks God, he can set his own pace, determining his own withdrawals and interruptions.

But, in the Divine religion, it is God Who comes to man. God is the great disturber. Man is not a twig in a torrent; he is free in the face of the summons of Divinity, either to create his own character or else to rebel against what is ultimately his peace and perfection. Man can set limits to the pace when he is in search of God, but when God pursues, there is a relentlessness. It is an extremely uncomfortable feeling to be pursued by the Hound of Heaven. As Claudel said, "The agonies that go on inside the soul far surpass in intensity the battles of the world. Here it is the heart, and not the face, that issues from the conflict smeared with blood."

The Hound of Heaven is God—a daring symbol used to indicate the inescapable character of the pursuit. The title may have been suggested by Shelley's *Prometheus Unbound,* in which occur the words "heaven's winged hound." "The Hound of Heaven" is the story of escapism. Escapism is the avoidance of confrontation with Divinity, a running away from the Hound of Heaven. It is a flight, a continuous rationalization adopted in order to escape responsibility. Escapism may take on many forms: in youth it may be found in the restlessness of uncontrolled passion; in maturity, it may lie in absorption with business or the pursuit of power and prestige. Very often, what is avarice in old age is nothing but the sublimation of the lust of youth.

Sometimes the escapists are so conscious of the falsity of their position that they attribute escapism to those who surrender to the Hound of Heaven. When a thousand men are running toward an abyss into which they are about to throw themselves, someone going in the opposite direction, away from destruction, may seem to them to have lost the way.

The major means of escape in the poem "The Hound of Heaven" are four:

1. The unconscious mind.
2. Illegitimate love or sex.
3. Children.
4. Naturalism or science.

The first is escape within the mind itself, which Thompson compares to a labyrinth. The unconscious mind is very often a kind of hell, a self-damnation before damnation, a whirlpool or an abyss. Many a modern author says that he or she writes a book, not in order to remember, but in order to forget.

Until recently, man had managed to have various escapes outside of himself, but the plunge into the unconscious self is the last and final flight from God. The new psychology offers man an escape from the responsibility of being guilty, almost an escape from the responsibility of being human. In the Garden of Paradise, man hid from God in the garden; now man hides within himself. In this state he regards it as bad taste to speak of God.

The popularity of depth psychology has given man a chance to live in another dimension than the purely horizontal one of the earth. In the days of faith, man lived in a three dimensional *universe:* heaven was above, hell below, and the earth between the two was a mere anteroom in which he would say aye or nay to eternal destiny. As these eternal verities slipped away, there was left the flat surface of the earth; an escape was sought by picturing three dimensions inside the mind; for heaven there was substituted superego; for earth, there was the ego; and for hell there was the id. The most important part of the mind was now the cavernous depth of the unconscious that man could dig into, explore, and analyze, in the hope of unearthing new mysteries or else of stirring up latent energies and powers that would bring peace. Thompson describes the serpentine ways of the mind, with its fears and glooms, in his opening words:

> I fled Him down the nights and down the days;
>   I fled Him, down the arches of the years;
>   I fled Him, down the labyrinthine ways
>   Of my own mind, and in the mist of tears
> I hid from Him, and under running laughter.
>   Up vistaed hopes I sped;
>   And shot, precipitated,
> Adown Titanic glooms of chasmèd fears,
>   From those strong Feet that followed, followed after.

Modern man makes every possible attempt to explain away the Hound of Heaven. "It is just a father complex," he says. "It is all in the mind." But the search for peace within self is doomed to failure. The two loneliest places in the world are a strange city and one's own ego. When man is alone with his own thoughts and with his false independence from the Love who made him, he is keeping bad company. True peace can come only by the breaking of this circle of egotism. But the feet of the Hound of Heaven pursue us, wherever we are.

> But with unhurrying chase,
> And unperturbèd pace,
> Deliberate speed, majestic instancy,
> They beat—and a Voice beat
> More instant that the Feet—
> "All things betray thee, who betrayest Me."

In literature few represent this escape better than Franz Kafka, who was born in Prague on July 3, 1883. He was gradually alienated from the world in which he lived, from the business in which he worked, and finally, alienated by tuberculosis from the woman he intended to marry. To him there was no such thing as individual personality; hence many characters in his books are known merely by initials, for instance, Joseph K. The author centered his narratives within his own mind. Although Kafka was an explorer of human conditions, his world was his own mind; but as he plunged inward to the lonesome self he did not burn himself in his own flame.

His consciousness of God seemed to aggravate his own moral isolation, in which he, too, felt the pursuit of the Hound of Heaven. There was no escaping from the Eternal, even by running backward. "A man was astonished how easily he went the eternal way, he happened to be rushing backward along it."

Love is the next lair in which the poet sought to escape the Hound of Heaven. The love here is depicted as illegiti-

mate love, such as Thompson had for the woman who befriended him, a hopeless beggar on London's streets, whom
he described as a "flower fallen from the budded coronal of
Spring." In the wider context, the escape stands for those
carnal and lustful pleasures that man enjoys when he becomes a law unto himself, an "outlaw" from God.

Sex is represented by Thompson as a little casement window in the shape of a heart, like one that he saw once in the
home of a girl he was courting in northern England. The
vines that cling to the window shutter symbolize the vagrant and restless loves. In contrast with that window is the
great, strong wind that symbolizes the boundless love of
the Hound of Heaven. But the poet feared that God was in
competition with the human heart, and that to be in love
with God meant the surrender of human love. Unmindful
he was that He Who has the Flame also has the spark, He
who is Infinite Love understands *all* love, however small
and imperfect. Despite his fight, he found that heaven's
love was like a great wind that closed the window of sex
each time he thought he could escape through it. But the
poet says that he was not as skilled in escape as the Hound
was skilled in pursuit.

> *I pleaded, outlaw-wise,*
> *By many a hearted casement, curtained red,*
> *Trellised with intertwining charities;*
> *(For, though I knew His love Who followed,*
> *Yet was I sore adread*
> *Lest, having Him, I must have naught beside)*
> *But, if one little casement parted wide,*
> *The gust of His approach would clash it to.*
> *Fear wist not to evade, as Love wist to pursue.*

An illustration of this escape is provided by the French
poet Arthur Rimbaud. He was born on October 20, 1854,
and from his seventeenth to his twentieth year he wrote poetry of outstanding beauty. But at the age of twenty he
abandoned poetry completely. Rimbaud was a precocious
boy with golden hair, blue eyes, and full lips—the kind of

face that one always associates with innocence. But his boy-
hood innocence soon degenerated into a pattern of vicious-
ness, vileness, and dissipation. He became cruel, egotis-
tical, vicious, drunken, and perverted.

Expressing the nineteenth-century desire to be free from
all shackles and to identify liberty with license, and in a
thoroughly drunken and sulky condition, he went to live
with his poet friend, Verlaine. The liaison soon wrecked
Verlaine's marriage. At that time, he would invent stories
that were so lewd, and attribute to himself such repulsive
actions, that those who overheard him in restaurants would
walk out in disgust. Then came the yearning for innocence.
In his work, *A Season in Hell*, he said: "I am no longer in
love with boredom, frenzies, debauches, madness—how
well I know its outburst and disasters—all my burden is
laid down."

Though he had flouted and blasphemed God, nevertheless, he was always conscious of Him. But it was the God-
consciousness of the damned. Finally he gave up the old
visions that surrounded him, particularly the vision of hell,
and he retained the vision of angelic beauty. He finally
received the sacraments, and the lost poetry came back. He
said: "Reason has been born within me. The world is good.
I shall give life my blessing, I shall love my brethren. These
are no longer the promises of a child. God is my strength,
and I praise God."

The next escape of Thompson's poem is by way of children. Though Thompson had none, he was very fond of
them, and in them saw the innocence he had lost. At the
time Thompson wrote "The Hound of Heaven," he was
recovering from the dope habit. At a rest home he met a
little girl, whose last name is unknown. In a poem dedicated to her, she is called Daisy. He said later that "she did
not know the hell that was in my soul; she only knew that
softness was in my gaze." The poem is about the hopeless
bliss that an innocent child awakens in the heart of a man
who has lost his way of life:

> *She listened with big-lipped surprise*
> *Breast-deep 'mid flower and spine:*
> *Her skin was like a grape whose veins*
> *Run snow instead of wine. . . .*

> *Her beauty smoothed earth's furrowed face.*
> *She gave me tokens three:—*
> *A look, a word of her winsome mouth,*
> *And a wild raspberry.*

Then comes the sad note: innocence never seems to know that it is loved, and quickly Daisy will leave, forgetting all—but he will never forget.

> *The fairest things have fleetest end,*
> *Their scent survives their close:*
> *But the rose's scent is bitterness*
> *To him that loved the rose. . . .*

> *She left me marveling why my soul*
> *Was sad that she was glad;*
> *At all the sadness in the sweet,*
> *The sweetness in the sad.*

In another poem, dedicated to little Olivia, the seventh of the Meynell children, [Thompson had been befriended by Alice and Wilfred Meynell] he expresses a fear of loving because it makes the heart capable of being hurt:

> *I fear to love thee, Sweet, because*
> *Love's the ambassador of loss;*
> *White flake of childhood, clinging so*
> *To my soiled raiment, thy shy snow*
> *At tenderest touch will shrink and go.*
> *Love me not, delightful child.*
> *My heart, by many snares beguiled,*
> *Has grown timorous and wild.*
> *It would fear thee not at all,*
> *Wert thou not so harmless-small.*
> *Because thy arrows, not yet dire,*
> *Are still unbarned with destined fire,*
> *I fear thee more than hadst thou stood*
> *Full panoplied in womanhood.*

But in the great poem he tells how he sought to escape from the Hound of Heaven through children:

> *I sought no more that, after which I strayed,*
> *In face of man or maid;*
> *But still within the little children's eyes*
> *Seems something, something that replies,*
> *They at least are for me, surely for me!*
> *I turned me to them very wistfully;*
> *But just as their young eyes grew sudden fair*
> *With dawning answers there,*
> *Their angel plucked them from me by the hair.*

The final escape is through a naturalism that is either a poetic and pagan revelry in nature or else a more scientific interest in its laws:

> *Across the margent of the world I fled,*
> *And troubled the gold gateways of the stars,*
> *Smiting for shelter on their clangèd bars. . . .*
>
> *I said to Dawn: Be sudden—to Eve: Be soon;*
> *With thy young skiey blossoms heap me over*
> *From this tremendous Lover!*
> *Float thy vague veil about me, lest He see!*
> *I tempted all His servitors, but to find*
> *My own betrayal in their constancy,*
> *In faith to Him their fickleness to me,*
> *Their traitorous trueness, and their loyal deceit. . . .*
> *Drew the bolt of Nature's secrecies.*
> *I knew all the swift importings*
> *On the willful face of skies;*
> *I knew how the clouds arise*
> *Spumèd of the wild sea-snortings;*
> *All that's born or dies*
> *Rose and drooped with; made them shapers*
> *Of mine own moods, or wailful or divine;*
> *With them joyed and was bereaven.*
> *I was heavy with the even,*
> *When she lit her glimmering tapers*
> *Round the day's dead sanctities.*
> *I laughed in the morning's eyes.*

I triumphed and I saddened with all weather,
　　Heaven and I wept together,
And its sweet tears were salt with mortal mine;
Against the red throb of its sunset-heart
　I laid my own to beat,
　And share commingling heat; ·
But not by that, by that, was eased my human smart.
In vain my tears were wet on Heaven's grey cheek.
　For ah! we know not what each other says,
　These things and I; in sound I speak—
Their *sound is but their stir, they speak by silences.*
Nature, poor stepdame, cannot slake my drouth;
　Let her, if she would owe me,
Drop yon blue bosom-veil of sky, and show me
　The breasts o' her tenderness:
Never did any milk of hers once bless
　My thirsting mouth.
　Nigh and nigh draws the chase.
　With unperturbèd pace,
　Deliberate speed, majestic instancy;
　　And past those noisèd Feet
　　A Voice comes yet more fleet—
"Lo! naught contents thee, who content'st not Me."

This description fits those who abandon the old authori-
ties and take refuge in science. By the beginning of the
twentieth century, many had begun to doubt science as a
substitute for value. The more they studied its regulated
knowledge, the greater became the sense of man's abysmal
limitations. Even the physical laws were uncertain, and
there was hardly any scientific theory of the last thirty years
that still remained unchallenged. Furthermore, science
seemed to create a chaos in which man felt himself infinitely alone. Added to this was the difficulty to the individual of reducing himself to a merely mechanical agent. To
abandon oneself to science was to invite degradation. Those
who had pursued science admitted its inadequacy. Darwin
regretted very much that his dedication to science had
killed entirely his taste for both music and poetry, which he

had loved as a university student. Wallace, the naturalist, said to his wife at his death: "Not even the consolation and joy of one of the loveliest women ever made is enough to bring solace to me now: I see before me a Light, which I should have pursued, but which I have not now enough strength to reach out and grasp."

H. G. Wells, above all others, expressed the escape of science. Drugs would cause tiny creatures to grow very quickly to a giant size; rats would become wolves. Progress would inevitably result from a planned world of eugenics, mechanized labor, scientific diets, scientific education. The world was to be made up of airships, propellers, and men in shorts. Wells summoned men to a citizenship of a world that was not limited and boxed in by Creation and the Day of Judgment, but which had unlimited possibilities. Man would become a kind of god, and there would be no more disease or death.

But at the end, he saw the futility of it all, and because he ignored the Hound of Heaven, he fell into despair. Man, who came from the cave and became scientific, would go back into a cave, which was an air-raid shelter. Because he had never been humble enough to recognize the Hound in pursuit, his hopelessness was complete: "In spite of all my disposition to a brave-looking optimism, I perceive that now the universe is bored with man, is turning a hard face to him, and I see him being carried less and less intelligently and more and more rapidly . . . along the stream of fate to degradation, suffering, and death." He who began by picturing man as a biological accident now ends by picturing him as a biological catastrophe. The star-begotten superman has let us down, and there is no Hound in pursuit.

Looking back on a wasted life, Thompson saw all the treasured honey of his life spent, and no new life to show. Then he compared himself to Samson, who, in the Temple of Dagon, the Philistine god, reached out his giant arms and shook the pillars until the roof fell in and he and the

Philistines perished. So the hours of Thompson's life were likened to the pillars he had pulled down upon himself, and now he lay beneath the ruins. It is noteworthy that he did not blame his father, his mother, or his failure at medicine; he took the full responsibility. The ruins were his, and not those of Oedipus or Electra.

> *In the rash lustihead of my young powers,*
> *I shook the pillaring hours*
> *And pulled my life upon me: grimed with smears,*
> *I stand amid the dust o' the mounded years—*
> *My mangled youth lies dead beneath the heap.*

A moment comes when there are no carnal desires left, when all the staffs upon which he had leaned now pierce his hand: the Hound of Heaven has caught up with him in his emptiness. None of those things in which he has trusted can now act as a shield against the Sword of Love.

> *Naked I wait Thy love's uplifted stroke!*
> *My harness piece by piece Thou hast hewn from me,*
> *And smitten me to my knee;*
> *I am defenseless utterly. . . .*

If his emptiness and barrenness had been abnormal, at this point he should have gone to a psychiatrist. But being normal, he wanted to be saved from the ruins. And at this precise point the struggle began. Everyone wants to be saved on three conditions:

1. That there will have to be no admission of guilt or sin.
2. That it be done in our way, not God's.
3. That it be done at not too great a cost. We must not be denied a preserve of forbidden fruit.

But there is no peace without war, and the Hound of Heaven now appears, demanding sacrifice of all that is evil in us. He who summons appears in blood-stained garments and crowned with thorns, "enwound with glooming robes purpureal, cypress-crowned." Then follow all the questions a soul asks before it makes the surrender, questions that are not asked so much for the sake of answers, as to delay the moment of decision.

First, is His love like one of those weeds that draw up all the moisture about it and thus prevent any other flower from blooming? Does He kill other joys in promising joy?

> *Ah, is Thy love indeed*
> *A weed, albeit an amaranthine weed,*
> *Suffering no flowers except its own to mount?*

Changing the metaphor, he now inquires from the "cypress-crowned" King if He can do nothing with a soul unless he subject it to the burning penance. Is His love like a piece of wood that must be thrown into the fires of self-denial and penance before it can become charcoal and be fit to be used in drawing a portrait?

> *Ah, must—*
> *Designer infinite!—*
> *Ah; must Thou char the wood ere Thou canst limn with it?*

Shelley has put the same thought in these words: "Is there no drinking of pearls except they be dissolved in biting tears?"

Thompson fears the surrender. He knows that the pulp of his youth has been a failure; will his old age be a failure too?

> *The pulp so bitter, how shall taste the rind?*

The final query is the most dramatic of all. Each winter the farmer spreads fertilizer upon the field to prepare for a richer harvest in the springtime. Is the love of Christ like that too? Must there be the Cross before the crown, death before life?

> *Whether man's heart or life it be which yields*
> *Thee harvest, must Thy harvest fields*
> *Be dunged with rotten death?*

Though it is not generally known, Nietzsche, in his loneliness and beyond all his denials, invoked the company of the God he had denied [*Thus Spake Zarathustra*]:

Away!
There fled he surely,
My final, only comrade,
My greatest foe,
Mine unfamiliar—
My hangman God . . .
—Nay! Come thou back!
With all thy great tortures!
To the last of all lonesome ones,
Oh, come thou back!
All my hot tears in streamlets trickle
Their course to thee! . . .
Oh, come thou back!
Mine unknown God! My pain!
My Final Bliss!

Man's ideas of God are not always accurate. Therefore, the atheism of a man such as Nietzsche and his consequent denial of Christianity contain a truth insofar as they reject a false idea of God. Sometimes this rejection is a necessary step toward one's return to God.

There is something hidden in man that is like the brand that was put upon Cain when he killed his brother Abel, the mark of mercy that shows that man, even when he is evil, is protected by God.

Man is like the horned toad, a very ugly animal, which has a constant drive to return to its origins. Some people have taken a horned toad fifty miles away from home and marked it in order to be sure that, if it returned, it would be the same toad. After weeks and weeks it always comes back to the rock under their house. Man is like that toad, twisted and grotesque, torn away from God, but really wanting to go home. As the trees twist and turn in the forest in order to be in the sunlight, so man is constantly twisting and turning in order to recover his origin and return to his home.

Those who think that religion is an escape should try the Cross. There are various kinds of cheap mysticism, expressing themelves in drama and poetry in which the soul is in perpetual search of God. There is, however, seldom any depth to these because they allow the heart to be complacent. Thompson takes the reverse step: it is not a soul searching for God but, far more terrible, God searching for the soul. Very few people know what they are letting themselves in for when this happens. There can be nothing leisurely about what follows. In the cheaper mysticism of man's approach to God everybody knows the questions but nobody wants to know the answers.

The questions are now answered by the Hound of Heaven:

> "Strange, piteous, futile thing.
> Wherefore should any set thee love apart?
> Seeing none but I make much of naught" (He said),
> "And human love need human meriting:
>   How hast thou merited—
> Of all man's clotted clay, the dingiest clot?
>   Alack, thou knowest not
> How little worthy of any love thou art!
> Whom wilt thou find to love ignoble thee,
>   Save Me, save only Me?
> All which I took from thee I did but take,
>   Not for thy harms,
> But just that thou might'st seek it in My arms.
>   All which thy child's mistake
> Fancies at lost, I have stored for thee at home:
>   Rise, clasp My hand and come!"

Finally come some of the most consoling words ever written to those who suffer. Inspired by the fact that there would never be a shadow if there were no light, and hence never a sorrow were there not a Hand to wipe away the tears, the poet asks:

> Is my gloom, after all,
> Shade of His hand, outstretched caressingly?

Pleasure

BECAUSE PLEASURE is the supreme goal of all egotistic living, it is fitting that we should know something of its laws. The very fury with which modern men and women seek pleasure is the strongest proof that they have not found it; for if the streets of our city were filled with clanging ambulances, and the hospitals were jammed to capacity, and doctors and nurses were running about madly, there would be a strong suspicion that health had not yet been found. Pleasure as a life goal is a mirage—no one reaches it. But it is possible to enjoy stable, refreshing pleasures provided that one knows their laws.

The first law of pleasure is that it is like beauty: it is conditioned by contrast. A woman in white, if she has any esthetic sense, would rather stand before a black curtain than a white one. Similarly, every pleasure, to be enjoyed, must come as a sort of treat, as a surprise. The kind of pleasure that evokes laughter is an example: incidents that are not funny on the street are hilarious in Church because of their contrast with the seriousness of the ritual—a man with his hat on the side of his head in the street does not provoke laughter, but a bishop with a miter on the side of his head does.

The condition of having a good time is that one shall not be always trying to have a good time. There is no fun in life if everything is funny. . . . Many people miss pleasure because they seek nothing else, thereby removing the first condition of enjoyment, which is contrast. In the liturgy of the Church, there is a constant contrast between joy and sacrifice, between fast and feast. Even during the seasons of Lent and Advent, when there are penance and pain, the

Church inserts a Laetare and a Gaudete Sunday, on which we are called to rejoice. She does this, first of all, to remind people that penance is not perpetual and, secondly, to prevent them from getting into a psychological rut.

The second law of pleasure is that no pleasure ever becomes our permanent possession until it has passed through a moment of pain. No one ever gets his second wind until he has used up his first wind; one never enjoys reading the Latin classics until he has survived the tedium of grammar and declensions; to swim is a thrill, but only after the shock of the first cold plunge. Even the joys of eternity are conditioned by this law, for unless there is a Good Friday in life, there will never be an Easter Sunday; unless there is a crown of thorns, there will never be the halo of light; and unless there is a Cross, there will never be the empty tomb. In our temporal concerns, too, the law prevails. In marriage, it is only after the first misunderstanding has been survived that people begin to discover the beautiful joy of being together.

The third law of pleasure is this: Every quest for pleasure is fundamentally a striving for the infinite. Every pleasure attracts us because we hope, by savoring it, to get a foretaste of something that will exceed it in intensity and joy. One bird, one star, one book should be enough to fill the hunger of a person, but it is not; we find no satisfaction in anything because our appetites are formed for everything. Like a great vessel that is launched, man moves insecurely in shallow waters, being made to skim the sea. To ask man to stop short of anything save the infinite is to nullify his nature; our greed for good is greater than the earth can gratify. All love of poetry is a cry, a moan, and a weeping; the more sublime and the truer it is, the deeper is its lament. If the joy of attaining something for which we longed ravishes the mind for an hour, it reverts, by evening, to the immensity of its still-unfulfilled desires.

Our hunger for the infinite is never quieted; even those disillusioned by excess of pleasures have always kept in their imagination a hope of somewhere finding a truer source of satisfaction than any they have tried. Our search for the never-ending love is never ended—no one could really love anything unless he thought of it as eternal. Not everyone gives a name to this infinity toward which he tends and for which he yearns, but it is what the rest of us call God.

The pursuit of pleasure is thus a token of man's higher nature, a symptom of his loneliness in this world. Torn between what he has, which surfeits him, and the far-off Transcendent, which attracts him, every worldly man stands in grave danger of self-hatred and despair until he finds his true Infinite in God. As Pascal put it: "The knowledge of God without a perception of man's misery causes pride, and the knowledge of man's misery without a perception of God causes despair. Knowledge of Jesus Christ constitutes the middle course because in Him we find both God and our own misery."

Until a man has discovered the true Infinite, he is invariably led from subjectivism—the setting up of his ego as the absolute—to hedonism—the philosophy of a life given solely to sensate pleasures. When a man starts with the assumption that his selfish wishes must be held supreme, that nothing beyond the ego is significant, then it follows that the only standards by which he will be able to judge the worth of any experience are its pleasurableness and its intensity. The more he feels something, the truer and more admirable it will be.

There is a fallacy, however, lurking behind the hedonist's assumption that the motivation of every action is pleasure, for if this were the case, no hedonist would be moving about today; he would have lain on the ground and refused to stir the first time he fell down and hurt himself as a child. A baby with barked shins does not get up and try, again, to toddle, out of a search for pleasure, but because its drive to develop human capacities overcomes its desire for the pleasure of lying supinely on the floor. Pleasure is actually a by-product of duty, and it evades direct pursuit. It is like the bloom on the cheek, as Aristotle has told us; the bloom is not something men try to develop but is the by-product of a healthy organism.

Working

VERY FEW PEOPLE in this age do the kind of work they like to do. Instead of choosing their jobs from choice, they are forced by economic necessity to work at tasks that fail to satisfy them. Many of them say, "I ought to be doing something bigger," or "This job of mine is important only because I get paid." Such an attitude lies at the bottom of much unfinished and badly executed work. The man who chooses his work because it fulfills a purpose he approves is the only one who grows in stature by working. He alone can properly say, at the end of it, "It is finished!"

This sense of vocation is sadly lacking nowadays. The blame should not be placed on the complexity of our economic system, but on a collapse of our spiritual values. Any work, viewed in its proper perspective, can be used to ennoble us; but a necessary prelude to seeing this is to understand the philosophy of labor.

Every task we undertake has two aspects—our purpose, which makes us think it worth doing, and the work itself, regarded apart from its end-purpose. We play tennis to get exercise; but we play the game as well as possible just for the joy of doing the thing well. The man who argued that he could get as much exercise by sloppy technique on the courts would have missed an understanding of the second aspect of all activity, the accomplishment of the task in accordance with its own standards of excellence. In the same way, a man working in an automobile factory may have, as his primary purpose, the earning of wages; but the purpose of the work itself is the excellent completion of the task. A worker should be aware of the second purpose at all times—as the artist is aware of the aim of beauty in his or her painting. . . .

Today the first aspect of working has become paramount, and we tend to ignore the second . . . so that many workers lead half-lives in their laboring hours. They are like gardeners, ordered to grow cabbage to give them sauerkraut juice, but indifferent as to whether their plots are weeded properly or their cabbages are healthy vegetables. This is a mistaken attitude: God Himself worked when He made the world and then, viewing it, He called it good.

The legitimate pride in doing work well relieves it of much of its drudgery. Some people, who have held to this craftsman's standard, get a thrill from any job they do. They know the satisfaction of a job well done whether they are engaged in caning a chair or cleaning a horse's stall or carving a statue for a cathedral. Their honor and their self-respect are heightened by the discipline of careful work. They have retained the old attitude of the Middle Ages, when work was a sacred event, a ceremony, a source of spiritual merit. Labor was not then undertaken merely for the sake of economic gain, but was chosen through an inner compulsion, through a desire to project the creative power of God through our own human effort.

No task should be undertaken in a spirit that ignores either of these two primary aspects of work. To link together the two things . . . the joy of making a table well with the purpose of making it at all, which is to earn a living . . . the following principles should be kept in mind:

1. Work is a moral duty and not, as many people imagine, a mere physical necessity. St. Paul said, *"The man who refuses to work must be left to starve."* When work is seen as a moral duty, it is apparent that it not only contributes to the social good, but also performs further services to the worker: it prevents the idleness from which many evils can

arise, and it also keeps the body in subjection to the reasoned will.

2. *"To work is to pray."* The well-regulated life does not defer prayer until work has been accomplished; it turns the work itself into a prayer. We accomplish this when we turn to God at the beginning and completion of each task and mentally offer it up for love of Him. Then, whether we are taking care of a child or making carburetors, turning a lathe or running an elevator, the task is sanctified. No amount of piety in leisure hours can compensate for slipshod labor on the job. But any honest task, well done, can be turned into a prayer.

3. A medieval economist, Antonio of Florence, summed up the relationship of work to life in the happy formula: *"The object of making money is that we may provide for ourselves and our dependents. The object of providing for self and others is that one may live virtuously. The object of living virtuously is to save our souls and attain eternal happiness."*

Work should, in justice, receive two kinds of reward—for it is not only individual, but also social. John Jones, who works in a mine, is tired at the end of the day: this is his individual sacrifice. For it he receives his wages. But John Jones has also, during the day, made a social contribution to the economic well-being of the country and the world. For this social contribution, John Jones today is given nothing . . . although he has a moral right to a share of the social wealth his work creates. We need a modification of the wage system so that the worker may share in the profits, ownership, or management of an industry. When labor leaders and capitalists thus agree together to give labor some capital to defend, there will no longer be two rival groups in industry; labor and management will become two cooperating members working together, as our two legs cooperate to help us walk.

Idling

A GREAT and distinguished psychologist once said that the tragedy of man today was that he no longer believed he had a soul to save. To such a group Our Lord addressed His beautiful parable of the laborers in the vineyard. Toward the close of the day the master of the vineyard went to the marketplace and said: "Why stand you here all the day idle?" In certain places of the east this custom still prevails, men gathering in front of mosques and public places with shovels in their hands, waiting to be hired.

This story has a spiritual application and refers to various kinds of idlers. In addition to those who idle in the literal sense, there are mere loafers with nothing to do. Many are idle in the sense of being industrious triflers, wearied with toils that accomplish no real worth. Many are idle because of constant indecision, and others become frustrated and worried, not knowing the purpose of life. To the human eye, there are not many idlers, but as the Eye of Heaven looks down to earth it must be like a vast marketplace wherein few labor. To the Divine, all such activity as the acquiring of wealth, marrying, and giving in marriage, buying and selling, studying and painting, are all means to the supreme and final end, which is the saving of one's soul. Every expenditure of human strength that makes what is a means an end, which isolates living from the goal of living, is a busy idleness, a sad and mournful unreality.

Despite this new and harsh definition of idleness that our Divine Lord gives, there is nevertheless much hope in the story, for some were hired at the eleventh hour and received just as much as those who had labored all the day. It is never too late for God's grace. It is a peculiar psychological fact that those who turn to God late in life generally consider all their previous life wasted. St. Augustine, reflecting on his wasted youth, said: "Too late, O ancient Beauty have I loved Thee." There are no hopeless cases; no life is too far spent to be recouped; no lifelong idleness precludes a few minutes of useful work in the vineyard of the Lord, even the last few hours of life, as was the case with the penitent thief.

When the Lord gave everyone at the end of the day the same wages, those who had borne the heat and burdens of the sun complained that those who came in at the eleventh hour received just as much. To which Our Divine Lord retorted: "Does your eye see evil because I do good?" The thought of reward does not enter into the heavenly service. Those who lead a moral life for forty years and then protest the latecomers' salvation have the spirit of the hireling. With all the true acts of the spiritual man, the inspiration is love and not a desire of reward. One cannot speak of the rewards of a true love in marriage without insulting the husband and wife. One cannot associate compensation with the affection that twines a child's arms about a mother's neck, or that keeps her waiting in vigils that outwatch the patient stars. One can not associate reward with the heroism of a person who would risk his or her life to save another. In like manner the servitors of daily piety and religion are as full of the charm and fascination and glory of self-forgetting devotion as any of these.

Physical idleness deteriorates the mind; spiritual idleness deteriorates the heart. The joint action of air and water can turn a bar to rust. Therefore at every hour in the marketplace, man must ask himself: "Why stand I here idle?"

Malign Neglect

WHAT IS IT that dries up the wells of repentance but the neglect of meditating on the heinousness of sin? What makes devotion well-nigh impossible but the neglect of prayer? What makes God seem so far away and so unreal but the neglect of living in His Holy Presence? What is it that drags a soul down to hell but the neglect to lift itself up to heaven? Let a man be solely at ease in himself, satisfied with what he is, consenting to the customs of the world, drawing in the unwholesome breath of refined evil and letting his moral inclinations run their natural course without check or stay, and he will most surely ride onward, with an easy and gentle motion, down the broad current of eternal death, for in the language of Paul," How shall we escape, if we neglect?"

Even in this life there is a terrible penalty for neglect. That penalty is the warping and the atrophying and the dulling of those faculties that were meant to feed on the things of God. God gave us a mind to know Him, a will to love Him, and a body to serve Him. If these energies of body and soul are neglected by not lifting them up in adoration of the Father from whom all gifts come, nature takes a terrible revenge. Something happens to us that happens to the lower animals, namely, we lose the use of these faculties and also the high objects toward which they should have been directed. . . .

And so, the penalty of neglect is the surrender of even the gifts we have. It is this lesson that our Blessed Lord revealed in the parable of the talents. "And to one he [a master] gave five talents and to another two and to another one." He that received the five talents traded and gained another five. In like manner, he that received the two gained another two. "But he that had received the one, going his way, digged into the earth and hid his lord's money." But when the reckoning day came, he who had received the five talents and he who had received the two talents and had earned another five and another two were admitted into the joy of the Lord. But he who had done nothing with the gift that had been given him, but merely hid it in the earth, had to suffer the penalty of the forfeiture of the talent, for the Lord said: "Take ye away therefore the talent from him." The deprivation was the natural consequence of his sloth. As the arm of a man, which is never called into exercise, loses its strength by degrees, and its muscles and its sinews disappear, even so the powers that God gave us, when unexercised, fail and fade from us. "For to everyone that hath shall be given and he shall abound: but for him that hath not that also which he seemeth to have shall be taken away."

Our land is filled with many men and women who have neglected their talents, whose spiritual faculties have dried up through sheer indifference, and who now no more think of God than they think of the political situation in Timbuktoo. The eternal aspirations of their souls are crushed, each inlet to heaven is barricaded, every talent is squandered, every faculty of the divine so bent on things of earth as to lose all relish for those of spirit. Daily and hourly they lose their sensitivity as regards the great realm of the soul. Just as the deaf are dead to the harmonies of life, such as the sigh of a waterfall and the rhythm of poetry; just as the blind are dead to the beauties of nature, such as the colors of a rainbow and the smile of a child, so too these atrophied souls are dead to the sweet whisperings of the Holy Spirit and blind to the dazzling vision of Jesus in the monstrance. It was of such souls, who neglected hearing the word of God and seeing the vision of His Son, our Blessed Lord spoke when He said: "Seeing they see not, and hearing they hear not, neither do they understand."

Sin

It would be well for our generation to remember that the fires of Sinai still burn in the history of men and nations, that its dread thunders still roll across the centuries, and that the cross that once was raised in defiance of sin will not be taken down until sin is vanquished and the Cross itself becomes the badge of eternal glory and triumph. And in order that our day may know that sin is not just an arbitrary tag tacked onto human actions by the Church or that it is not a mere fall in the evolutionary process, it might be profitable to inquire into the nature of sin by asking what nature thinks of sin, what conscience thinks of sin, and what God thinks of sin. Nature tells us that sin is death; conscience tells us that sin is guilt; and God tells us that sin is an offense against His divine love.

Nature says that sin is death, a definition that Sacred Scripture confirms: "The wages of sin is death." Death in the natural order is the domination of a lower order over a higher order, for the universe is made up of various levels or hierarchies one subordinated to the other, such as the chemical, the vegetative, the animal, the human, and the divine. If, for example, a rose is placed in a room filled with poisonous gas, it will die just as soon as the lower order, namely the chemical, gains mastery over the higher order, which is that of life.

The human body often dies through a slow wearing away and oxidation of its organism. At that precise point where there is a balance of forces in favor of the chemical process of oxidation as against the vital process, death ensues. Now, man has not only a body but also a soul. As the life of the body is the soul, so the life of the soul is God. When, therefore, the body dominates the soul, the laws of the world dominate the laws of Christ, the flesh dominates the spirit, and the things of time dominate the things of eternity, there is a domination of a lower order over a higher order, and that domination or death we call sin. Sin, then, is a death in the strict sense of the term, namely the death of the life of God in the soul. In this sense it is the crucifixion over again, for as often as we sin we crucify Christ again in our hearts. Every soul is therefore a potential Calvary and every sin an actual cross. . . .

Nature tells us that sin is death, but conscience tells us that it is guilt, and that as such it is totally different from anything in the animal order and therefore something that is not a mere episode in the passage of nature and a thing that can be left behind, dead and done for. Nothing is more typical of the sense of human guilt than its power of asserting itself with unbated poignancy in spite of the lapse of time. Society may forgive the transgressor, but he does not forgive himself; his friends may cease to blame him, but he does not cease to blame himself, others may forget it, but he does not forget. He knows he cannot forgive himself, but that he must be forgiven; and his horror-crammed memory cries out. . . .

How can we explain this sense of guilt and this indelible remorse except in reference to a Person who has claims of love upon us? How explain this pain of the soul except as a deordination against the God of justice and love? If a magnetic needle were endowed with feeling and it pointed south instead of north, it would be in "pain" because of not pointing in the direction of its true nature. If a bone becomes dislocated, the whole body suffers because the bone is not where it ought to be. In like manner, if the heart and mind and soul of man, by a free act of choice turn not to the God of love and mercy, but away from Him to the things of self, he too suffers pain and remorse because he is not where he ought to be—in the arms of God.

Old Errors with New Labels

WHEN ONE HAS READ one book on morals by any "new" thinker of our day, he has read them all. Two dominant ideas run through each of them: the first is the decay of old traditions through the advance of modern culture; the second is a plea for a new morality suitable to the way people live today.

The first argument is generally couched in some such language as this: "We do not live in a patriarchal society. We do not live in a world that disposes us to believe in a theocratic government. And therefore insofar as moral wisdom is entangled with the promises of a theocracy, it is unreal to me. It is the unconscious assumption that we are related to God as creatures to a creator, as vassals to a king, as children to a father, that the acids of modernity have eaten away." All these things have ceased to be consistent with our normal experience of ordinary affairs. Men no longer believe seriously that they are governed from heaven and that anarchy will result from all this confusion unless by conscious effort they find ways of governing themselves.

The second part of these books is generally consecrated to the elevation of humanism to a system of morals. Starting with the premise that the history of every man is a history of his progress from infantilism to maturity, they conclude that a goal for moral effort can be found in the notion of maturity. "To replace the conception of man as the subject of a heavenly king, which dominates the ancestral order of life, humanism takes as its dominant pattern the progress of the individual from helpless infancy to self-governing maturity. . . .

What is to be thought of this type of book? Two general criticisms occur to us, one referring to the section that deals with the "modernity" of the modern mind; the other referring to the second section, which treats of the new morals of "disinterestedness" or "maturity." We should say that the first part on the modern mind is too unmodern, and of the second part, on the morals of "maturity," that it is too immature and that the morals of "disinterestedness" are too selfish. When it is argued that the modern man can no longer live under the ancestral morality and the theocratic religions, and that a new morality must be found for him, one is really stating something very old and ancient. There are new men in the world, but there is still the "old man" in the sense that human nature has not changed. All such an author has done is to develop a man's lip-worship, or better still, to reburnish the golden calf.

AGNOSTICISM

AGNOSTICISM IS AN EVIL when it contends not only that an individual mind knows nothing, but also that no other mind knows anything. In this sense it is cowardly because it runs away from the problems of life. Only about ten percent of the people think for themselves. Columnists and headline writers think for the greater percent of the remainder. Those who are left are the agnostics, who think agnosticism is an answer to the riddle of life. Agnosticism is not an answer. It is not even a question.

There is, however, a sense in which agnosticism is desirable. In fact, a healthy agnosticism is the condition of increase of knowledge. A man may be agnostic in either one of two ways, either by doubting the value of things *below* him in dignity or by doubting the value of things *above* him in dignity. Modern agnosticism doubts the things *above* man and hence ends in despair; Christian agnosticism doubts the value of things *below* man and hence ends in hope.

These statements admit of universal application. The universe may be compared to a temple made up of a vestibule, a sanctuary, and a holy of holies. Josephus in his *Antiquities* tells us that it was Jewish belief that the temple of Jerusalem with its three divisions was modeled on the plan upon which God built the universe, which too had its vestibule, its sanctuary, and its holy of holies.

The vestibule of creation or the material world is the world of the sun, moon, stars, plants, animals, and men—in a word, every sensible thing. The sanctuary of creation is the world of causes, of science, philosophy, and natural law. The holy of holies of creation is the world of mystery and revelation, such as the Trinity and the Incarnation. The same key that unlocks the vestibule of creation does not unlock the sanctuary of creation nor does the world of causes open the holy of holies. There are three keys for the temple. The first key that unlocks the world of matter is the five senses, by which we taste, see, touch, smell, and hear the material world and thus enter into communion with it. The second key that unlocks the world of causes, or purposes, is the key of reason, which enables us to penetrate the inner meaning and purpose of things. Finally, the key that unlocks the holy of holies of creation is the delicate key of faith.

THE CRISIS IN MORALS

THERE SHOULD BE A VACATION for certain overworked words, and in particular the word *crisis*. What "service" is to a Kiwanis booster, the word *crisis* is to moralists. This latter class have used it so often as to prove without doubt that Robert Louis Stevenson was right in saying that not by bread alone do men live but principally by catchwords. It is hardly possible to pick up a magazine today without reading an article by some self-styled ethicist on "The Crisis in Morals."

The repeated use of the word *crisis* in reference to morals is interesting, for it reveals a tendency on the part of many modern writers to blame the abstract when the concrete is really at fault. They speak, for example, of the problem of crime, rather than of the criminal; of the problem of poverty, rather than of the poor; and of the crisis in morals, when really the crisis is among people who are not living morally.

The crisis is not in ethics but in the unethical. The failure is not in the law, but in the lawbreakers. The truth of this observation is borne out by the failure of such writers to distinguish between the problem of making people conform to standards and that of making standards conform to people. Instead of urging people to pass the test, they alter the test. Instead of inspiring them to hold to their ideals, they change the ideals. In accordance with this logic, they urge that morals be changed to suit those who cannot live morally, and that ethics be changed to please those who cannot live ethically.

All this takes place in accordance with the democratic principle of certain philosophers, who are prepared to construct any kind of philosophy that man desires. If men want ghosts, the democratic philosophers, who know the will of the populace, will write a philosophy justifying ghosts; if the man in the street wants to follow the line of least moral resistance, philosophers will develop for him the justifying philosophy of "self-expression"; if the man of affairs has no time for the thoughts of eternity, then philosophers develop for him the philosophy of "space-time."

There are ultimately only two possible adjustments in life: one is to suit our lives to principles; the other is to suit principles to our lives. "If we do not live as we think, we soon begin to think as we live." The method of adjusting moral principles to the way men live is just such a perversion of the due order of things. Just suppose this logic were applied in the classroom. Boys and girls find it difficult to spell *knapsack* and *pneumonia,* because the spelling of these words is not in the line of least phonetic resistance. Others, too, find it very hard to learn the multiplication table. Many a budding liberal mathematician cannot crush the urge to see that three times three equals six. Now here is a real "crisis" in spelling and mathematics, a kind of intellectual anarchy much akin to the moral anarchy described by our intelligentsia.

How meet the "crisis"? One way to meet it is the way to meet any crisis, that is, to write a new speller and a new mathematics entitled *A Preface to Spelling* or *Crisis in Mathematics.* This is precisely what has taken place in the field of morals. Instead of making men conform to principles of morality, they change the principles. This kind of philosophy would never have permitted the prodigal son to return to his father's house. It would have settled the "crisis" by finding a new and handsome name for the husks he was throwing to the swine, and called it progress away from antiquated modes of morality.

THE THEISM OF ATHEISM

THE ARGUMENTS for the "new God" are generally twofold: first, the times demand it, and secondly, science requires it. Two false assumptions underlie these arguments, and the first is the confusion between a *fact* and an *idea.* There is a world of difference between "God" and "the idea of God." If I see a canary and call it a giraffe, I must revise my idea to suit the fact, the canary remaining a canary all the while. But if I am an architect, I may revise a house to suit my idea of the house or of an ideal house. In the first case, change the idea to fit the fact; in the second, I change the fact to suit the idea. The two are not the same; in fact, the one condition that makes it possible for me to change the fact to suit my idea is that I be the creator, or cause, of the fact.

Applying this to God, the demand for a new God must mean either one of two things: either we must change the idea of God to suit God, or else we must change God to suit our new idea of God. In the first case, to change the idea to suit God is meaningless if God is unchanging. If He is unchanging, it is nonsense to say that God was one thing in the days of Israel and is another in the days of science. This is just like saying that two apples plus two apples made four apples in the days of Isaiah, but do not in the days of Einstein.

In the second case, if we must change God to suit our idea, then we create God. Now this God we create is greater or less than we are. If He is greater than we are, then the greater comes from the less; if He is less than we are, then it is folly to speak of Him as a God.

As for the necessity of coining new names for God, it is incomprehensible to a thinking mind that philosophy and civilization can be enriched by ceasing to think of God as Life, Truth, Beauty, and Love, and beginning to think of Him as a blind and whirling space-time configuration dancing dizzily in an Einstein universe, plunging forward along a path of which He is ignorant, toward a goal of which He knows nothing whatever. It is much easier to worship the God who made life than the God who is a "space-time epochal occasion."

Another assumption that vitiates the logic for the new God is that it hypostatizes science. "Modern science repudiates God," it is said. Now just what is "science"? Renouvier used to say: "I should very much like to meet that person every one is talking about—that person Science." They talk of science as if it were just as real as themselves; they draw portraits of *its* conclusions, sketches of *its* godlessness; they state demands of *its* new visions, when all the while there is no *it*—there is only a *their* and *theirs*—and that means *scientists,* which is as different a thing from science as "John" is different from "humanity."

BROAD-MINDEDNESS

AMERICA, it is said, is suffering from intolerance. It is not. It is suffering from tolerance: tolerance of right and wrong, truth and error, virtue and evil, Christ and chaos. Our country is not nearly so much overrun with the bigoted as it is overrun with the broad-minded. The person who can make up his or her mind in an orderly way, as a person might make up a bed, is called a bigot; but a person who cannot make up his or her mind, any more than one can make up for lost time, is called tolerant and broad-minded.

A bigoted person is one who refuses to accept a reason for anything; a broad-minded person is one who will accept anything for a reason—provided it is not a good reason. It is true that there is a demand for precision, exactness, and definiteness, but it is only for precision in scientific measurement, not in logic.

The breakdown that has produced this unnatural broad-mindedness is mental, not moral. The evidence for this statement is threefold: the tendency to settle issues not by arguments but by words; the unqualified willingness to accept the authority of any one on the subject of religion; and, lastly, the love of novelty.

Voltaire boasted that if he could find but ten wicked words a day he could crush the "infamy" of Christianity. He found the ten words daily, and even a daily dozen, but he never found an argument, and so the words went the way of all words and the thing, Christianity, survived. Today, no one advances even a poor argument to prove that there is no God, but they are legion who think they have sealed up the heavens when they have used the word *anthropomorphism*. This word is just a sample of the whole catalogue of names that serve as the excuse for those who are too lazy to think. One moment's reflection would tell them that one can no more get rid of God by calling Him anthropomorphic than he can get rid of a sore throat by calling it streptococci. . . .

Not only does the substitution of words for argument betray the existence of this false tolerance, but also the readiness on the part of many minds to accept as an authority in any field an individual who becomes a famous authority in one particular field. The assumption behind journalistic religion is that because a man is clever in inventing automobiles he is thereby clever in treating the relationship between Buddhism and Christianity; that a professor who is an authority on the mathematical interpretation of atomic phenomena is thereby an authority on the interpretation of marriage; and that a man who knows something about illumination can throw light on the subject of immortality or perhaps even put out the lights on immortality. There is a limit to the transfer of training, and no one who paints beautiful pictures with the right hand can, in a day and at the suggestion of a reporter, paint an equally good one with the left hand. The science of religion has a right to be heard scientifically through its qualified spokesmen and spokeswomen, just as the science of physics or of astronomy has a right to be heard through its qualified representatives. Religion is a science despite the fact that some would make it only a sentiment.

Religion is not an open question, like the League of Nations, whereas science is a closed question, like the addition table. It has its principles, natural and revealed, which are more exacting in their logic than mathematics. But the false notion of tolerance has obscured this fact from the eyes of many who are as intolerant about the smallest details of life as they are tolerant about their relations to God. . . .

Another evidence of the breakdown of reason that has produced this weird fungus of broad-mindedness is the passion for novelty, as opposed to the love of truth. Truth is sacrificed for an epigram, and the Divinity of Christ for a headline in the Monday morning newspaper. Many a modern preacher is far less concerned with preaching Christ and Him crucified than he is with his popularity with his congregation. A want of intellectual backbone makes him straddle the ox of truth and the ass of nonsense, paying compliments to Catholics because of "their great organization" and to sexologists because of their "honest challenge to the youth of this generation." Bending the knee to the mob and pleasing people rather than God would probably make them scruple at ever playing the role of a John the Baptist before a modern Herod. . . . Rather would we hear: "Friend, times are changing! The acids of modernity are eating away the fossils of orthodoxy. If thy noble sex urge to self-expression finds its proper stimulus and response in no one but Herodias, then in the name of Freud and Russell accept her as thy lawful wife to have and to hold until sex do ye part."

The attitude of the Church in relation to [broad-mindedness] may be brought home by the story of the two women in the courtroom of Solomon. Both of them claimed a child. The lawful mother insisted on having the whole child or nothing, for a child is like truth—it cannot be divided without ruin. The unlawful mother, on the contrary, agreed to compromise. She was willing to divide the babe, and the babe would have died of broad-mindedness.

HUMANISM

MODERN PAGANISM is doing the same thing the Christian world has always done, but is doing it for a different reason. It has retained the external form of things but emptied their content and meaning. Christian terms and practices are retained, consecrated words of revealed religion are used—but they are retained and used in the same fashion that a new firm trades under the old name, in order to win the good will of its former customers.

The Christian world, for example, recommends fasting; the modern world fasts, too, under the name of dieting, not to make the soul beautiful, but rather to make the body beautiful. The Christian world recommends examination of conscience; the modern world does the same, under the guise of psychoanalysis. The Christian world recommends telling one's sins to a confessor; the pagan world recommends telling them to the world. In the first instance, however, the reason for the confession is to elevate the soul by purification; in the second, it is to ease the body by sublimation. Another example of this tendency is furnished us by our movie world. Hollywood is fascinated by the Cross of Christ, just as Christians are, but not because the Cross is the prelude to the empty tomb, but rather because it is the prelude to a full purse: it is good business.

The world thus becomes blighted not only by bad things but also by good things; a patronage is shown toward the better things of life that at times becomes more intolerable than persecution. In this connection, Mr. Chesterton has written: "By its own radical incapacity for restraint or dignity or honorable privacy, it is spoiling all the good things as instruments of good. The virtues it is too weak to practice it is sufficiently strong to weaken. All that is hard in fact it will make soft with fiction, and make a cant even of death and pain and the last reserves of humanity."

In keeping with this general attitude, to do Christian things for an unchristian reason, is to be noted a very old movement that is thought to be very new, namely, Humanism. Humanism has been defined as "the endeavor to keep the best spiritual values of religion while surrendering any theological interpretation of the universe." In its broadest sense it is an endeavor to have Christianity without Christ, godliness without God, and Christian hope without the promise of another life.

THE COSMICAL RELIGION

It will be recalled that when Einstein left the field in which he was one of the world's greatest masters and entered the field of religion, he declared that the religion of the future will not be a religion of fear, or of morality, but what he called a cosmical religion—a religion in which man enters into communion with the great universe round about him.

One of the principal difficulties in the way of the cosmical religion is that it leaves no room for that which religion necessarily involves, namely, love. No man will ever love anything unless he can fight for it, and no man will fight for a cosmical religion. I can imagine medieval knights with plumes flying in the air and spears glistening in the sun going out to battle in defense of their earthly Venus, but I cannot imagine astronomers, with telescopes flying like plumes and measuring rods glistening like spears, going out to battle for the astronomical Venus. I know men in whose veins flows the milk of human kindness who are willing to lay down their life for their fellowman, but I know of no scientist who will lay down his life for the

Milky Way. I know missionaries who will spend themselves and be spent for the soul of a single Bengalese, but I wonder if even Einstein would be willing to lose his finger for the spark of Betelgeuse.

It will be no answer to say that the men will lay down their lives for the Milky Way and hence will lay them down for science, for the Milky Way is not science any more than a Tom Thumb golf course or green cheese or buttermilk is science. To equate the Milky Way with science is like equating a thousand gallons of water with the Annapolis school spirit or six hundred and forty acres of land with patriotism. The Milky Way is a thing; science is a thing related to a mind and particularly as regards its quantity and its measurement. No man would ever lay down his life for the Milky Way, for the simple reason that he will never sacrifice himself for anything that is below him in dignity and worth. A man will sacrifice himself for love of truth, but truth is something quite different from a planet.

Human beings do not die for things alone but for what they believe about things. No scientist ever died for a bug. He died for the sake of humanity, which that bug was stinging. No one ever laid down his life for the stars, but some will lay down their lives for the truth that the stars bring. It is, therefore, not matter but the spirit that summons the best in man, the spirit of learning, the spirit of truth, the spirit of love—and all these are above the individual man in dignity and worth.

Being void of love, the cosmical religion must ever be unsatisfying. The human heart never can and never will love anything it cannot put its arms around, and the cosmos is too big and too bulky. That is why, I suppose, the immense God became a babe in order that we might encircle Him in our arms. And just as there is no love in the cosmical religion, neither is there truth. Truth does not mean going out to the cosmos. It means the cosmos coming into the mind. Truth is not the heavens by themselves, but rather the heavens in the head, which is the primary condition of truth.

THE GODLESS UNIVERSITY

To LEAVE GOD out of a university curriculum is to leave out the First Cause and the intelligibility of all that is, and to leave out the First Cause is to deny God; it is to inculcate a contrary prejudice. Leaving God, the source of moral obligation, out of a university curriculum is not just merely negation; it is a privation. It is not merely the absence of something, like lack of color on a wall, but it is a privation, like the plucking out of an eye. The young minds in many of our universities, by a process of refined skepticism, are not being permitted to know the beauties that lie beyond the solar system. It was just such ignorance of the whole totality of environment that explains a pathetic remark that a young student of one of our large universities made to me after having heard a sermon on the love of God: "That is not possible; if such a lovely thing had ever been, they would have told me about it." The point I am trying to make is that they have not been told, and hence the proper definition for many a modern university is "a place where five thousand students are looking for a religion and something to satisfy their hearts, and know not where to go to find it."

Would it not be well to establish universities in this country dedicated to the purpose not of learning but of unlearning? Have not the false philosophy and the false morality that certain universities have been guilty of in the last two hundred years created a distinct problem in the realm of education, namely, that of undoing what has been done badly? The time has come when a certain intellectual disinfection or sterilization has become necessary in order that health may be restored to thinking society. Just suppose that we could endow a university in America that would unlearn the notion that drenching a mind with physics makes a man religious; suppose we had a university department that would unlearn the false pragmatic philosophy of our country, which tends to prove that all proof is worthless; suppose we had a department of religion that would unlearn the false notion that because all religions are alike in certain elements, they therefore have the same common root and foundation and are all of human origin; suppose we had a university for unlearning the idea that progress is just mere change and complexity, instead of development in the right direction; and a school for unlearning all the false history that has been taught under the inspiration of Gibbon.

If such a university could rise within our land, wherein professors would set minds right along the lines of sanity and would root out the misconception that novelty is truth and that morality is something more than taste—that university, I say, would be doing the same service for our country that a board of health does for our city, for it would help to keep clean those mental arteries that supply the mind and the heart. If we honor those scientists who, by their knowledge, industry, and effort, have held back the ravages of disease and death, why should we not honor those other men who keep back the ravages of error? For after all, if disease is possible, it may be equally true that error is possible, and the greatest of all diseases. Such a university will come into being, perhaps, as soon as we realize that our country is suffering not so much from falsehood as from the unbearable repetition of half-truths.

EVOLUTION

THERE ARE . . . only two possible theories concerning the nature and dignity of man: one is that life is a push from below, and the other that it is a gift from above. According to the first, man is supposed to act like a beast because he came from one; according to the second, he is expected to act like God because he is made in His own image and likeness.

The source of our dignity is not to be sought by looking for a *man in a tree* but rather by looking to the *Man on the Tree.* The man in the tree is the beast swinging from its tail in the selfish joy of its bestiality. The Man on the Tree is Christ Jesus in the ecstatic beatification of His redemption. The man in the tree is the beast-man. The Man on the Tree is the God-man. The man in the tree looks forward to a progeny of the children of animals, and the Man on the Tree looks forward to a progeny of the children of God. The man in the tree looks back to the earth whence he sprang. The Man on the Tree looks upward to the heavens whence he descended. To the man in the tree, all the other trees of the forest bear only the burden of leaves. To the Man on the Tree, all the other trees of the forest bear the burden of penitent thieves.

When the man in the tree dies, not even the leaves chant a requiem. When the Man on the Tree dies, even the earth yawns and gives up its dead, for it is the tree that matters now as in the beginning when man balanced a fruit against a garden.

PAGANISM

NEW PAGANISM may be defined as an outlook on life that holds to the sufficiency of human science without faith and the sufficiency of human power without grace. In other words, its two tenets are: scientism, which is a deification of the experimental method, and humanism, which is a glorification of a man who makes God to his own image and likeness.

New paganism is not the same as the old paganism. The most important differences between the two are these: the old paganism was a confusion. New paganism is a divorce. The old paganism did not deny God; in fact it asserted supreme powers, such as Zeus and Jupiter and the "Unknown God of Athens." What it did, however, was to confuse divinity and humanity, matter and spirit, God and man, to such an extent as to reduce them to a kind of unity. Thus it was that idols of gold and silver or marble and brass were called gods. There was much that was reprehensible in this kind of theology, but there was also something that was noble.

Why did the pagans make their gods in sensible forms like statues? Merely because in their ignorance they could make no distinction whatever between spirit and matter? May it not be more likely that in making their gods visible in matter, they were dimly expressing an instinctive yearning in the human heart for an Incarnation, or a God among men? May it not be that Bethlehem was the realization of those crudely expressed pagan ideals? And the very fact that idolatry passed out of the world with the knowledge of the Incarnation proves in some way that the human heart has had its cravings satisfied and its ideals realized.

New paganism, on the contrary, does not confuse the human and the divine—it separates them, it divorces them. It runs a sharp sword of cleavage between the things that God joined together and forbade to be put asunder, that is, such tremendous realities as God and the cosmos, nature and grace, faith and science, body and soul, morality and conscience, husband and wife, maternity and Providence, divine action and human liberty. After having divorced the two, new paganism immediately throws away the better half and lives worse with the other half. That is why today there is religion without God, Christianity without Christ, and psychology without a soul. That is why there are behaviorism, humanism, and all the other new labels. . . .

The second difference between the old and the new

paganism is that the old paganism worshipped the vital forces of nature and entered into vital communion with them and the cosmos by some sort of ritualistic magic that belongs to the domain of religion. New paganism continues to worship the forces of nature, but it enters into communion with this cosmic order not by a ritualistic magic that belongs to the realm of religion, but by a mathematical formalism that belongs to the domain of science. The old paganism with its ritualistic magic had the advantage of admitting the worshipper into some dim borderland of the unknown and providing him with an inspiration and an awe that are foreign to the new paganism, with its clockwork cosmos of Pointer-readings and shadowy configurations of space-time. The old paganism found a God, though it was only an unknown God. New paganism finds a God—and its name is man.

The third difference resides in the nature of the two kinds of paganism. The old paganism was the perversion of *natural* lights and misuse of reason by those who could have come to a knowledge of the invisible God from the visible things of the world. This was the basis of St. Paul's reproach to the Romans. New paganism, on the contrary, is a perversion of *supernatural* lights, the putting out of the flame of Christianity and the light of faith and the revelation of Christ Jesus. The old paganism put out the light of the candle of reason; new paganism put out the light of the sun of faith. The only way to understand the degradation to which man had fallen is to know the heights from which he had fallen, and no one will deny that it is impossible to fall from a greater height than the hope and life that Christ brought to this world, and in this sense the fall of new paganism is the greater.

The Four Columns

IF WE HAD NOT ABANDONED absolute truth, if we had not adopted the stupid moral philosophy that freedom means the right to do whatever you please, even the right to destroy freedom, we would have no fifth columnists.

That is why I say the fifth columnist is possible only because there are already fourth columnists, and these constitute our danger from within. What are these four columns?

The first columnists are those educators and publicists who reject a universal norm of morality in favor of a relative morality based either on expediency, pleasure, profit or selfishness of the individual; in other words, a rejection of the principle that right is right if nobody is right, and wrong is wrong if everybody is wrong. . . .

The first column undermines justice; the second column undermines charity. The second columnists are those who sin against charity and include all those who sin not only by rejecting the solidarity of mankind, because begotten of a common origin and redeemed by our Divine Lord, but also by rebelling against the fraternal spirit and tolerance that should exist among citizens of the same country.

In this second column are those in the ranks of capital and labor who through avarice on the one hand and envy and greed on the other turn the nation into a warring camp at the very moment we talk about a war from the outside.

In this second column, too, are those individuals who are guilty of anti-Semitism, anti-Catholicism, bigotry, atheism, and immorality, who by their hatreds are not murdering bodies but slaughtering souls with eternal destinies and for which they will one day have to answer before the judgment seat of Almighty God.

The third columnists are those lawyers, jurists, and teachers who, by divorcing civil authority from dependence on the law of God, make law only an instrument for action or the social expression of the way beings live, rather than the way they ought to live.

In the third column are those so-called educators who complain against the release time from school for religious instruction in the nonsensical plea that it means the union of Church and State.

It is interesting to note that the persons who most opposed religion for the young as being un-American are often the same ones who draw money from American taxpayers to tie us up with anti-American activities.

Let me say to these third columnists that there is no danger in this country of the union of Church and State, but there is danger of the union of atheism and the State.

If that is what they want, then let them say so, and we will fight back in the name of the Declaration of Independence—Washington and Lincoln—in a word, in the name of America.

The fourth columnists are those who either explicitly or implicitly adhere to the philosophy of "self-expression" and reject the necessity of discipline, authority, and self-sacrifice as the condition of individual and national betterment.

In this fourth column are those who think they should get everything for nothing in America and still have the right to complain about the quality; those who refuse to face the responsibility of spending and thus mortgage America's future; those who consider education a social necessity rather than an intellectual privilege; those labor leaders and those capitalists who shout persecution as soon as one of their own is convicted of injustice by the government; those parents who are raising a bumper crop of spoiled children because they see too many exhibitions and learn too few inhibitions; those who sue the school and the board of education if a teacher scolds for an act of wrongdoing by their "darling child" who can do no wrong; and finally those who pamper the rapacious egotism of their children and thus prevent the formation of good habits.

God and Caesar

IN THESE DAYS when everyone talks of rights and few of duties, it is important for us Americans to recall that the Declaration of Independence is also a Declaration of Dependence. The Declaration of Independence asserts a double dependence: dependence on God and dependence on law as derived from God.

Where do we get our rights of free speech? Where do we get freedom of conscience? Whence is derived the right to own property? Do we get these rights and liberties from the State? If we did, the State could take them away. Do we get them from the federal government in Washington? If we did, the federal government could take them away. Whence comes the right to life, liberty, and the pursuit of happiness?

Read the Declaration of Independence and there find the answer: "We hold these truths to be self-evident, that all men are created equal, that they are *endowed by their Creator* with certain unalienable Rights, that among these are Life, Liberty, and the pursuit of Happiness." Notice these words: *The Creator has endowed men with rights and liberties;* men got them from God! In other words, we are dependent *on God,* and that initial dependence is the foundation of our independence.

Suppose we interpret independence, as some liberal jurists do, as independence of God; then rights and liberties come either from the State, as Bolshevism contends, or from the dictators, as Nazism and Fascism believe. But if the

State or the dictator is the creator of rights, then the State or the dictator can dispossess men of their rights. That is why in those countries where God is most denied, man is most tyrannized, and where religion is most persecuted, man is most enslaved. It is only because we are dependent on God that we are independent as persons from the total will of any man on earth.

Let us not think that by denying God we will have purchased independence. The pendulum of the clock that wanted to be free from its point of suspension found that, on becoming independent of its suspension, it was no longer free to swing. The Communists and the Nazis and the Fascists who denied God as the source of their freedom got in the end the inglorious freedom of State prisoners.

Democracy is based not on the divine right of kings but on the divine right of persons. Each person has a value because God made him, not because the State recognizes him. The day we adopt in our democracy the already widespread ideas of some American jurists that right and justice depend on convention and the spirit of the times, we shall write the death warrant of our independence. When watchmakers set watches according to their whims and not according to a fixed point of reference, such as the sun, we will no longer have the right time; when aviators build machines in repudiation of the laws of gravitation, we will no longer fly; and when we deny God as the foundation of our rights, we shall no longer have rights. The Declaration of Independence, I repeat, is a Declaration of Dependence. We are independent of dictators because we are dependent on God.

Because we are dependent on God, it follows that it is religion's first duty to reserve that relationship between man and his Creator. Religion and democracy, therefore, are not the same. Some religious leaders never once in their discourses mention the name of God but actually define religion as democracy. Certain alarmists, when a personal representative of the president was sent to the Holy Father, shrieked against union of Church and State—but they do not protest against the identification of religion and democracy, which is an insult to both religion and democracy.

If religion is democracy, then let us drop religion and become State servants; if democracy is religion, then let us scrap democracy and enter a monastery. Religion is not democracy. The two are as different as soul and body. Religion is primarily for the salvation of man's soul, and democracy is primarily for the prosperity and common good of the nation. God is not Caesar, and Caesar is not God. Have our so-called religious leaders forgotten: "Render therefore to Caesar the things that are Caesar's; and to God, the things that are God's" (Matthew 22:21).

Communism

THERE IS CONSIDERABLE CONFUSION in our American life about Communism, too much emotional hatred of Communism, and not sufficient thinking and reasoning about it.

But Communism is intrinsically wrong, independently of Russia's foreign policy. The foreign policy of Russia is a tactic; it is by the philosophy of Communism that Russia is to be judged.

The two basic principles of Communism that we select for presentation are

1. Economic determinism.
2. Communist notion of man.

Economic determinism sounds very learned, but it means, very simply, that culture, civilization, religion, philosophy, art, morals, and literature are all *determined* by economic methods of production. The latter is the base on which all else rests.

For example, if the method of production at a given period of history is based on private ownership of property, such as we have here in our democracy, the Communist argues that literature, art, and philosophy are nothing but a superstructure or a defense of private enterprise. "Your literature would be so written," the Communists say, "as to justify slavery, colonialism, capitalism, and the right of property owners to submerge the workers."

"Morals, in like manner," the Communists say, "in private enterprise would be so constructed as to defend ownership." As Lenin wrote, "We deny all morality taken from noneconomic class conceptions." Take the seventh and tenth commandments—"Thou shalt not steal" and "Thou shalt not covet thy neighbor's goods." The Communists say, "Can't you see these two commandments are based upon private property? Why should anyone prohibit stealing except in a society where there is personal ownership of the methods of production? When the state owns everything, there is no need of that morality, for everyone will be so prosperous there will be no need of stealing."

"Religion is based upon the economics of private enterprise, too," contend the Communists. "It is an opiate given to the workers to make them content with being exploited. It leads them to believe that there is another world to make up for all the injustices of this one." The Communists add, "If you change your method of production and, instead of having private enterprise, put all property in the hands of the State, then the superstructure changes. There will then be Communist literature, Communist morals, Communist art, and Communist philosophy."

Communist literature will attack capitalism, make fun of America, and prove that Russia invented everything from flying machines to radar.

Communist morals will see but one wrong, namely, injuring or hurting state property or in any way betraying the revolutionary class.

Art, too, becomes Communistic. During the days when

we Americans were foolishly having a honeymoon with Russia, there was a considerable amount of art developed that was Communist inspired. Remnants of it can be seen in some hotels and public buildings. The art is unmistakable, for it shows great, tremendous, muscular men with little heads (no brains), pushing wheels, pulling at ropes, tugging at plows; *i.e.,* man was made for production; his origin is economic; therefore so is his destiny.

What is the fallacy of economic determinism, which means that economics determines everything? The first fallacy of economic determinism is that Karl Marx, who studied philosophy and should have known better, confused what is known as a *condition* with a *cause.* For example, the window is a *condition* of light, but the window is not the *cause* of light. We are willing to admit that economics, to some extent, does condition literature and art. But it certainly does not *cause* literature and art.

If economics is the cause of culture and religion, why, in the pre-Christian era, were different cultures and religions produced by the same economic methods of production? There was no difference between the economic methods of production among the Jews and those among the Hindus or the Chaldeans, but their civilizations were different; their religious and moral concepts were different, the Hebrew having the highest moral concept that was known to man in the pre-Christian era. Since their economic methods of production were identical, it cannot be said that economics was the cause of the difference in cultures.

There was no change of economic methods in the Roman Empire when it became Christian from when it was pagan. But the civilization and the art and the religion and the morality were totally different in the two periods. Therefore, it is not the economics that determines civilization. The way a violin is made does not determine the music that will be played on it.

Economics has gone to the head of the Communists like wine to an empty stomach. Notice that whenever the Communists try to convince us of their superiority, they make moral judgments about us. They say we are "immoral," "unjust," "unethical," and "bad," while they are right and good. These moral judgments do not belong in the economic category. Whence comes their moral worth, if reality be not moral? If economics is at the base of reality, how can it be said that any system is "right" and another "wrong"? If religion be a product of economic method of production, how could it be an opiate? Finally, if changes in morality, art, and culture are due to changes in methods of production, *what causes changes* in the methods of *production?* They are more often due to invention, and invention is an intellectual or a spiritual cause. Those who believe in an ethical order independent of economics can condemn exploitation, but the materialism of Communism cannot do it without repudiating the whole system. They have no right to use the words "right" and "wrong," but only "private" and "social." If everything is economically determined, right and wrong, truth and error have no existence, for they do not fit in an economic category.

Communism is strong only when it borrows some of the moral indignation that has been inherited from the Hebraic-Christian traditions; Communism is weak when it departs from that tradition. Communism has bootlegged and smuggled into its system the decency and morality that have come from the great Hebraic-Christian tradition of the Western world and then uses them to pass judgment on the world. Moral indignation is needed against injustice, but Communists have no basis for using it.

This is a reminder of how we ought to meet Communism on the "Voice of America" and elsewhere, namely, not to talk about the supremacy of our economics. Whenever we talk about the supremacy of economics, we pay tribute to the Communists' error of the primary value of economics. Communists are speaking to the rest of the world on the basis of ethics, which their system repudiates. We, who have moral ideals, are speaking to the rest of the world in terms of economics. They are using the language that we ought to be using.

The second basic principle of Communism is that man has value only inasmuch as he is a member of a class. In one of his earlier writings, Karl Marx, who is the father of Communism, said, "We have already destroyed the outer religion; now we must destroy the inner religion," that is, man's spiritual nature.

Then follows this very remarkable statement in which Marx very correctly tells us the essence of democracy. Marx knew the basis of democracy far better than many who live under its blessings. Marx said that democracy is founded on the principle of the "sovereign worth of a person." "This, in its turn," he continued, "is based upon a postulate, a dream and an illusion of Christianity, namely, that every man has an immortal soul." In the first edition of his work on capital, Marx says, "Persons of and by themselves have no value. An individual has a value only inasmuch as he is the representative of an economic category, 'the revolutionary class'; outside of that, man has no value."

Molotov developed this idea by saying that "bread is a political weapon." We believe in food for the hungry, regardless of who they are. Molotov in good Marxist fashion argued that bread be given only to certain people, namely, those who follow Communist revolutionary ideas.

Some years ago, Heywood Broun told me of a cartoonist employed by one of the Communist papers in New York. The cartoonist developed cancer and was obliged to give up work. Broun went to the Communists and asked if they would not give him some pension to help pay his hospital bills. The answer that he received from the Communists was, "He is of no use to us. He is no longer a member of the revolutionary class, and therefore for us he does not exist." That was good Communism, but it is not good humanitarianism. Once you start with the principle that the person has no value, but only the revolutionary class has, then liquidation becomes inevitable.

Man is then likened to lower forms of life in which an individual fly, an individual gnat, an individual ant is of no consequence; what is of importance is the species.

Marx and Communism have turned the supremacy of the species into the supremacy of the class. Once admitted, it follows that what happens to an individual person is of no concern. The revolutionary class of Communism alone has value. Communism is an aggressive religion of the species.

This explains how Russia uses her satellite people in war. Communist tanks run over the bodies of their wounded. No one would even kick them out of the path of the great machines because they are no longer of worth. It also explains their war tactics in Korea. The first line of attack rushed into battle to be cut down. The second line, which was unarmed, carried mattresses and threw themselves on barbed wire to be shot. The third group had guns and gave battle.

This liquidation of man in the modern world will not be arrested simply by protests of horror. We must recognize the evil of this Communist philosophy and begin affirming, in the United States, the worth of a person as a creature of God.

As Hitler put the emphasis upon *race*, as Mussolini put it on the *nation*, so the Communists put it on a *revolutionary mass*. The hour has struck to affirm the power and worth and vocation of the individual. That means returning to what Marx rightly saw as the basis of democracy, namely, the truth that every man has an immortal soul. What we are attempting to do now in our Western world is foolishly to preserve the fruits of Christianity without the roots. Personality has a religious basis. A person is a *subject*, not an *object*. A person has more worth than the universe: "What doth it profit a man if he gains the whole world and loses his soul?" A person realizes himself and comes to relative perfection in society, but only because he has within himself a principle independent of a society, namely, a soul. This soul has rights anterior to any state or dictator, parliament or king. As our Declaration of Independence puts it,

"The Creator has endowed man with certain unalienable rights." The world must move away from mass civilization by restoring value to the person. The Lord of the Universe saw value in the lowest kind of criminal and addressed him in the second person singular: "This day *thou* shalt be with me in Paradise." This promise was the foundation stone of democracy.

Communists are right in saying this world needs a revolution, but not their cheap kind, which merely transfers booty and loot out of one man's pocket into another's. We need the kind of revolution that will purge out of man's heart pride and covetousness and lust and anger. The true battle against Communism begins in the heart of every single American. The revolution must begin in man before it begins in society. The Communist revolution has been a basic failure; it is not revolutionary enough; it leaves hate in the soul of man. We need not fear Communism as much as we need fear being Godless. If God is with us, then who can be against us?

Amputation, Mortification, Limitation

I ONCE HEARD of a man who boarded the Pennsylvania Railroad in Washington, went into the dining car, and ordered anchovies. There were no anchovies. He said to the steward, "I am the anchovy king of America. I spend seventy-five thousand dollars a year shipping anchovies on the Pennsylvania Railroad; and I come into your dining car and cannot find a single anchovy. Is that good business relationship?"

As soon as the train got to Baltimore, the steward immediately telegraphed ahead to Wilmington, "Rush anchovies!"

They put anchovies on at Wilmington, had them all ready

to serve at Philadelphia. The anchovy king, when he saw them before him, said, "I will not eat them; I would rather be mad."

People who are always wanting their own will are unhappy. The self-centered are the self-disrupted. The man who is self-seeking eventually ends up by hating himself. That is why such a person often tries to "get away from himself" through alcohol, dissipation, and drugs. The self one has to live with can be one's own greatest punishment. To be left forever with that self that we hate is hell. He who starts loving only self ends by hating himself; he becomes like a mansion lying forlorn, spacious, and empty.

The other law that gives primacy to the things of the spirit is what might be called the law of self-perfection. This involves a certain amount of self-restraint, effort, and discipline to bring the body captive to the mind as the horse is mastered by the driver. As soon as one speaks of self-restraint, one is met by a certain nonthinking group who say, "But you should not repress yourself." If there were ever any nonsense in the world, it is the notion that repression is always wrong. It assumes that nothing should ever be repressed. This is to forget that if you repress evil, good comes up; if you repress the idea that you are going to rob a bank, honesty asserts itself; if a soldier represses the temptation that he ought to sleep while he is on guard, duty asserts itself. The problem is not whether there will be repression or not; it is rather what will be repressed—goodness or evil!

Amputation refers to that which is intrinsically evil, *mortification* refers to a mixture of good and evil; *limitation* refers to good. In the physical order, amputation would correspond to an operation for the removal of cancer or a malignant growth. Mortification, which refers to that which is a mixture of good and evil, might be likened to a fever; the fever is not cured by cutting off the head. Limitation would apply to a good thing, such as eating caviar.

Amputation. Some evils that afflict human nature cannot

be overcome except by a sudden and self-inflicted death. Alcoholism, for example, starts with the free act; the free act becomes a habit; the habit becomes a reflex; and then much of the energy that might have been used by the will to resist the habit goes into the reflex act. The result is that the alcoholic seems to have lost power to resist evil. The question now arises whether it is better with God's grace and with the cooperation of the will to break evil habits off gradually or to amputate them. Our Divine Lord, who knew human nature better than anyone else, recommended amputation: "If your hand should cause you to sin, cut it off and throw it away." Prolonged gratification is no compensation for gradually diminishing indulgence. If the evil is not eradicated at once, there are both a lingering pain and a diminishing pleasure. Total abstinence is a biological phenomenon as well as a moral recommendation.

Suppose we were talking about wife beating. That is a habit that is intrinsically evil. Certainly it is not to be recommended that it be broken gradually. A husband will not make much sense if he says, "I will break off the habit gradually, but every Thursday from two to three I want the right to beat my wife, and every Friday from seven to seven-thirty I want the right to give her a black eye." Few have many great sins, but one disease is enough to kill a man and bring him to his grave. Precipitate flight from chains that enslave is what a man would do in the face of a tyrant. The same recommendation is counseled in the face of vice.

Mortification is to be recommended where there is a mixture of good and evil. The eye is good, but it is bad for the eye to look at a light that is too bright. The ear is good, but it is bad for the ear to subject itself deliberately to a sound that might break the eardrum. Knowing this, one limits the operation of the faculty to what is good and cuts off that which is evil. Applying this to the development of character, as the eye should not look at everything, so neither should the brain look at everything. Though reading is good, one will not put garbage inside the brain. When the wrong kind of ideas get into the mind, they seep down into the unconsciousness and, later on, come out in evil acts.

Hearing is good, but the ear will refuse to listen to God-lessness, backbiting, slander, and evil suggestions. Helping the neighbor is right, but one will also cleanse the good deed of evil motives, for example, giving money in order to be seen and praised by the neighbor. Sociability is good, but one will avoid evil companions; desiring prosperity is good, but desiring to achieve it by cheating the neighbors is evil.

No character ever develops without a certain amount of punishment and resistance and mortification to that which is evil. It will hurt a bit, just as the violin, if it were conscious, would scream with pain when the violinist tightens the strings. But the violinist would say, "My dear string, this is to give you a better tone." If a block of marble were conscious, it would protest when the chisel strikes, but the sculptor would say, "There is a beautiful form inside of you, and all you have to do is cut away that which is gross, and the inner beauty will be revealed."

Limitation refers to that which is good. Wine, caviar, ice cream, lobster, filet mignon are all good. They could become evil only by abusing them or by taking so much as to destroy our health. A cocktail is good, but ten cocktails taken in succession would be evil. Not long ago I received a letter from someone who said, "I used to take five or six cocktails; now I will take just one. In place of the others, I will send the money to you to help your poor people in India." (Hope others follow that good example.) Character is developed by limiting the area of legitimate pleasures. Limiting the good that we enjoy is actually a form of concentration; it is very much like paying more attention to the rose than to the thorn.

It is necessary every now and then to impose hard things upon ourselves lest we develop faults in a given avocation. I first started teaching in England, which proved that I was very kind to my fellow countrymen and to students. Most teachers begin their profession in their own native country, and the students suffer. But though I tried teaching in another nation before I tried it on my fellow countrymen, I must have been very poor at it. The class that I taught was dogmatic theology in a seminary in London. Some years later, I met one of the students, and he asked if I were still teaching. I told him that I was then teaching philosophy, and he said, "I hope you are a better teacher now than you were then."

The point, however, that I wish to bring out is that there were two things I saw very clearly on which I would have to limit myself. The first was to read notes; the second was to sit at my desk while reading the notes. It was very clear if I ever did either of these two things, I would never be successful as a teacher. It was very hard to get the subject matter so well in my head before class that I could talk on it intelligently to the students; it was less hard, once it was already in my head, to stand instead of sit. But in virtue of limiting two good things, namely, reading and sitting, I made myself a teacher much less insufferable than I would have been otherwise.

Health and Holiness

THE ACCUMULATED WISDOM of the human race has always acknowledged that there was some kind of relationship between peace of soul and health. "A healthy mind in a healthy body" is only an abbreviation of a statement from the Latin poet Juvenal, who wrote in his *Satires*, "We should pray for a sane mind in a sound body." A more modern poet, Francis Thompson, wrote, "Holiness is an oil that increases a hundredfold the energies of the body, which is the wick." The Austrians had a proverb: "A sad saint is a sorry sort of a saint."

Today, however, medicine and psychiatry are combining to prove that there is some intrinsic relationship between holiness and health. The French tradition of medicine has always believed in a long interrogation of the patient in order to view the drama of his human life. Recently there has been published a treatise by the well-known Swiss psychiatrist Dr. Paul Tournier, entitled *The Healing of Persons,* which is a contribution to a synthesis of modern psychology and the Christian faith. He holds that the physical problems of a person's life often correspond to mental problems, and both of these, in turn, to spiritual problems. There is no physical reform possible without a moral reform. And there is no moral reform without a spiritual renewal. This boils down to saying that behavior and a mode of life are very important factors in determining health. Symptoms, he holds, may be exaggerated forms of normal defense reactions; they are abnormal so far as disease is concerned, but they may be normal so far as the defensive reaction is concerned.

A confirmation of this idea comes from Dr. Swain of Boston, who wrote of 270 cases in which the patient was cured on being freed from fear, worry, and resentment. His conclusion was that sixty percent of arthritis cases had their origin in moral conflict. Everyone is familiar with the conclusions of Dr. K. A. Menninger, who stresses the influence of the state of mind on the condition of those suffering from high blood pressure. The latter often seems to be a sort of physical expression of a moral hypertension that paralyzes it. Dr. Alexis Carrel, speaking of the alarming increase of neurosis and psychosis over the last hundred years, states that this increase "can be more dangerous for civilization than infectious diseases. Mental diseases by themselves are more numerous than all other diseases put together." Dr. Tournier holds that "all functional disturbances and, *a fortiori,* all neuroses, may be seen to involve thus a secret flight into disease. This, of course, is not to say that the disease itself is imaginary. . . . How many women there are who have a migraine every time they receive an invitation to visit their hostile in-laws."

Some years ago, Dr. C. G. Jung made a statement that has been quoted many times: "During the past thirty years, people from all civilized countries of the earth have consulted me. . . . Among all my patients in the second half of life—that is to say, over thirty-five—there has not been one whose problem in the last resort was not that of finding a religious outlook on life. It is safe to say that every one of them fell ill because he had lost that which the living religions of every age have given to their followers, and none of them had really been healed who did not regain his religious outlook."

The vocation of a doctor may have been very much underrated. The ideal is not just to cure a patient of neuralgia or phobias, but also to be at one and the same time an educator, a politician, a person of God, a philosopher, and a theologian, not in the sense that he or she takes over completely any of these functions, but rather that he or she recognizes that every sick person in the world has, to some extent, a combination of three disorders: physical, psychic, and spiritual.

Mental Fatigue

THERE ARE TWO GENERAL REASONS why people are fatigued mentally. First, because they have no target; second, because they have too many targets.

By no target, we mean no philosophy of life. They would not have a gadget in the house for ten minutes without discovering its purpose, and yet they will live with themselves for ten, thirty, sixty years and not know why they are here or where they are going. Nothing so much creates boredom as the meaninglessness of life. If you give a boy a BB gun and a target, he is not so dangerous. If you give him a BB gun and no target, he is likely to shoot out the school window.

If you give people atomic bombs without a philosophy of life, you will start a world war. A boiler that has lost the purpose imposed upon it by an engineer is in danger of explosion. A society that has lost the goals and destiny imposed upon it by right reason and moral law becomes chaotic, revolutionary, and chilled with cold wars. Naturally, when minds lose the purpose of living, they lose the energy to work toward a goal. If a traveler loses interest in visiting Paris, the output of his energy in that direction declines.

Many, having lost the target of life, also lose interest in shooting arrows. This accounts for the tendency of many to deny they have freedom of will. Two of the most popular theories among the bored today are the Marxian and the Freudian. Marx holds that we are economically determined; Freud, that we are biologically determined. Despite all the talk about freedom today, the plain fact is that many are bored with freedom. That is why they are willing to surrender it to a dictator, as Marxism demands, or else are willing to deny any personal responsibility, as Freudianism suggests, by denying moral guilt. Minds are tired principally because they have lost the pattern of life and, therefore, find it no longer worth living; or else, because seeing no purpose, they can see no reason for spending energy to save themselves from blind fatalism and deep, cavernous despair. . . .

A second reason for fatigue can be too many targets. People are unable to determine for themselves any fixed philosophy of life. One year they are reactionaries, with their feet firmly planted in cement. The next year they are liberals, with their feet firmly planted in midair. They read a best seller and for a month are idealists. Next month they read a book on materialism, and they become materialists. Suppose you got on a train with your mind made up to go to

Chicago, and got off after an hour and decided to go to New Orleans. Then you traveled one hundred miles and changed your mind, saying, "No, I will go to San Francisco." You traveled another hundred miles and said, "No, I will go to Indianapolis." If you did this long enough, you would go crazy. One university drove pigs crazy that way. They put their food in a certain slot, and after the pigs learned to go to that slot, they changed the slot. This went on indefinitely, the pigs getting a terrible disappointment from wrong slots, until they went crazy. The poor pigs would never go crazy by themselves. But man could drive them crazy by perverting their instincts and habits.

Something like that is happening to human beings. They are fatigued and exhausted from want of a permanent, overall purpose in life. Can you imagine basketball players enjoying a game if the basket moved from one side of the gymnasium to the other whenever they took a shot? Minds are bored, worried, exhausted, and burdened with ennui because life is purposeless. If there is no meaning to life, there is not much use in living.

There are three ways to achieve power and to overcome fatigue:

1. Have a master idea.
2. Strengthen the will.
3. Have recourse to outside power.

Have *a master idea*. The mind is strengthened by a strong idea. An English professor of psychiatry tested weight lifters. The three men averaged lifting 101 pounds. He hypnotized them and told them they were strong. They lifted 142 pounds, or almost half more weight. Because they got the idea of strength, they became strong. He hypnotized them again and told them that they were weak. They lifted only 29 pounds. The idea of weakness induced weakness in action. The mind was exhausted before the body. At the time of the San Francisco earthquake, 30 people who had been in bed for 30 years got up and walked. The idea that they had to do something about their condition produced appropriate action. . . .

The ideomotor theory of psychology means that an idea tends to work itself out in action. You watch a football game from the stands. You can see an opening for the ball carried around right end. You instinctively move your body in that direction, simply because the idea prompted it. Get wrong ideas in your head and they come out as bad actions. It is nonsense to say that it does not make any difference what you think or believe, it all depends on how you act. If you think about robbing a bank, you will end up robbing one. Keep the mind clean, and the body will keep clean.

The first master idea to possess is to realize we were made for happiness. But in order to be happy, we have to satisfy the higher part of our being, namely, our intellect and our will. We strive for Perfect Truth and Perfect Love, which is God. The master idea then is that we are made to know, love, and serve God in this life and be happy with him forever in the next. The body then becomes the servant of the mind, the senses minister to reason, and reason to faith. No one who loves this master idea is ever unhappy, even amidst the trials and vicissitudes of life. Energy multiplies to achieve it, by goodness to neighbors, patience, charity, meekness, resignation, and some of the other forgotten virtues, such as courtesy and sacrifice. Life becomes full of zeal, and even though sometimes one may do wrong, one nevertheless always has the map. There are many people who get off the road and stay off because they have no road map. So long as you have a master idea, you can get back. There are two classes of people in the world: those who fall down and those who stay down. A pig falls in the mud and stays in the mud: a lamb falls in the mud and gets out of the mud.

Strong reasons make strong actions. To occupy yourself with love of God and neighbor is never to be idle. Hell is full of the talented, but heaven, of the energetic. As sanctity declines, energy declines. Many today do not *believe* enough to be great. Mediocrity is the penalty for loss of faith.

Strengthen the will. Hardly ever does an educator today speak of training the will. A little boy asked his mother, "May I have another piece of cake?"

The mother said, "You have already had eight pieces."

"I know, Mother, but just let me have one more piece, please, please, please."

And the mother said, "All right."

Then the little boy said, "You haven't any will power at all, have you?"

There is a world of difference between willing and wanting. Most people *want* to be good, but they do not *will* to be good. Augustine said, before he became a saint, "Dear Lord, I want to be pure; not now, but a little later on." That was before he became a saint!

Many an alcoholic *wants* to be better; few *will* to be better. It is unfortunate today that some regard alcoholism as a disease like cancer. It may end as a disease, but it begins with an act of the will, namely, to take a drink. The repeated acts of the will become a habit, and the habit becomes enslavement. But even then there is left a little beachhead of human will that one can lay hold of and enlarge until the person is rehabilitated.

If people are told that they are animals or machines, they lose the sense of inner power to become better. A person is a slave of bad habit so long as he accepts the slavery. Why is it that those who constantly warn us of the danger of repressing our sex instincts never warn us about the danger of repressing our will to be better?

Character is like chiseling a statue; one has to knock off huge hunks of selfishness, which requires self-discipline. Only then does character begin to emerge. We mistakenly believe everything can be acquired without effort: for example, "How to learn French without studying vocabulary," or "How to learn to play the piano without reading notes," or "How to make money without working."

We never receive our second wind until we use up the first. God does not give us new graces until we exhaust ourselves in spending those already received. The condition of receiving new power is the resolute will to give power to others. We try to escape intellectual effort by reading picture magazines and novels exclusively and discover in the end that our power to think clearly has been lost. As George Bernard Shaw once said, "Our language is the language of Shakespeare, Thompson, and Milton, and we sit and croon like bilious pigeons."

Maybe our refusal to exercise our body could atrophy our muscles. Could the great increase of heart trouble be due to the fact that few exercise their hearts by hard exercise? I wonder if a ditchdigger ever developed angina pectoris?

Power is bought only in terms of willed service. Nonexpression of the will in effort and self-discipline has caused far more ravages than self-expression.

Have recourse to outside power. The exercise of the will is right, but it is wrong if we think that we can do everything by our own will. We cannot lift ourselves by our own bootstraps or by the lobes of our ears. Those who rely only on their will generally become aggressive, domineering, selfwilled, dictatorial, and proud. Human will has to depend on something else. The basic trouble with atheism is that it breathes in the same air that it breathes out.

There has to be another source of power outside our will. We do not nourish ourselves; we are dependent on the plant and animal world outside. No organism is self-contained; it thrives only by contact with an environment that is nonself. We need air for our lungs and light for our eyes. When we are born, our mind is like a chalkboard, on which nothing is written. Our five senses pour into the mind raw material, from which our intellect, like a great X-ray, abstracts ideas, which we combine into judgments and reasoning processes.

Our spirits, too, are continuous with a larger spiritual world. We are not cisterns, but wells; we grow less by our own power than by assimilation of outside forces. Our intellect and will both need to cooperate with this power of God. Once it gets into our intellect, it becomes faith; in our will, it becomes power. Divine energy, or truth and love, does not originate in us but flows through us. As we establish contact with the atmosphere, which cannot be seen or tasted by breathing, so we establish commerce with the divine source of power by prayer and the sevenfold channels that the good Lord himself offers to our depleted human forces. Unite a dedicated will with this divine energy, and a character is transformed into inner peace and outer service. "I can do all things in Him Who strengtheneth Me."

Unfortunately, many have lost fire and enthusiasm. What has become of great patriots, of an intense devotion and love of country? A country is strong when it has faith in right; it is weak when it loses faith. Only a restoration of our firm belief in God will shake off indifference and apathy and a sense of opiate that makes us cold to international injustices.

Communism is a "faith," a "philosophy of life" based on hate and confiscation. Communism can be overcome only by another faith, a faith in God, a faith in His moral law, and a faith in the providential destiny of our country.

Treasures of the Subconscious

HAS PSYCHOLOGY REVEALED totally the mystery of the subconsciousness? Besides these libidinous instincts, repressed desires, drives to pleasure and sex, and the collective myths of our human ancestry, is there not another drive? Our consciousness and anthropology reveal a great treasure in the depth of our being. The subconsciousness need not be just a cesspool, something we are so ashamed of that it takes constant prodding to bring it to the surface; it is not always a sewerage and drainage system full of the muck and rot of our lives.

Besides the id there is another neglected area for which we have to find a name. Since Freud used the Latin word *id* to signify the cellar of repressed desires, we will use a Greek word *pneuma* to describe the other aspect, though we could use the Hebrew word *ruah*.

Both the id and the pneuma are in the subconscious levels of our mind; through them pass suggestions, desires, urges, drives, and impulsions that seek entrance into the conscious level of life and conduct. They are also the same in that there is a little censor at the top of the stairs who can keep down the dynamisms, drives, and thrusts of the pneuma if it does not like them. In fact, there are seven censors battling against the pneuma: egotism, lust, greed, anger, laziness, intemperance, and jealousy. But there is one big difference; the id is principally concerned with the drive to pleasure. The pneuma is concerned with a drive toward peace, harmony, integration, and happiness. There is in us a double drive: one toward giving release to our carnal nature, the other giving freedom to our deeper spiritual nature. One is an urge to flaunt conscience and the moral law and to be bad; the other is to grow in goodness and love of neighbor; one is to exalt our own ego, the other to serve neighbor and to crush our selfishness.

We are, therefore, solicited in two ways: one toward release of what is egotistic, the other toward a harmony and a perfection of our nature. In other words, we are tempted also to be good.

How far we have gotten away from the total understanding of our subconscious mind will be clear from one word. When I say the word *temptation,* what images and ideas are conjured up in your mind? "Sex"? "Get drunk"? "Rob"? "Steal"? and so on? Why do we always associate the word with what is rotten, immoral, and antisocial? Why does the subconsciousness always have to be considered a Gehenna or a drainage ditch? Why do we assume that every solicitation we have is something we would be ashamed to admit in polite society? Analyze yourself, and you will find this astounding fact—that you have more temptations to be good than you have to be bad.

How many times have you been tempted to help a poor family, and how often you felt sad if you did not and happy when you did? How often you were tempted to give up excessive drinking, bad temper, stealing, to "see what is in the Bible," to be kinder to your wife, gentler to your children, less cranky with your employees, less sarcastic to your neighbor, to try praying, to share your wealth with the hungry, to be more interested in community welfare? It is not only devils who walk up those stairs to the conscious mind; the stairs are really like Jacob's ladder with angels on every rung. And as regards repression, we knock more good thoughts over the head than we do bad thoughts. If, as some say, repression of our primitive instincts is wrong, why is not the repression of our meaningful instincts also wrong?

Why must we think of our subconscious always as a garbage pail instead of a dinner table? Why conceive that the energy of electric power is to give us a shock and not to light and heat? Are there only snakes underground, or do we also find gold? Do not the depths of the soil shoot up oil and fountains of water, as well as being the centers of earthquakes? The time has come when psychiatrists must see the subconscious not just as a mudhole where pigs love to wallow but also as a runway where planes take off for a flight into the sky. The subconscious may be a basement, but it is one not only where we throw out refuse, but also where we keep our groceries, our hobbies, and our playroom, and our wine.

What about the origin of this pneuma that transmits urges and drives from the subterranean part of our lives? Where does it come from? As psychiatrists say, the id has its origin outside us; so does the pneuma. The id, they say, is due either to contacts with our environment or more remotely with our animal ancestry, or it is a cultural lag in the evolutionary process, a result of the collective unconsciousness of the race.

As the origin of the id is external—that is, not wholly of our making—and yet that through which all our drives function, so the origin of the pneuma is external, even much more so, though it, too, functions through our subconsciousness. In fact, it is very mysterious, something like the wind that is invisible and yet strong. We pass over naming the source of the pneuma to concentrate on its silent, enigmatical intrusion into our subconsciousness.

How often we have been moved by an inspiration to change our lives; we know that it does not come from ourselves, for when we have it, we say, "I don't know what made me do this." A truck driver in Los Angeles, speeding down a highway, saw a large cardboard carton ahead of him. Generally, he said, he would drive over it and crush it, for it gave him a sense of power. But this time, he suddenly swerved to avoid it, stopped, got out of his truck cab, and went back to take it off the highway. Lo and behold, it was moving! A little boy had crawled into it and was propelling himself across the road. When asked what made him do it, the driver answered, "God! Because I never acted that way before."

How often a soldier in battle will be suddenly inspired to crawl out of a trench in the face of murderous shellfire to rescue a wounded buddy in a veritable no-man's land. Braver than ever before in his life, he is praised for his rescue but will disdain it, saying, "Anyone else would have done it. I deserve no credit." In other words, "I did not do it—*something else moved me.*"

A characteristic of the upsurgence of the subconscious mind is what might be called sensing a crisis. H. G. Wells expressed it well: "At times in the silence of the night, and in rare lonely moments, I come upon a sort of communion of myself and something great that is not myself. . . . It takes on the effect of a sympathetic person, and my communion has a quality of fearless worship." What is present is a kind of dissolving of the elements of consciousness, as if some new chemical had been poured into the soul and there begins to be a surrender to what the individual believes to be a higher power.

Thus, there pass through the subconscious mind inspirations, insights, new values, and motivations that never before were entertained. They did not come from ourselves, and if we correspond with them, they completely remake us. They change fear into love, indifference into enthusiasm, hate into service. This *pneuma does not belong to our nature as such,* though the id does. But it is so constantly introduced into our impoverished nature that it seems to be a part of our life. When it touches us, it seems to affect principally our intellect and our will: the intellect, by enlightening us to see a truth we never saw before, and our will by giving us a power to do something we never had the strength to do before.

But the healing and elevating power of the pneuma always sets up a counterresistance on the part of our disordered human condition. We are not easily persuaded to give up our sinking ship. The id revolts against the pneuma, and the pneuma against the id, making our hearts the battleground. The egotistic self is threatened with its conceits, lusts, intemperance, anger, and the like. To die to them is not easy, even though the prospect of peace is so appealing and desirable. But once the pneuma is at the helm of the ship, the psychic regions are filled with an indescribable joy and delight.

Just as not everyone gives way to the sexual license that the id may suggest, so not everyone accepts the temptation of the pneuma to reorganize one's life. But when one does, among many effects that might be mentioned we concentrate on but one—a complete change of life's direction.

If I take a ball and roll it across the floor, it will move in one direction unless diverted by a superior power. So, too, our lives very quickly become grooved through habit. They will roll by mere inertia in that same direction of crime, insensibility, mediocrity, emptiness, banality, unless some outside power or force alters their direction.

A law runs through nature that the lower is taken up into the higher. Chemicals are taken up into plants, plants into animals, and animals into man. Everywhere there is an upsurge to life. Lower life is meant to be born to a higher life. But there is one condition—the carbons, phosphates, oxygen, nitrogen, and other chemicals are never privileged to live in a plant kingdom unless two things happen: The plant must intercept them, incorporate them into itself, and the chemicals, in their turn, must die to their lower nature. It is as if the grass and the trees and the roses said to the chemicals, "Unless you die to yourself, you cannot live in my kingdom. You must be reborn from above."

Plants, in their turn, can become one with the sentient, mobile life of the animal if the animal comes down to them, descends to their lower life, and takes them up into itself. The plant, in its turn, must be pulled up from the roots. The same is true of the lower orders living in our body—to become one with the living, thinking, loving being, man must humble himself and go down to their lower state; they in turn must submit to the sacrifice of the knife and the fire, and thus the law is fulfilled: "Unless you die to yourself you cannot live in my kingdom. You must be born again from above."

Now the pneuma that works inside us is a summoning presence, a kind of alien intruder, but one that always respects our freedom. Animals do not consult plants nor carry on a dialogue with them before using them as food. But the pneuma does not violently possess us; it solicits quietly, it tempts, it leads us into a desert, it begs us to die to what is lower. Once we freely consent to absorb the élan and drive of the pneuma, there is a peace that the world cannot give and a joy that surpasses all understanding. Most of us miss the exhilaration because we prefer to move in the horizontal areas of monotony instead of the vertical heights where there are new knowledge and deeper love.

There is not a single person in the world who has not experienced both the id and the pneuma, though greater priority is given to the id than the pneuma because it titillates the flesh and makes no demands on the ego. The id belongs to what William James has called the once-born; the pneuma to those who are twice-born. We have three ways of knowing: One is by our senses, such as the clasp of a hand. The second is by abstract ideas and scientific training, such as the science of physics. Over and above both feeling and intellect, there is another kind of knowing that a husband and wife have after many years of married life— they have come to know each other by loving each other. This kind of knowledge the pneuma gives, only its love is more intense.

A new heart is created within us by a response to the pneuma. From the fleshy heart, there goes forth blood to the body and then a return flow to it. The heart understood psychologically is also understood as the center from which flows our mental and moral activity. From it comes all our character and worth, and to it returns all our good merits; but the heart can also be the center of depravity that corrupts the whole circuit of life. "Out of the heart come forth evil thoughts, murders, adulteries, fornications, thefts, false witnesses."

A boy in a family could not be induced to keep himself clean: dirty fingernails, hair hanging like a mop, clothes unpressed, dirty shoes. The parents begged, pleaded, coaxed, and even tried to bribe him into cleanliness. It did no good. But one day he appeared clean, brushed, and neat. He did not slam the door as he went out. What made the difference? He was in love with Suzie! This is the key to pneuma, the Spirit that reorients life; it is essentially love but not an earthly love.

As there are compulsive drinkers and compulsive addicts

in the id world, so there are compulsive lovers of humanity and compulsive lovers of love in the pneuma world. We are no longer in the presence of demons and pink elephants, but of a Light that unfailingly allows us to follow footprints in the darkest forest of life.

I knew a man in London who told me that he had been an alcoholic for years; so enslaved was he that he would take off his shoes at the saloon door and sell them for a drink. This particular year he was seated on a bench at Hyde Park, musing about his miserable condition. Suddenly he felt a strong urge to reform his life. He professed ignorance as to where the resolution came from, but he said that it was not from himself. Following this inspiration was easy, but putting it into practice was difficult. He went into a church, and there came over him immediately an intense craving for drink. He ran to the rear of the church to escape, but he knelt down at the door. From that time on, the goal of his life was changed. He now spends his time caring for his fellow alcoholics in the same London dive where he lived for years. The day the inspiration seized him, he knew only one thing—it came not from himself. He had been hellbent, and suddenly he was, after a struggle, on the heavenbent road to inner happiness. The pneuma confronted him on the inside of his being, but it came from the outside. It was as if another Presence were in his life, acting like a radar bringing him to the port of peace.

Another example is given by the Russian novelist, Tolstoy. His despairing nature drove him to the thought of suicide. Then, as he put it, something contrary to his mood seized him:

"I felt [says Tolstoy] that something had broken within me on which my life had always rested, that I had nothing left to hold on to, and that morally my life had stopped. An invincible force impelled me to get rid of my existence, in one way or another.

"Yet, whilst my intellect was working, something else in me was working too, and kept me from the deed—a consciousness of life, as I may call it, which was like a force that obliged my mind to fix itself on another direction and draw me out of my situation of despair.

"During the whole course of this year, when I almost unceasingly kept asking myself how to end the business, whether by the rope or by the bullet, during all that time, alongside all those movements of my ideas and observations, my heart kept languishing with another pining emotion. I can call this by no other name than that of a thirst for God."

We have in our subconscious a mass of dead ideas, lifeless hopes, faded childhood memories, and lost faiths. We would like to get back to their innocence and joy, but they are cold and sepulchered. Then what was crucified by us suddenly rises from the dead; what was cold is now hot; what was crystal now becomes a living cell. What was on the periphery of life now becomes a center; what we ignored now is valued. And we know very well that this old building in which we lived, with its leaky plumbing and cracked walls, did not suddenly become a mansion without some builder from the outside. If my life is traveling in the direction of "confusion worse confounded," and all of a sudden changes its course, with new goals, then the Latin maxim applies: *Nihil movetur nisi per aliud movetur.* "Nothing is moved unless it is moved by another." The new mental arrangement of ideas, the sudden thrust of some alien motor efficacy, demands a source outside of me and yet working inside me and principally through my subconsciousness.

The classic playboy of all antiquity was Augustine, who combined the greatness of the intellect with a sexual abandon that he justified by rationalization. One day the dissension between his sex life and his higher aspirations became so intense that he picked up St. Paul's Letter to the Romans; in it he read that not in wantonness, immorality, strife, and envy do we work out salvation. It acted as a thunderbolt in his soul with his wasted young life. Changing the direction of his life after the impact of the pneuma, he cried out: "Too late, O Ancient Beauty, have I loved Thee!"

A spiritual knowledge under the pneuma is arrived at so quickly that the intellectual is left behind; one is not able to find a cause for the change in any previous thought. No one goes from the life of sin to holiness without some intervening cause that is sufficient to account for the change. There has been what is nothing less than a divine-human encounter. A power enters into the subconsciousness that regenerates, changes direction, alters the moral character, making precious what was previously vile and vile what was previously precious.

No new faculties are created. They are just regenerated. What happens may be likened to putting a lamp inside a Japanese lantern. It was nothing but a crisscross of crazy patterns. Once the light was put in it, there was a unification of color and line so that a pattern was revealed. The change may also be likened to a new kind of vision. We have the same eyes at night as we have in the day, but we cannot see at night because we lack the light of the sun. So a new light is given that enables us to see things that before we could not see.

There is never any violation of personality. No invasion is there like to what has been described as possession. But there is a *surrender* of self to Another. Looking back on the evil that one has done, one never sees it as a violation of the law, but rather as hurting someone we love. A new master center takes possession of personality and gives it what Frankl calls "a will to meaning." The whole life begins to be organized, not merely as a sum of parts but rather as a whole, very much the same as the melody that is heard very differently from the distinct notes on the paper.

Id requires analysis because the mind is all mixed-up. The pneuma synthesizes. To analyze the waters that pour into a sinking ship is not to save the ship; to plow by constantly looking back to see if the furrow is crooked may make life even more zigzag. Under probing, the true essence of life vanishes. Our physiological life demands harmony, the tiny cell choosing from its environment what it is able to assimilate; the psychological demands similar peace. A regulator, a kind of thermostat, is at the center of our organism, seeking to establish constants, such as temperature, blood pressure, and digestion. The automatic control is ever working to synthesize harmony and meaning.

So, too, there functions in the depths of our being another kind of regulator, or constant, summoning us back to order and to peace. Little warning lights begin to flicker as they do in the cockpit of a plane when anything is wrong, such as an unlocked door or an overheated motor. That is, organized sensitivity to the body becomes spiritual sensitivity in the conduct of our lives. A carpenter uses a gauge containing a colored liquid. He lays it on a board to see if it is level. Once he finds it off center, he begins to make the adjustment and correction. So, too, in us is an adjuster that makes us rediscover inner peace and the true center, even in the midst of errors and excesses.

It has been moved medically that the power of healing wounds at a certain age increases when the temperature of the body is raised by four degrees. It is conceivable that the power of the pneuma, which increases the joy and the love in a person, may also accelerate the healing of the anxiety and chaos in the depths of being.

Now, what is this pneuma? Pneuma is the Spirit, the Spirit of God, the Spirit of Christ. As my body lives, thanks to my soul, so my soul begins really to live, thanks to the Spirit. Because this Spirit comes from outside us and is not either of our making or of our deserving, it is free or gratis or what is commonly called grace. The id draws to pleasure of the flesh; the pneuma to the joys of the spirit. It might be well to cut down on the temptations of the id and begin giving way to the temptations of the pneuma.

Fig Leaves and Fashions

IN ORDER TO UNDERSTAND the theology of dress, one must go back to the primal story of Adam and Eve, in which is revealed a tremendous mystery about man's dignity. After the Fall of the first parents, Scripture says: "Then the eyes of both were opened, and they became aware of their nakedness; so that they sewed fig leaves together and made themselves girdles."

Evidently, before the Fall there was an absence of clothes, but there was no nakedness. After the Fall, there was an absence of clothes, plus a sense of nakedness. Hence, in the original state of man, the two states were not identical. Nakedness implies the absence of clothes; but before sin the absence of clothes did not imply nakedness. What was veiled before was now unveiled. Something that had been covered was now uncovered. The body after the Fall is something that has been stripped, or in our language, naked. *The body had existed in a different state before the Fall from that after the Fall.*

An example of this kind of uncovering is to be found in some actors. For years they have trod the stage and received the adulation of an audience; then comes a time when their talents can no longer find an outlet; they suffer a kind of "fall." There is a story of an actor who for years played the role of Abraham Lincoln with distinction. While enjoying good fortune, he dressed like the rest of men when he was outside the theater. But after he had fallen from prestige, and had been "driven out of his Paradise," he always appeared on the street in his stage costume of Abraham Lincoln. Other actors said of him that he would never be happy until he was assassinated. He thus covered up the shame of what he had undergone. The actor when stripped of theatrical glory still wore its trappings. So, too, the body, when stripped of its dignity as a result of the Fall, put on clothes.

The inside and the outside of man existed in a different way after the Fall from the way they existed before. Man has a body and soul. Before the Fall, the soul had an inner radiance, a grace, a glory, a brilliance, a splendor, a beauty that shone through the entire body, clothing it in light. It must have been something like unto the body of Our Blessed Lord at the moment of the Transfiguration, when the brilliance of the sun shone round about Him, making it impossible for the Apostles to look upon Him.

The clothing of the body before the Fall was this inner radiance of grace shining through. Where there is innocence from the moral point of view, there is no sense of nakedness. Virtue was the *habitus,* or habit or garment, but when the grace and the inner glory were lost, then the body no longer had that radiant beauty that it had possessed before. It perceived itself naked because it had lost innocence. Immediately, there was felt the necessity of covering up the nakedness. The dignity of the body went with the glory that it had lost, and its indignity was nakedness. Clothes, therefore, are an expression of inner nakedness, a compensation for something that has been surrendered. The body, once discovered and stripped of grace is an object of shame. Immediately a veil has to be thrown over its nudity. Clothing therefore is an expression of respectability, and not of innocence.

The truth of this relationship between inner and outer beauty goes deeper than clothes. It will often be discovered that, the greater the inner nakedness of someone, that is, the less virtue and goodness and humility there are in the soul, the greater will be the display on the outside. The more glory that there is on the inside and the more grace, the less concern there will be for what is on the outside. As Shakespeare said: "Assume a virtue, if you have it not." Those who lack a quality often make it appear as if they possessed it. A person who is not well educated but who would like to appear so uses a vocabulary that is pretentious. A poor person who wishes to appear rich may dress well; a rich person need not necessarily do likewise.

Those who have many external trappings soon fall into the error of believing that *having* is *being,* and that, because they have something, therefore they are somebody.

It was Carlyle who first used the expression "clothes-horse" to imply that the body was nothing but a prop on which to hang decorations. Luxurious garments at one time used to be piled on top of one another to achieve the maximum of gorgeousness. This reached a climax in the extremely gaudy dress of Louis XV and Louis XVI. Clothes are everything; man is only a coat hanger. Behind it all is the philosophy that man has no inner worth, no inner grandeur, but he must appear to possess them. The want of "being" is compensated for by the excess of "having."

Adam and Eve when they perceived themselves to be naked, stripped of the inner radiance of grace, clothed themselves with fig leaves and then, later on, with the skins of animals. In each instance, that which covered the shame was baser than man himself, belonging either to the plant kingdom or to the animal kingdom—things that are fit for the adornment of the body but not for the soul. The coat of skins cost a life to cover man's shame. This suggests, for the first time, that it might cost a life to cover all the shame of all humanity. The animals who were killed had no part in the guilt of Adam and Eve, and the One who was going to be killed to cover the sin of humanity Himself had no part in our guilt. It is as if God were saying to men, "You are right in making clothes for yourselves. It was your soul that once clothed your body; now you have put the body above your soul, and you must hide the shame of it." In the eyes of God there is nothing to be ashamed of when the soul clothes the body, but there is a great deal to be ashamed of when the body is put before the soul. That is why the body has to be covered and hidden; like a murderer concealing his victim, we try to hide our crime.

But where there is inner grace, a participation in the Divine Nature, a God-likeness in the soul, there is no need to compensate for it on the outside. This explains the beautiful ceremony of the clothing of nuns. A young woman who gives herself to God presents herself at the altar dressed in all the finery she can afford. She is allowed to wear any jewels she pleases and is often attired in a kind of wedding gown; unlimited trappings are permitted. Once she has made her surrender to God and promised to serve him for life as a spiritual spouse, she retires into the cloister and puts on the humble habit of her community. The assumption behind this ceremony is that, while she was yet in the world, she had to exaggerate her lack of inner worth by external pomp and splendor; but once her soul is crowned with grace, goodness, and virtue, then there is less need of the external. There is a kind of return to the Garden of Eden, where outer display was unecessary because real worth shone through.

The theology of clothes is illustrated in the ceremony of baptism. When a child is baptized, the grace that was lost in the Fall is restored. A white robe or garment is placed on the child with the words: "Receive this white garment which mayest thou keep unspotted until the day when thou dost appear before the tribunal of Our Lord and Savior Jesus Christ." The whiteness and the simplicity of the garment represent the grace that was lost; they provide a reminder of the inner radiance that once suffused the whole human body. When the prodigal son returned home, he was given a robe by his father, which symbolized a return to the inner clothing of grace. Our clothing was meant to be the light of grace and virtue and heavenly innocence. Earthly clothing is the covering up of the nakedness caused by the absence of our real clothing.

Clothing therefore tells the story of inner and outer worth. It is a symbol of lost innocence, a memento of a former glory. There are therefore two fashions: the passing fashion of the world and the enduring fashion of the spiritual. In the final reckoning it will not matter how we are dressed on the outside; one can go into the kingdom of heaven in rags; but it makes an eternity of difference as to how we are dressed on the inside.

The importance of that inner fashion was revealed in our Lord's parable of the wedding feast. Thousands came in from the highways and the byways. When the King looked over all who came, he saw a man there who had on no wedding garment. The Greek word used in the Gospel implies that the omission was his own deliberate fault, a determination not to wear it. The wedding garment stood for that inner radiance of grace, charity, and innocence that was lost in the Fall. On this earth there are occasions that demand white tie and tails or formal gowns. These will not get us into heaven. For that, we will need the white robe of grace.

The Apostolate of Beauty

FRANCIS QUARLES has taken a view of beauty that seems a little base:

> *Gaze not on beauty too much,*
> *Lest it blind thee;*
> *Nor too near,*
> *Lest it burn thee.*
> *If thou like it, it receives thee;*
> *If thou love it, it disturbs thee;*
> *If thou hunt after it, it destroys thee.*

This view looks upon beauty as a temptress, and generally a bodily one. It forgets that beauty is more universal than tempting flesh. Beauty is nestling in the rosebud, walking like starry sentinels across the encampment of night, smiling in the cheek of a lily, rolling onto the surf in the measured harmonies of the wild waves. Beauty, when seen this way, is a gift, not a danger.

Everything beautiful in the world is a reflection of the divine beauty. As Augustine put it, "All that loveliness, which passes through men's minds into their skillful hands, comes from that supreme loveliness, which is above our souls. For it my soul sighs day and night. From that supreme Beauty, those who make and seek after exterior beauty derive the measure by which they judge of it, but not the measure by which it should be used." For a long time in his life, he had failed to see that the beauty of earth was like a ray of the sun. When finally he traced back the beams of light to the great furnace of light, he cried out, "Too late I have loved thee, O Beauty of ancient days, yet ever new! Too late have I loved thee! And lo, thou wert within, and I abroad searching for thee. Thou wert with me, but I was not with thee."

One wonders if it be not true that of all the gifts that God gives, the one for which he receives thanks last and least of all is the gift of beauty. God gives wealth; those who receive it will often use it for holy purposes. God gives power of speech or music, and the gift is repaid in influence and song. But very often when beauty is given to a human, the good Lord gets back only old bones. One wonders if any parent ever thanks God for a beautiful child or if a beautiful woman ever thanks God for the gift of beauty.

When human beauty is allied with virtue, then it becomes one of the most powerful means of an apostolate for Good. As Shakespeare put it:

> *Oh, how much more doth beauty beauteous seem*
> *By that sweet ornament which truth doth give!*
> *The rose looks fair, but fairer we it deem*
> *For that sweet odor which doth in it live!*

"The beauty of the king's daughter is from within." Real beauty is from inside. An otherwise beautiful face is ruined by an ugly soul. That kind of beauty never makes anyone better; it becomes a rose to be trampled on. But the beauty of soul that shines through the prison bars of the flesh produces a hush of devotion and a spiritual admiration in others.

Beauty without virtue is like a fair flower that has an offensive odor. But the true beauty bathes in that light without which nothing is beautiful. Beauty is a gift of God, like the rain. He allows the rain to fall upon the just and the wicked, and He gives beauty not only to the good, but even to the wicked. Wicked beauty strikes the eye, but the inner beauty of grace wins the soul.

Roses in God's Garden

WHY SHOULD THERE NOT BE HEARTS in the world like St. Agnes, who could say before her martyrdom when an earthly love was presented to her: "The kingdom of the world and every ornament thereof have I scorned for the love of Jesus Christ, my Lord, whom I have seen and loved, in whom I have believed and who is my love's choice"? Why should there not be young men and women who would put their whole selves at the disposal of God, for the value of every gift is enhanced if it exists solely for the one to whom it is given, fulfills no other purpose, and remains unshared? Why should there not be hearts so much in love with God that they should build walls around themselves, not to keep themselves in, but to keep the world out? Why should there not be Marys and Magdalenes at the foot of the Crucifix of the twentieth century as well as at the foot of the Cross of the first? Why should there not be hearts whose first love is their last love, which is the love of God?

Why should there not be roses in God's garden? In an earthly garden is an earthly rose that has its own father and mother, brothers and sisters, hopes and aspirations for the future, its own joys and sorrows, its own laughter when there is sunshine, and its own tears when there is dew. Out into the garden comes a human hand that plucks the rose and destroys its life. The rose has a life and a right to live that life, and yet no injustice is done nor murder committed, for the hand of man is above the rose in dignity and worth and may use the rose for his own sweet purposes.

In the human family is a human rose with its own real father and mother, brothers and sisters, hopes and aspirations for the future, its own real laughter, and its own real tears. From out the high heavens there comes the Hand of the Everlasting Gardener who plucks the human rose and destroys its life, insofar as its human environment is concerned, for that young man or woman has a human life and the right to live it. But there is no injustice done nor murder committed, for as the hand of man is above the earthly rose, so the Hand of God is above the human soul, and may use it to His own sweet purposes—and God's purposes are always sweet.

But it may be asked, what benefit accrues to the poor rose that is plucked from the earthly garden? It is put into a crystal vase, refreshing waters are poured on it from day to day; it is touched by human hands, it may even be pressed to human lips, and like another John may be privileged to tabernacle its crimson head upon the breast of the Eucharistic Emmanuel. Its earthly life is shortened, yes. But what a beautiful life it now begins to lead with man!

In like manner, when God plucks the young human heart from the garden of the human family, it is placed in the crystal vase of His Church, refreshing waters of sanctifying grace are poured on it from day to day, it is touched by the hands of the saints and the Mother of God, and is pressed in daily communion to the Heart of Christ. Its human life is shortened, yes. But what a beautiful life it now begins to lead with God!

What a Saint Is Not

THERE HAS BEEN MUCH FLIPPANCY, written and spoken, about sanctity. It is also important to know what a saint is not. Oscar Wilde said, "The only difference between a saint and a sinner is that every sinner has a past and every saint has a future." Someone else has said, "A saint is a dead sinner revised and edited." A popular misunderstanding is, "He doesn't smoke, he doesn't drink, he doesn't swear, he's a saint."

Another false conception of a saint is that he is one who is completely separated from the world. Sanctity does not depend upon *where* we are; it depends on what we are thinking about. Holiness has no relation whatever to geography. A conductor in a New York subway could be a saint just as well as Simeon Stylites on a pillar.

Neither does sanctity consist in great penances; flagellation or sleeping on spikes for mortification of the flesh is not necessarily associated with sanctity. Mortifications must always be the means to an end, not an end in itself. St. Paul said that "if he should deliver his body to be burned, and have not love, it profited him nothing." That is the difference between a Communist and a saint; the Communist may give his body to be burned, but it will be out of hate, not love for God and forgiveness of man. There was one monk in a monastery who decided during Lent to live on nothing but crusts; he upset the routine of the whole monastery. There is not much need in the twentieth century for wearing hair shirts for sanctity because there are enough people around us who take the place of hair shirts; we can sanctify our lives by bearing their boredom.

Neither does sanctity consist in pious gestures, artificial

tones of voice, beatific expressions, or the sprinkling of conversation with texts from Sacred Scripture. Our Blessed Lord said, "Not everyone that sayeth, 'Lord, Lord,' will enter the kingdom of heaven." Some motion-picture actresses portraying saints believe that holiness has something to do with the open mouth gasping for breath; this is a confusion of holiness with adenoids.

Neither does sanctity consist in sadness or a long face, for Our Blessed Lord told us that when we fast we are not to wear a long face. No saint is ever sad; one of the conditions of sanctity is joy. The saint always rises above difficulties with humor and gladness and joy. In the last century Don Bosco was telling a monsignor in the chancery about a religious order that he hoped to found, and that he would send missionaries and establish houses for boys all over the world—which is true today. The monsignor thought Don Bosco had gone mad and decided to put him into an insane asylum. Calling a cab, he asked Don Bosco to get in with him for a ride. Don Bosco knew what he was up to, so when the carriage drove up, he said that he would not dare step into a cab ahead of the monsignor. He asked him to get in first; when he got in, he slammed the door and told the driver, who was a good friend of his, to drive the monsignor as quickly as possible to an insane asylum because he was mad and there was not a moment to be lost. The more the monsignor shouted and shrieked, the more the driver was convinced he *was* mad. He was really locked up, and it took the chaplain of the insane asylum to get him out.

What a Saint Is

Turning now to the positive side of what constitutes sanctity, we enumerate three basic principles:

1. *Divine standard.* The mediocre are always self-satisfied and boast that they have done enough. That is because they judge themselves by their neighbors. A saint, however, judges himself, not by human standards, but by the Divine. The Pharisee, who judged himself by his neighbor, thought himself superior to them all because he fasted several times a week; the Publican in the back of the temple, judging himself by the mercy of God, struck his breast and asked for mercy.

If a painting is observed and studied by candlelight, it may seem to be very perfect, but if it is brought under the sunlight, one sees bad composition, defective coloring, or uneven proportion. So it is with human life. When it is judged by the candlelight of the mediocrity and ordinariness of our neighbor, we flatter ourselves that we are really a good portrait; but in the glare of the Divine Light we see our imperfections. That is one of the reasons why all saints, who measure themselves by the Infinite, are absolutely convinced of their nothingness. Thomas Aquinas said all that he had written was a straw when he was bequeathed a vision of the truth of God. There is a sublime paradox in the fact that a saint is constantly getting back to zero. It is at this point that a saint gets closest to the Infinite, since it was from nothingness that we all came.

2. *Diffused goodness.* A leprous physician cannot heal. Only wise men can impart wisdom; only the holy can diffuse holiness. A man can bring out of his heart only the treasures that are locked therein. Saints diffuse holiness because they reflect the life of Christ as color reflects light. If a thing reflects no light, it is black; if it reflects part of the light, it is blue, indigo, or red. If it reflects all rays, it is white. This is why Scripture describes the saints in heaven as wearing white robes.

As the rays of the sun are so rich that we cannot see their many splendors unless they are shot through a prism, which causes them to break into the seven rays of the spectrum, so, too, the life of Christ, which the saints reflect, is so infinitely good that it takes an infinite variety of saints shot through the prism of love and penance to reflect the holiness of the Son of God. Sinners are always alike; saints are always different. They therefore break up the monotony of life.

3. *Total surrender.* Love is not shown by gifts, but by a complete surrender through an act of will. The gift of the lover without the love of the giver is bare; that is one of the reasons why we take price tags off gifts, in order that there be no proportion between the thing and our love. The only thing in all the world that is really and absolutely our own is our will. Talents, wealth, power, beauty, prestige—all of these God can take away because they are His gifts, but the one thing God will not take away is our will. This is eternally our own; therefore, it is the only perfect gift that we can ever give. The saint gives the will so totally and absolutely that he desires nothing else but the will of God.

There is something in the manner of the saint toward God like unto a dog toward its master. The dog has habitual attention toward the master, sleeps with one eye open, knows the sound of his voice, is always in readiness for his command; the dog never enjoys a walk alone but always has to be taken and, in the midst of all distractions of sniffing, the master is still the center of attention. No pain or punishment that the master may inflict upon the dog ever alienates the dog; the master is always right. The dog puts its tail between its legs and comes to the master for forgiveness.

So the saint knows that, even when God permits him to take bitter medicine, the medicine comes from an all-loving Father. Like the vessel that Magdalene brought unto the feet of the Savior, he pours out his dedication, not drop by drop, but breaks the vessel of the ego and the self in order that the perfume of his consecration may fill the world. But this sanctity never implies a separation from neighbor, for the saint knows that, as he cannot go to God without others, so he cannot go to others without God. St. Augustine says, "I cannot live in myself if I do not live in God."

There is one point in which we are all like unto saints, and that is in the expenditure of energy. A saint does not put forth any more energy in being a saint than the head of an advertising agency does to get business, or an athlete does in training for a fight, or a college boy does to get into a fraternity, or a woman does to get into a size-ten dress each spring. The difference lies in their sense of values. The simple truth is that it does not require much time to make a saint; it requires only much love. The difference, however, is that we are escapists, and the saints are not. The saints go all the way, but we hold back. With Augustine, before his conversion we day, "Dear Lord, I want to be a saint—not now, but a little later on." Jacques Rivière said, "Take from me, O Lord, the temptation to be a saint." Laurence Housman wrote:

> O, Tempt me not! I love too well this snare
> Of silk and cords. Nay, love, the flesh is fair;
> So tempt me not! This earth affords
> Too much delight;
> Withdraw be from my sight
> Lest my weak soul break free
> And throw me back to thee.

Most of us have our arms on our breasts, not to form a cross, but to protect the trivial treasures we would not give up.

Our consolation is that God is the only One in the universe who will take our old bones. The world does not want old bones, just young ones, but God will take all the tangled skeins of a wrecked and ruined life to weave out of them the beautiful tapestry of saintliness and holiness.

The Divine Sense of Humor

ONE CLASS OF PEOPLE who have the divine sense of humor
are saints. I do not mean canonized saints, but rather
that great army of staunch and solid Christians to whom
everything and every incident speak a story of God's love.
A saint can be defined as one who has a divine sense of
humor, for a saint never takes this world seriously as the
lasting city. To a saint the world is like a scaffolding up
which souls climb to the kingdom of heaven, and when the
last soul shall have climbed up through it, then it shall be
torn down and burned with a fervent fire, not because it is
base, but simply because it has done its work—it has
brought souls back again to God. A saint is one who looked
out upon this world as a nursery to the Father's heavenly
mansion and a stepping stone to the kingdom of heaven. A
saint is one to whom everything in the world is a sacrament. In the strict sense of the term, there are only seven
sacraments, but in the broad sense of the term everything
in the world is a sacrament, for everything in the world can
be used as a means of special sanctification.

A saint is one who never complains about the particular
duty of his state in life, for he knows full well that "all the
world's a stage, and all the men and women merely
players." Why, then, should he who plays the part of a king
glory in his tinsel crown and tin sword and believe that he
is better than someone else who plays the part of a peasant,
for when the curtain goes down they are all men? So, too,
why should anyone, who in this world happens to enjoy
the accident of either honor or wealth, believe he is better
than someone else who may possess neither gold nor
worldly learning? Why should he glory in his tinseled

crown and tin sword, and believe that he is better than someone else who plays a less important role in the great drama of life? For when the curtain goes down on the last day, and we respond to the curtain call of judgment, we will not be asked what part we played, but how well we played the part that was assigned to us.

A saint, then, is one who has learned to spiritualize and sacramentalize and ennoble everything in the world and make of it a prayer. No occupation is too base for such spiritualization, nor is any suffering too hard for such ennobling. It is only those who have not this highly developed sense that let the opportunities of daily life pass by without either making of them a prayer or drawing from them a divine lesson. Centuries ago, according to a story perhaps apocryphal, in the streets of Florence there stood a beautiful piece of Carrara marble that had been cut and hacked and ruined by some cheap artist. Other mediocre artists passed it by and bemoaned that it should have been so ruined. One day Michelangelo passed it by and asked that it be taken to his studio. He there applied to it his chisel, his genius, and his inspiration. He drew out of it the immortal statue of David. The lesson contained herein is that there is nothing so base or low that it cannot be reconquered, that there is no duty however menial that cannot be retrieved for sanctity, and that there is nothing that is cast down that cannot be lifted up.

Sacramentalizing the Universe

THE UNIVERSE is a great sacrament. A sacrament in the strict sense of the term is a material sign used as a means of conferring grace, and instituted by Christ. In the broad sense of the term everything in the world is a sacrament inasmuch as it is a material thing used as a means of spiritual sanctification. Everything is and should be a stepping stone to God. Sunsets should be the means of reminding us of God's beauty as a snowflake should remind us of God's purity. Flowers, birds, beasts, men, women, children, beauty, love, truth, all these earthly possessions are not an end in themselves; they are only means to an end. The temporal world is a nursery to the eternal world, and the mansions of this earth a figure of the Father's heavenly mansions. The world is just a scaffolding up which souls climb to the kingdom of heaven, and when the last soul shall have climbed through that scaffolding, then it shall be torn down and burned with fervent fire, not because it is base, but simply because it has done its work.

Man therefore partly works out his salvation by *sacramentalizing the universe;* man sins by refusing to sacramentalize it or, in other words, by using creatures as selfish ends rather than God-ward means. Manichaeism is wrong because it considers matter as an evil instead of a "sacrament." Epicureanism is wrong because it considers pleasure as a God, instead of a means to God. Sacramentalizing the universe ennobles the universe, for it bestows upon it a kind of transparency that permits the vision of the spiritual behind the material. Poets are masters in sacramentalizing creation for they never take anything in its mere material expression; for them things are symbols of the divine. Saints surpass poets in that gift, for saints see God in everything, or better, see God through everything. The poor, the lame, the blind to them are transparent like a windowpane; they are revelations of Christ as Christ himself told us they really were: "I was sick and you visited me."

Sanctifying the Moment

ONE REMEDY for the ills that come to us from thinking about time is what might be called the sanctification of the moment—or the now. Our Lord laid down the rule for us in these words: "Do not fret, then, over tomorrow; leave tomorrow to fret over its own needs; for today, today's troubles are enough." (Matthew 6:34) This means that each day has its own trials; we are not to borrow troubles from tomorrow because that day, too, will have its cross. We are to leave the past to Divine Mercy and to trust the future, whatever its trials, to His Loving Providence. Each minute of life has its peculiar duty—regardless of the appearance that minute may take. The now moment is the moment of salvation. Each complaint against it is a defeat; each act of resignation to it is a victory.

The moment is always an indication to us of God's will. The ways of pleasing Him are made clear to us in several ways: through His Commandments, by the events of His incarnate life in Jesus Christ our Lord, in the voice of his Mystical Body, the Church, in the duties of our state of life. And, in a more particular way, God's will is manifested for us in the now with all of its attendant circumstances, duties, and trials.

The present moment includes some things over which we have control, but it also carries with it difficulties we cannot avoid—such things as a business failure, a bad cold, rain on picnic days, an unwelcome visitor, a fallen cake, a buzzer that doesn't work, a fly in the milk, and a boil on the nose the night of the dance. We do not always know why such things as sickness and setbacks happen to us, for our minds are far too puny to grasp God's plan. Man is a little like a mouse in a piano, which cannot understand why it must be disturbed by someone playing Chopin and forcing it to move off the piano wires.

When Job suffered, he posed questions to God: why was he born, and why was he suffering? God appeared to him, but instead of answering Job's questions, He began to ask Job to answer some of the larger questions about the universe. When the Creator had finished pouring queries into the head of the creature, Job realized that the questions of God were wiser than the answers of men. Because God's ways are not our ways—because the salvation of a soul is more important than all material values—because divine wisdom can draw good out of evil—the human mind must develop acceptance of the now, no matter how hard it may be for us to understand its freight of pain. We do not walk out of a theater because the hero is shot in the first act; we give the dramatist credit for having a plot in his mind; so the soul does not walk out on the first act of God's drama of salvation—it is the last act that is to crown the play. The things that happen to us are not always susceptible to our minds' comprehension or wills' conquering, but they are always within the capacity of our faith to accept and of our wills' submission. . . .

Every moment brings us more treasures than we can gather. The great value of the now, spiritually viewed, is that it carries a message God has directed personally to us. Books, sermons, and broadcasts on a religious theme have the appearance of being circular letters, meant for everyone. Sometimes, when such general appeals do appear to have a personal application, the soul gets angry and writes vicious letters to allay its uneasy conscience: excuses can always be found for ignoring the divine law.

But though moral and spiritual appeals carry God's identical message to all who listen, this is not true of the now moment; no one else but *I* am in exactly these circumstances; no one else has to carry the same burden, whether it be sickness, the death of a loved one, or some other adversity. Nothing is more individually tailored to our spiritual needs than the now moment; for that reason it is an occasion of knowledge that can come to no one else. This moment is my school, my textbook, my lesson. Not even our Lord disdained to learn from his specific now; being God He knew all, but there was still one kind of knowledge He could experience as a man. St. Paul describes it: "Son of God though He was, He learned obedience in the school of suffering" (Hebrews 5:8).

Pain and Suffering

OUR CAPACITY FOR PAIN is greater than our capacity for pleasure. Suffering reaches the point where we feel we can endure it no longer, and yet it increases and we endure it. But pleasures very quickly reach a peak and then begin a decline. Age decreases the capacity for pleasures. Though pain never turns into a pleasure, a pleasure can turn into a pain. Tickling may be funny at first, but it can also become excruciatingly painful. Our capacity for pain is greater because the good Lord intended that all pain should be exhausted in this world. The divine plan is to have real joys in the next life.

Because so many in our world suffer anxieties that grow like fire, or a loneliness that spreads like a desert, or else experience heartaches, disappointments, bereavements, and scorpion thrusts of pain, we thought it fitting to say something of the philosophy of suffering and evil.

Our subject will be divided into three parts:

1. What pain or suffering does to us.
2. How to meet it.
3. Why there is suffering.

The first effect of pain is that it makes us concentrate on ourselves. A toothache creates a barrier between us and the outside world; pain makes us so attentive to the ego as to kill our social instincts. If you have the colic, it is hard to be altruistic. We often invoke our sickness as an excuse for our selfishness, egotism, and impatience. But this concentration on the ego can be "for better or for worse," just like marriage. I was going to say something about this analogy, but I will not. . . .

As Franz Werfel expressed it, "Sickness invites us to heaven or to hell." It invites us to hell, and makes us worse, when it intensifies selfishness; it makes us bitter and disgruntled, or tyrants demanding constant attention. Such is the tyranny of sickness. Some persons in hospitals are constantly ringing for a nurse. As W. C. Fields once put it, "They take a turn for the nurse."

Sickness can also liberate a man from his selfishness and so transform his soul as to reveal the mystery of his being. At least one thing pain can do is to cut down the opportunities for sinning and thus prepare the soul for virtue; it also gives one an opportunity to study oneself, to examine one's conscience, to inquire into the purpose of life. Sickness prevents many a man from being a scoundrel and gives him a chance to mend his ways. Many a man who is a sinner is unable to sin when he is flat on his back. There is much more opportunity for sinning when one is well than when one is ill.

Once offered as a sacrifice, pain can liberate the soul and turn a curse into a blessing. This better-or-worse quality of pain finds its two most perfect examples in the two thieves who were crucified on Calvary on either side of our Divine Lord. Actually, there seems to have been no difference between these two thieves, at the beginning. They were sentenced for the same crime; they were both equally criminal; they both blasphemed; they both suffered crucifixion. Then something happened. Pain forced them to concentrate on the ego. The thief on the left became worse. Pain, unsanctified, can scar, spoil, and scorch the soul. The thief on the left asked to be taken down. "Save thyself, and us too, if thou art the Christ." He wanted to be taken down in order that he might go on with the dirty, sordid business of stealing.

The thief on the right, though he began with cursing, soon saw his own pains as the just reward of his sins and protested against the gibes of his brother thief. "Hast thou no fear of God, when thou art undergoing the same sentence? And we justly enough; we receive no more than the due reward of our deeds; but this man has done nothing amiss."

Then he turned to our Lord and said, "Remember me when thou comest into thy kingdom." The answer came back, "I promise thee, this day thou shalt be with me in Paradise." "Thou"—it was the affirmation of democracy, the declaration of the worth of a single individual. That thief died a "thief," for he stole Paradise. Paradise can be stolen again!

The next question related to pain is *how to meet it*. There are actually three solutions about pain. One is the Stoic solution, which is to grit your teeth and bear it. The second is the Buddhist, which holds that all pain and suffering come from desire. If we could extinguish all our desires, we would eventually reach a point of tranquillity where we would be absorbed into the great Nirvana of unconsciousness. The third solution is the Hebraic-Christian philosophy of pain, which believes that pain and suffering can be transcended.

Suffering is transcended through love. Pain without love is suffering or hell. Suffering with love is sacrifice. Love does not have the power to diminish it. After losing money, a person often says, "I hope some poor person found it." The love of the poor softens the loss. A mother sits up all night with a fever-stricken child, but it is not suffering to her; it is love and sacrifice. No work is hard where there is love. Students who do not love a subject never do well in that subject. If then we can bear so much out of human love, how much more patient will we be out of love for God. As parents sometimes give bitter medicine to a child, so, too, the Heavenly Father gives it for some greater good. We know that somehow a Cross fits into the plan and purpose of this sinful world; otherwise, He would not have allowed his Divine Son to be crucified.

Never losing our love of God, we can then find reasons for supporting pain. If we have ruined our health by excesses, we impose upon ourselves dietary laws and avoid delicacies out of love for our health. One can do the same with the soul. One can say, "I will accept this particular suffering in order to make reparation for my own faults." Or we can also offer up our suffering for others. We live in a universe in which we help other people. Though some wear the best of woolens, they did not raise the sheep. Most of us do not raise the vegetables that we eat. We share in the communion of workers. So we can transfer and communicate to others the merits of our sufferings, offered in union with the Cross.

Doctors will graft skin from one part of the body to the face, if the face is burned. Those suffering from anemia receive a transfusion of blood from another member of society to cure them of that disease. If it is possible to transfuse blood, also one can transfuse sacrifice. If it is possible to graft skin, one can also graft prayer. We have blood banks for our own soldiers, that their lives may be saved through our sacrifice of blood. Pain, agony, disappointments, injustices—all these can be poured into a heavenly treasury from which the anemic, sinful, confused, ignorant souls may draw into the healing of their wings.

Thus through love of God suffering becomes sacrifice. The great mystery of the world is not what people suffer; it is what they miss when they suffer. They could be minting coinage for their own salvation and the salvation of the world. The tragedy of wasted pain! The unsanctified tears! The dull aches, the nauseating pains, the infuriating double-crosses! How much of these are wasted and thereby converted into curses because those who suffer them have no One to love! Life may be like a game of cards; we cannot help the hand that is dealt us, but we can help the way we play it. The lovelessness of lives is always the fault of the soul; the pain of life is not always such. The secret is to bring our little crosses under the shadow of the Cross, "Whom Love made life, Life made pain, and Pain made death."

That brings us to our final question and, of course, I cannot give the complete answer to the why of pain and suffering. One of the very best stories of the problem of suffering is contained in the Hebraic tradition in the Old Testament in the Book of Job. Job was a very wealthy man who lived in a large house with much land. He had seven sons and three daughters. He had thousands and thousands of oxen, sheep, and camels, and every one of his children had a country home.

The Sabeans came in and took his oxen; the Chaldeans came and stole his camels. Lightning struck his sheep; lightning struck the house of the eldest son, and he was killed. Then Job finally developed some ailment that covered him with sores from head to foot. His answer was that the Lord gave and the Lord takes away; "praised be the Lord."

His wife could not understand anybody who could say that, and she said, "Curse God and die." Poor Job, in addition to all his troubles, had the worry of a troublesome wife. . . .

Job had some comforters, and they came to see and console him. They first sat for seven days, according to Oriental custom, saying nothing.

Here was poor Job, whose wife would not allow him in the house, seated on a dunghill, cleaning his sores. After seven days, his comforters began to speak, and their solutions all boiled down to this: "Job, do you know why you are suffering? It is because you are not leading a good life." They were saying that there is an equation between economics and piety, and there are many who believe that. "So Job, if you are no longer prosperous, it must mean that you are no longer pious."

Job was not conscious of any sin, and Job rebelled against that suggestion, and rightly so. But Job did not know the answer either, and he began to ask himself many questions. "Why this loss; why this suffering; why this pain; why was I ever nestled at my mother's breast; why did I ever see the light of day?" He yearned that God might come and answer all of his questions.

Suppose the Book of Job stopped there. What a wonderful opportunity for a Broadway drama! Here is Job, suffering, asking all of these questions, and a Broadway dramatist would have made God walk across the stage and say, "Job, what are your questions?" God would answer them all, and the mysteries of the universe would clear.

And yet the Divine Dramatist does not operate that way. Actually, out of the whirlwind does come the voice of God, and God speaks and he says, "Now it is my turn to ask questions and yours to answer them. From what vantage point wast thou watching when I laid the foundations of the earth? Tell me, since thou art so wise, was it thou or I designed earth's plan, measuring it out with the line? How came its base to stand so firm, who laid its cornerstone? Was it thou or I shut in the sea behind bars? No sooner had it broken forth from the womb than I dressed it in swaddling clothes of dark mist, set it within bounds of my own choosing, made fast with bolt and bar. Thus far thou shalt come, said I, and no farther; here let thy welling waves spend their force. Tell me if such knowledge is thine, all its secrets; where the light dwells, where darkness finds its home; hast thou followed either of these to the end of its journey, tracked it to its lair? Didst thou foresee the time of thine own birth, couldst thou foretell the years of life that lay before thee? What sire gendered the rain or the drops of dew; what mother's womb bore the ice, the frost that comes from heaven to make water hard as stone, imprison the depths beneath its surface? Dost thou tell the daystar when to shine out, the evening star when to rise over the sons of earth? Can thy voice reach the clouds and bid their showers fall on thee; canst thou send out lightnings that will do thy errand and come back to await thy pleasure?"

And thus Job answered: "So vain a pleader, I have no suit to make; finger on lip I will listen."

The intelligence of Job was nothing compared with the mind of God, just as the mouse in the piano would never understand why anyone should sit down and play the keys of a piano. As the brain of a mouse is below that of man, so is the brain of man below the mind of God.

Finally, Job had everything restored to him sevenfold, because God never closes His door but that He also opens the window. That still did not quite answer the question because people might still ask, "Yes, but is there not such a thing as sacrifice in the world?" How do you explain that?

I tell you that if God in heaven had not come down to this earth in the form of a man and given us the supreme example of sacrifice, then it would be possible for fathers and mothers, men and women of countless ages, to do something greater, it would seem, than God himself could do, namely, lay down their lives for a friend.

Once He came, then never again could they say, "He does not know what it is like to suffer." He walked through the forest first and made the pathway and showed us that without Good Friday there would be no Easter Sunday. Never again can anyone say, "What have I done to deserve this?"

Death, Disease, War, and Famine

LOOKING OUT on the Four Horsemen spreading death, disease, war, and famine over the earth, we are tempted to ask: "Why does God let this happen?"

This is an incomplete sentence from the theological point of view. Finish it and it reads this way: "Why does God let this happen to Himself?"

What a different light this casts on the tragedy of war to realize that in some mysterious way Christ is living, suffering, thirsting, starving, and being imprisoned and dying in us, and that this war is His passion.

This does not mean that the historical Christ, who was born of Mary, suffered under Pontius Pilate, and is now glorified at the right hand of the Father, suffers again in that same human nature; for having died once He can never die again.

But it does mean that the Christ Who is the head of the body that is the Church, does suffer again.

Just as Our Divine Lord took a human nature from the womb of Mary overshadowed by the Holy Spirit, so on the day of Pentecost He took from the womb of humanity a corporate nature, or a Church overshadowed by the same Pentecostal Spirit.

Through that Church He still continues to teach, to govern, and to sanctify.

That is why the Church is infallible, because Christ the teacher teaches through it; that is why its authority is divine, because He the King governs through it; that is why the Sacraments are divine because He the Priest sanctifies through it.

This union of the head and the body is what St. Augustine calls the *Totus Christus,* the whole Christ, the Church that is the prolongation through space and time of the Incarnation.

The union of Christ and the Church is as intimate as the vine and the branches that have but one common life: "As the branch cannot bear fruit of itself unless it remain on the vine, so neither can you unless you abide in me" (John 15: 4).

In the analogy of St. Paul, the unity of Christ with us, and we with one another, is like the unity of hand and foot, head and body, all with all.

If someone steps on your foot, your head complains. St. Paul found out that this applies to the mystical body as well, when he was persecuting the Church of Damascus. The heavens opened and the glorified Christ said: "Saul, Saul, why dost thou persecute me?" (Acts 9:4).

In striking the Church, which was His Body, Paul was striking Christ; "I am Jesus whom thou persecuteth."

And did not Our Lord Himself say that anyone who would do anything to one incorporated to Him would be doing it to Him, for example, "And whoever receives one such little child for my sake receives me" (Matthew 18:5).

Did He not picture Himself as going through the world hungry, thirsty, imprisoned, and sick, and tell us that in serving them in His name we were serving Him: "Come, blessed of my Father, take possession of the kingdom prepared for you from the foundation of the world; for I was hungry and you gave me to eat; I was thirsty, and you gave me to drink; I was a stranger, and you took me in; naked, and you covered me; sick, and you visited me; I was in prison, and you came to me" (Matthew 25:34–37).

War as a Judgment of God

IN THE HISTORY OF ISRAEL God punishes both His own people and their enemies, but with a different kind of chastisement: *punitive* against the Assyrians, it ended in their desolation; *paternal* upon the Jews, it ended in their restoration.

May not those days be upon us once again? May not we all be under the judgment of God? Without changing a single word, Isaiah could repeat to our generation these frightening words: "Come near, ye Gentiles, and hear, and hearken, ye people. Let the earth hear, and all that is therein, the world, and everything that cometh forth of it. For the indignation of the Lord is upon all nations, and his fury upon all their armies" (Isaiah 34:1–2).

Could not this war be a chastisement of God upon us all, in two different ways: A chastisement upon evil nations that will end in their destruction; and a paternal correction to milk-and-water Christian nations, to their correction and amendment? God made use of the Assyrians to chastise his people, of the Persians to reestablish them, of Alexander and his successors to protect them. May not evil nations, which have borne the fruit of the godlessness that other nations have sown, be the fire of Divine Justice to remold those other nations into new vessels worthy to hold the oil of the charity and justice of God?

This idea of war as a judgment of God upon us all is not a soft theme, but it is a needed theme. If we resent the suggestion that we as a nation are not all we ought to be before God, it is because we, too, have been blind to justice. It is not easy to convince a nation that denies sin that the "wages of sin is death"; it is not easy to convince a people that denies the distinction between right and wrong that they may be wrong; it is not easy to awaken a people whose morality is relative to dictatorial barbarians, that they may not be angels. Too long have we who call ourselves Christians been nourished on the diluted sentimentalism of a liberal Christianity that stripped Christ of his justice and left him as a mere teacher of humanitarian ethics on a mountaintop. Adolf von Harnack, who gave us the ungoldly human Christ, has done more harm to souls than Adolf Hitler: the first Adolf gave us the crossless Christ without redemption; the second gave us its offspring, the double cross of the swastika with persecution.

Because I say war is a judgment of God, be not too hasty in saying God is revengeful. Let it be recalled that judgment as chastisement may be of two kinds: external and internal. This war [World War II] is of the second kind, not the first. An external punishment is arbitrary and capricious, like a spanking for an act of disobedience, for a spanking need not follow an act of disobedience; the modern mother might instead punish her child by saying: "Now just for that you may see only six murder movies this week instead of your usual seven."

Internal judgment or punishment, on the contrary, is bound up necessarily with the violation of law. For example, if I violate the laws of nature and do not eat for three days, I suffer a headache. There is nothing arbitrary about that headache. As a chastisement it is one with the refusal to eat. If you deliberately drink poison, you necessarily invoke nausea as a punishment; if you throw yourself from the thirty-fifth floor of a building you may be optimistic because you are alive at the eighteenth, but the sentence of death is already passed, though its execution be momentarily delayed. Go into the prisons, asylums, hospitals, and you will find nature squaring her accounts for violation of her laws. One can almost see there a judge seated in judgment.

Now, what is true of the physical law is true of the moral law: For every action there is a contrary and equal reaction.

Neglect the mind, and you condemn yourself to ignorance; neglect to exercise, and your muscles atrophy; neglect proper diet, and the body is dwarfed. Whence comes this judgment from nature, if it has not been placed there by Divine Justice? Search the Scriptures and read of the intrinsic relations between sin and punishment: "Be not deceived, God is not mocked. For what things a man shall sow, those also shall he reap. For he that soweth in his flesh, of the flesh also shall reap corruption. But he that soweth in the spirit, of the spirit shall reap life everlasting."

War as a Judgment of God does not mean that it is a punishment in the sense of being an arbitrary action on the part of God, but in the sense of being an execution of the law of justice. Men are visited with the effects of their own sins. In other words, sin brings adversity, and such adversity is the expression of God's chastisement of sin, brought about by the action of man himself.

The Meaning of Death

DEATH IS AN AFFIRMATION of the purpose of life in an otherwise meaningless existence. The world could carry on its Godless plan if there were no death. What death is to an individual, that catastrophe is to a civilization—the end of its wickedness. This is a source of anguish to the modern mind, for not only must man die, but also the world must die. Death is a negative testimony to God's power in a meaningless world, for by it God brings meaningless existence to naught. Because God exists, evil cannot carry on its wickedness indefinitely. If there were no catastrophe, such as the Apocalypse reveals, at the end of the world, the universe would then be the triumph of chaos. But the catastrophe is a reminder that God will not allow unrighteousness to become eternal.

Death proves also that life has meaning because it reveals that the virtues and goodness practiced within time do not find their completion except in eternity.

Man is much more afraid of dying in a train wreck or automobile accident than he is of dying on a battlefield or as a martyr to his faith. This proves that death is less terrifying and more meaningful when we rise above the level of the commonplace and lift ourselves into the realm of spiritual values.

That death is the end of evil is revealed too in the fact that the face of the dead is often more harmonious than the same face in life, as the sleeping face is more restful than the face awake. The ugly feelings and hates, eccentricities and discords, disappear in the presence of the dead, so much so that we use the expression, "Of the dead say nothing but good." In the face of the dead we give praise and adulation; we resurrect the good things and the charities, kindnesses and humor. All of these are recalled posthumously, making us wonder if death itself may not be the thrusting into the forefront of the good that we have done, rather than the evil. Not that both will not be recalled, but rather that as life brought out the debit side of our character, so death will also bring out the credit side. Death, in other words, is bound up with goodness.

Death is also bound up with love, or better, love is always bound up with death. He who accepts love accepts sacrifice. The ring of gold instead of the ring of tin is sacrifice, and sacrifice is a form of death. Beyond all of these minor sacrifices, the love is complete when it is most willing to accept for the beloved the sacrifice of death, as a soldier dies for his country. He who would attach too much value to life and run away from death runs away from perfect love. "This is the greatest love a man can show, that he should lay down his life for his friends."

Death also will individualize and personalize us, who are today brought together in crowds and groups. Death separates the soul from the body; in doing so, each and every person is searched. Then shall be revealed my true self—not the self I think I am. The soul will stand naked before God as it truly is. If it is not clothed with virtue, it will feel ashamed, as Adam and Eve did after their sin when they hid from God. It is curious that only after their sin did they feel naked and ashamed. The correlation between the nakedness of the soul and sin is manifested in the fact that the less people have of inner grace in this life, the more gaudily they dress; it is a kind of compensation for the nudity of their own souls. There shall then be only that *me* that sinned, that gave to the poor, that prayed, or that blasphemed. Then it will not be the *me* that lives, but the *me* that has lived, the *me* at the end of the day of life.

There will be no attorneys to plead the case, no alienists to argue that we were not in our right minds when we did wrong, there will be only one voice. It will be the voice of conscience that will reveal ourselves as we really are. We will thus be our own witness and our own judge. Nothing is as democratic as death—for in it each person votes and decides his or her eternity.

The Necessity of Judgment

THERE COMES A TIME in the life of every man when at the supreme and tragic hour of death his friends and relatives ask, "How much did he leave?" It is just at that split second God is asking, "How much did he take with him?" It is only the latter question that matters, for it is only our works that follow us. The story of life is brief: "It is appointed unto men once to die and after this the judgment" for "the Son of Man shall come in the glory of His Father with His angels, and then will He render to every man according to his works." In the general forgetfulness of the Christian religion, which has passed over our civilization like a foul miasma, this great truth that a judgment follows death has been ignored in the moral outlook of the universe. Our souls can profit much from meditation upon it and its two important features: namely, its necessity and its nature.

All nature testifies to the necessity of judgment. Everywhere below man nature reveals itself as passing sentence on those who refuse to obey her laws. We need only look around us in the hospitals, prisons, and asylums to see that nature, like a judge seated in judgment, is squaring her accounts with those who violate her laws. If the body has abused itself by excess, nature takes revenge and passes the judgment of disease and infirmity. If a fragment of a star breaks from its central core and swings out of its orbit, nature passes the judgment that it shall burn itself out in space.

Nature settles her account with natural things here and now. But the moral side of the universe has not made its lasting reckoning with every man on this side of the grave. There is too much anguished innocence; there is too much unpunished wrong; there is too much suffering of the good; too much prosperity of the evil; too much pain for those who obey God's laws; too much pleasure for those who disobey them; too much good repute for those who sin unseen; too much scorn for those who pray unseen; too many unsung saints; too many glorified sinners; too many Pilates who act as righteous judges; too many Christs who go down to crucifixion; too many proud and vain souls who say, "I have sinned and nothing has happened."

But the reckoning day must come, and just as once a year each business person must balance the accounts, so too that important hour must come when every soul must balance its accounts before God. For life is like a cash register in that every account, every thought, every deed, like every sale, is registered and recorded. And when the business of life is finally done, then God pulls from out the registry of our souls that slip of our memory on which are recorded our merits and demerits, our virtues and our vices—the basis of the judgment on which shall be decided eternal life or eternal death. We may falsify our accounts until that day of judgment, for God permits the wheat and the cockle to grow unto the harvest, but then, "in the time of the harvest, I will say to the reaper: gather up first the cockle and bind it into bundles to burn, but the wheat gather ye into my barn."

But what is the nature of judgment? In answer to this question we are more concerned with the particular judgment at the moment of death than with the general judgment when all nations of the earth stand before their God. Judgment is a recognition both on the part of God and on the part of the soul.

First of all, it is a recognition on the part of God. Imagine two souls appearing before the sight of God, one in the state of grace, the other in the state of sin. Grace is a participation in the nature and life of God. Just as one participates in the nature and life of one's parents by being born of one's parents, so too a person who is born of the Spirit of God by baptism participates in the nature of God—the life of God, as it were, flows through the veins, imprinting an unseen but genuine likeness. When, therefore, God looks upon a soul in the state of grace, He sees in it a likeness of His own nature. Just as a parent recognizes his own child because of likeness of nature, so too Christ recognizes the soul in the state of grace in virtue of resemblance to Him, and says to the soul: "Come ye blessed of My Father: I am the natural Son, you are the adopted son. Come into the Kingdom prepared for you from all eternity."

God looks into the other soul that is in the state of sin and has not that likeness, and just as a father knows his neighbor's son is not his own, so too God, looking at the sinful soul and failing to see therein the likeness of His own flesh and blood, does not recognize it as His own kind, and says to it as He said in the parable of the bridegroom "I know you not"—and it is a terrible thing not to be known by God.

The Fact of Hell

IF THERE IS ANY SUBJECT that is offensive to modern senti-
mentalists, it is the subject of hell. Our generation clamors
for what the poet has called "a soft dean, who never mentions hell to ears polite," and our unsouled age wants a
Christianity watered so as to make the gospel of Christ
nothing more than a gentle doctrine of good will, a social
program of economic betterment, and a mild scheme of pro-
gressive idealism.

There are many reasons why the modern world has
ceased to believe in hell, among which we may mention,
first, a psychological reason. If a man has led a very wicked
life, he does not want to be disturbed in his wrongdoings
by harsh words about justice. His wish that there be no
final punishment for his crimes thus becomes father to the
thought that there is no such thing as hell. That is why the
wicked person denies hell, whereas the saint never denies it
but only fears it.

Another reason for the denial of hell is that some minds
confuse the crude imagery of poets and painters with the
reality of the moral order behind the doctrine. Eternal realities are not always easy to portray in the symbols of time
and space, but that is no reason why they should be denied
by anyone, any more than the reality of America should be
denied because it is sometimes symbolized by a woman
bearing a flag of red, white, and blue.

A final reason is found in the reason that the doctrine of
hell has been isolated from the organic whole of Christian
truths. Once it is separated from the doctrines of sin, freedom, virtue, redemption, and justice, it becomes as absurd
as an eye separated from the body. The justice of this rea-

soning is borne out in the fact that men become scandalized about hell when they cease to be scandalized about sin. The Church has never altered one single iota the belief in an eternal hell as taught by her Founder, our Lord and Savior, Jesus Christ. In adherence to His divine testimony, the Church teaches, first that hell is a demand of Justice, and secondly, that hell is a demand of Love.

First of all, once it is recognized that the moral order is grounded on justice, then retribution beyond the grave becomes a necessity. All peoples have held it morally intolerable that by the mere fact of dying, a murderer or an impenitent wrongdoer should triumphantly escape justice. The same fate cannot lie in store for the martyr and the persecutor, Nero and Paul, the Judas and Christ. If there is a supreme Good to which man can attain only by courageous effort, it must follow that the man who neglects to make that effort imperils his felicity. Once it is granted that eternal life is a thing that has to be won, then there must always be the grim possibility that it may also be lost.

Even the order of nature itself suggests retribution for every violation of a law. There is a physical law to the effect that for every action there is a contrary and equal reaction. If, for example, I stretch a rubber band three inches, it will react with a force equal to three inches. If I stretch it six inches, it will react with a force equal to six inches. If I stretch it twelve inches, it will react with a force equal to a foot. This physical law has its counterpart in the moral order, in which every sin necessarily implies punishment. What is sin but an action against a certain order?

There are three orders against which a man may sin: first, the order of individual conscience; secondly, the order of the union of consciences, or the State; and thirdly, the source of both, or God. Now, if I sin or act against my conscience, there is a necessary reaction in the form of remorse of conscience that, in normal individuals, varies with the gravity of the sin committed. Secondly, if I act or sin against the union of consciences or the State, there is a contrary and equal reaction that takes the form of a fine, imprisonment, or death sentence meted out by the State. It is worthy of note that the punishment is never determined by the length of time required to commit the crime, but rather by the nature of the crime itself. It takes only a second to commit murder, and yet the State will take away life for such an offense. Finally, whenever I sin against God, and this I do when I rebel either against the order of conscience . . . I am acting contrary to One Who is infinite. For this action, there is bound to be a reaction. The reaction from the Infinite must, therefore, be infinite, and an infinite reaction from God is an infinite separation from God, and an infinite separation from God is an eternal divorce from Life and Truth and Love, and an eternal divorce from Life and Truth and Love is—hell! . . .

Hell is demanded not only by justice, but also by love. The failure to look upon hell as involving love makes men ask the question, "How can a God of love create a place of everlasting punishment?" This is like asking why a God of Love should be a God of Justice. It forgets that the sun that warms so gently may also wither, and the rain that nourishes so tenderly may also rot. Those who cannot reconcile the God of Love with hell do not know the meaning of love. There is nothing sweeter than love; there is nothing bitterer than love; there is nothing that so much unites souls and so much separates them as love. Love demands reciprocity; love seeks a lover, and when love finds reciprocity, there are a fusion and a compenetration and a union to a sublime and ecstatic degree. And when it is a question of the love of God and the love of the soul, that is the happiness of heaven. But suppose that love does not find reciprocity; or suppose that love does find it only to be betrayed, spurned, and rejected. Can love still forgive? Love can forgive injuries and betrayals and insults, and Divine Love can forgive even to seventy times seven. But there is only one thing in the world that human love cannot forgive, and there is only one thing in eternity that Divine Love cannot forgive, and that is the refusal to love. When, therefore, the soul by a final free act refuses to return human love for Divine Love, then Divine Love abandons it to its own self-ishness, to its own solitariness, to its own loneliness. And what punishment in all the world is comparable to being abandoned, not by the lovely but by the Love that is God?

Love forgives everything except one thing, and that is the re-fusal to love. A human heart pursues another and sues for its affection with all the purity and high ardor of its being. It showers the loved one with gifts, tokens of sacrifice, and all the while remains most worthy of a responding affec-tion. But if, after a long and weary pursuit, it has only been spurned and rejected and betrayed, that human heart turns away and bursting with a pent-up emotion in obedience to the law of love, cries out: "Love has done all that it can. I can forgive anything except the refusal to love."

Something of this kind takes place in the spiritual order. God is the Great Lover on the quest of His spouse, which is the human soul. He showers it with gifts, admits it into His royal family in the sacrament of baptism, into His royal army in the sacrament of confirmation, and invites it to His royal table in the Sacrament of the Everlasting Bread, and countless times during human life whispers to it in health and sickness, in sorrow and joy, to respond to His plaintive pleadings, abandon a life of sin, and return love for love. If, however, the human heart, after rejecting this love many times only to be reloved again, after ignoring the knock of Christ at the door of his soul only to hear the knock again, finally, at the moment of death, completely spurns and re-jects that Divine Goodness, then the God of Love, in obe-dience to the law of love, cries out: "Love has done all that it can. I can forgive everything, except the refusal to love." And it is a terrible thing to be through with love, for once Divine Love departs at death, it never returns:—that is why hell is eternal!—that is why hell is a place where there is no love!

Eternity

Go back in the storehouse of your memory, and you will find ample proof that it is always in those moments when you are least conscious of the passing of time that you most thoroughly enjoy the pleasures of time. How often it happens, for example, when listening to an absorbing conversation or the thrilling experiences of a much-traveled person, that the hours pass by so quickly we are hardly conscious of them.

What is true of a delightful conversation is also true of esthetic pleasures. I dare say that very few would ever notice the passing of time listening to an orchestra translate the beauty of one of Beethoven's works. In just the proportion that it pleases and thrills, it makes us unconscious of how long we were absorbed by its melodies. The contrary fact illustrates the same truth. The more we notice time, the less we are being interested. If our friends keep looking at their watches while we tell a story, we can be very sure that they are being bored by our story. A person who keeps an eye on the clock is not the person who is interested in his or her work. The more we notice the passing of time, the less is our pleasure; and the less we notice the passing of time, the greater is our pleasure.

These psychological facts of experience testify that not only is time the obstacle of enjoyment, but also that escape from it is the essential of happiness. Suppose we could enlarge upon our experience in such a way as to imagine ourselves completely outside of time and succession, in a world where there would never be a "before" nor an "after," but only a "now." Suppose we could go out to another existence where the great pleasures of history would not be denied us because of their historical incompatibility, but all unified in a beautiful hierarchical order, like a pyramid in that all would minister to the very unity of our personality. Suppose I say that I could reach a point of timelessness at which all the enjoyments and beauties and happiness of time could be reduced to those three fundamental unities that constitute the perfection of our being, namely, life, and truth, and love, for into these three all pleasures can be resolved.

Suppose first of all that I could reduce to a single focal point all the pleasures of life, so that in the now that never looked before nor after, I could enjoy the life that seems to be in the sea when its restless bosom is dimpled with calm, as well as the urge of life that seems to be in all the hill-encircling brooks that loiter to the sea; the life that provokes the dumb, dead sod to tell its thoughts in violets; the life that pulsates through a springtime blossom as the swinging cradle for the fruit; the life of the flowers as they open the chalice of their perfume to the sun; the life of the birds as the great heralds of song and messengers of joy; the life of all the children that run shouting to their mothers' arms; the life of all the parents that beget a life like unto their own; and the life of the mind that on the wings of an invisible thought strikes out to the hidden battlements of eternity to the life whence all living comes. . . .

Suppose that in addition to concentrating all the life of the universe in a single point, I could also concentrate in another focal point all the truths of the world, so that I could know the truth the astronomers seek as they look up through telescopes, and the truth the biologists seek as they look down through microscopes; the truth about the heavens, and who shut up the sea with doors when it did burst forth as issuing from a womb; the truth about the hiding place of darkness and the treasure house of hail, and the cave of the winds; the truth about the common things; why fire, like a spirit, mounts to the heavens heavenly, and why

gold, like clay, falls to the earth earthly; the truth the philosophers seek as they tear apart with their minds the very
wheels of the universe; the truth the theologians seek as
they use Revelation to unravel the secrets of God that far
surpass those that John heard as he leaned his head upon
the breast of his Master. . . .

Suppose that, over and above all these pleasures of life
and truth, there could be unified in another focal point all
the delights and beauties of love that have contributed to
the happiness of the universe: the love of a patriot for a
country; the love of the soldier for his cause; the love of the
scientist for a discovery; the love of the flowers as they
smile upon the sun; the love of the earth at whose breast all
creation drinks the milk of life; the love of mothers, who
swing open the great portals of life that a child may see the
light of day; the love of friend for friend to whom he could
reveal his heart through words; the love of spouse for
spouse; the love of husband for wife; and even the love of
angel for angel, and the angel for God with a fire and heat
sufficient to enkindle the hearts of ten thousand times ten
thousand worlds. . . .

Suppose that all the pleasures of the world could be
brought to these three focal points of Life and Truth and
Love, just as the rays of the sun are brought to unity in the
sun; and suppose that all the successive pleasures of time
could be enjoyed at one and the same now; and suppose
that these points of unity, on which our hearts and minds
and souls would be directed, would not merely be three ab-
stractions, but that the focal point in which all the pleasures
of life were concentrated would be a life personal enough to
be a Father, and that that focal point of truth, in which all
the pleasures of truth were concentrated, would not merely
be an abstract truth, but a truth personal enough to be a
Word or a Son, and that that focal point of love, in which all
the pleasures of love were concentrated, would be not
merely an abstract love, but a love personal enough to be a
Holy Spirit; and suppose that once elevated to that supreme

height, happiness would be so freed from limitations that it would include these three as one, not in succession, but with a permanence; not as in time, but as in the timeless— then we would have eternity, then we would have God! The Father, Son, and Holy Spirit; Perfect Life, Perfect Truth, Perfect Love. Then we would have happiness—and that would be heaven.

Would the pleasures of that timelessness with God and that enjoyment of life and truth and love that are the Trinity be in any way comparable to the pleasures of time? Is there anyone on this earth that will tell me about heaven? Certainly there are three faculties to which one might appeal, namely, to what one has seen, to what one has heard, and to what one can imagine. Will heaven surpass all the pleasures of the eye, and the ear, and the imagination?

First of all, will it be as beautiful as some of the things that can be seen? I have seen the Villa d'Este of Rome with its long lanes of ilex and laurel, and its great avenues of cypress trees, all full of what might be called the vivacity of quiet and living silence. I have seen a sunset on the Mediterranean when two clouds came down like pillars to form a brilliant red tabernacle for the sun and it glowing like a golden host. I have seen, from the harbor, the towers and the minarets of Constantinople pierce through the mist that hung over them like a silken veil. I have seen the chateau country of France and her Gothic cathedrals aspiring heavenward like prayers. I have seen the beauties of the castles of the Rhine. And the combination of all these visions almost makes me think of the doorkeeper of the Temple of Diana who used to cry out to those who entered: "Take heed to your eye," and so I wonder if the things of eternity will be as beautiful as the combined beauty of all the things I have seen. . . .

I have not seen all the beauties of nature. Others I have heard of that I have not seen. I have heard of the beauties of the Hanging Gardens of Babylon, of the pomp and dignity of the palaces of the Doges, of the brilliance and glitter of the Roman Forum as its foundations rocked with the tramp of Rome's resistless legions. I have heard of the splendor of the Temple of Jerusalem as it shone like a jewel in the morning sun. I have heard of the beauties of the garden of Paradise where fourfold rivers flowed through lands rich with gold and onyx, a garden made beautiful as only God knows how to make a beautiful garden. I have heard of countless other beauties and joys of nature that tongue cannot describe, nor touch of brush convey, and I wonder if all the joys and pleasures of heaven will be as great as the combined beauty of all the things of which I have heard. . . .

Beyond what I have heard and seen, there are things that I can imagine. I can imagine a world in which there never would be pain, nor disease, nor death. I can imagine a world wherein everyone would live in a castle, and in that commonwealth of castles there would be a due order of justice without complaint or anxiety. I can imagine a world in which the winter would never come, and in which the flowers would never fade, and the sun would never set. I can imagine a world in which there would always be a peace and a quiet without idleness, a profound knowledge of things without research, a constant enjoyment without satiety. I can imagine a world that would eliminate all the evils and diseases and worries of life, and combine all of its best joys and happiness, and I wonder if all the happiness of heaven would be like the happiness of earth that I can imagine. . . .

Will eternity be anything like what I have seen or what I have heard or what I can imagine? No, eternity will be nothing like anything I have seen, heard, or imagined. Listen to the voice of God: "Eye hath not seen, nor ear heard, neither hath it entered into the heart of man what things God hath prepared for them that love Him."

If the timeless so much surpasses time that there can be found no parallel for it, then I begin to understand the great mystery of the shape of the human heart. The human heart is not shaped like a Valentine heart, perfect and regular in

Bibliography

BOOKS QUOTED IN THE TEXT

A Declaration of Dependence. Milwaukee: The Bruce Publishing
    Company, 1941.

Footprints in a Darkened Forest. New York: Meredith Press, 1967.

For God and Country. New York: P. J. Kenedy and Sons, 1941.

God and War. New York: P. J. Kenedy & Sons, 1942.

Go to Heaven. New York: McGraw-Hill Book Company, Inc., 1960.

Guide to Contentment. New York: Simon and Schuster, 1967.

Life Is Worth Living. First Series. New York: McGraw-Hill Book
    Company, Inc., 1953.

Life Is Worth Living. Fourth Series. New York: McGraw-Hill Book
    Company, Inc., 1956.

Life Is Worth Living. Fifth Series. New York: McGraw-Hill Book
    Company, Inc., 1957.

Lift Up Your Heart. New York: McGraw-Hill Book Company, Inc.,
    1950.

Love One Another. New York: P. J. Kenedy & Sons, 1944.

Moods and Truths. New York: The Century Co., 1932. Reprinted in
    1950 by Garden City Publishing Co., Garden City, New
    York.

Old Errors and New Labels. New York: The Century Co., 1931.

Peace of Soul. New York: McGraw-Hill Book Company, Inc., 1949.

The Cross and the Beatitudes. New York: P. J. Kenedy & Sons, 1937.

The Divine Romance. New York: The Century Co., 1930.

The Eternal Galilean. New York: D. Appleton-Century Company, Inc., 1934.

The Life of All Living: The Philosophy of Life. New York: The Century Company, 1929.

The Moral Universe: A Preface to Christian Living. Milwaukee: The Bruce Publishing Company, 1936.

The Power of Love. New York: Simon and Schuster, 1965.

The Seven Last Words. New York: The Century Co., 1933.

The World's First Love. New York: McGraw-Hill Book Company, Inc., 1952.

Way to Happiness. Garden City, New York: Garden City Books, 1954.

BOOKS NOT QUOTED IN THE TEXT

Calvary and the Mass: A Missal Companion. New York: P. J. Kenedy & Sons, 1936.

Characters of the Passion. New York: P. J. Kenedy & Sons, 1947.

Children and Parents. New York: Simon & Schuster, 1970.

Communism and the Conscience of the West. Indianapolis: The Bobbs-Merrill Company, 1948.

For God and Country. New York: P. J. Kenedy & Sons, 1941.

Freedom Under God. Milwaukee: The Bruce Publishing Company, 1940.

God and Intelligence in Modern Philosophy: A Critical Study in the Light of the Philosophy of Saint Thomas. With an Introduction by G. K. Chesterton. London: Longmans, Green and Co., 1925.

God Love You. Garden City, New York: Garden City Books, 1955.

Liberty, Equality, and Fraternity. New York: The Macmillan Company, 1938.

Jesus, Son of Mary.

Life Is Worth Living. Second Series. New York: McGraw-Hill Book Company, Inc., 1954.

Life Is Worth Living. Third Series. New York: McGraw-Hill Book Company, Inc., 1955.

Life of Christ. New York: McGraw-Hill Book Company, Inc., 1958.

Missions and the World Crises. Milwaukee: The Bruce Publishing Co., 1963.

Philosophies at War. New York: Charles Scribner's Sons, 1943.

Philosophy of Religion: The Impact of Modern Knowledge on Religion. New York: Appleton-Century-Crofts, Inc., 1948.

Philosophy of Science. Milwaukee: The Bruce Publishing Company, 1934.

Preface to Religion. New York: P. J. Kenedy & Sons, 1946.

Religion Without God. New York: Longmans, Green and Co., 1928.

Seven Pillars of Peace. New York: Charles Scribner's Sons, 1945.

Seven Words of Jesus and Mary. New York: P. J. Kenedy & Sons, 1945.

Seven Words to the Cross. New York: P. J. Kenedy & Sons, 1944.

The Armor of God. New York: P. J. Kenedy & Sons, 1943.

The Cross and the Crisis. Milwaukee: The Bruce Publishing Company, 1938.

The Divine Verdict. New York: P. J. Kenedy & Sons, 1943.

The Mystical Body of Christ. New York: Sheed & Ward, 1935.

The Priest Is Not His Own. New York: McGraw-Hill Book Company, Inc., 1963.

The Rainbow of Sorrow. New York: P. J. Kenedy & Sons, 1938.

These Are the Sacraments. Described by Fulton J. Sheen. Photographed by Yousuf Karsh. New York: Hawthorn Books, Inc., 1962.

The Seven Virtues. New York: P. J. Kenedy & Sons, 1940.

The True Meaning of Christmas. New York: McGraw-Hill Book Company, 1955.

The Way of the Cross. New York: Appleton-Century-Crofts, Inc., 1932.

Thinking Life Through. New York: McGraw-Hill Book Company, 1955.

Three to Get Married. New York: Appleton-Century-Crofts, Inc., 1951.

This Is Rome: A Pilgrimage in Words and Pictures. Conducted by Fulton J. Sheen; photographed by Yousuf Karsh; described by H. V. Morton; with an Introduction by Fulton J. Sheen. New York: Hawthorn Books, Inc., 1960.

This Is the Holy Land: A Pilgrimage in Words and Pictures. Conducted by Fulton J. Sheen; photographed by Yousuf Karsh; described by H. V. Morton; with a Foreword by Bishop Sheen. New York: Hawthorn Books, Inc., 1961.

This Is the Mass. Described by Henri Daniel-Rops; celebrated by Fulton J. Sheen; photographed by Yousuf Karsh. Translated by Alastair Guinan; with an Introduction by Bishop Sheen. New York: Hawthorn Books, Inc., 1958.

Those Mysterious Priests. Garden City, New York: Doubleday & Company, Inc., 1974.

Victory over Vice. Garden City, New York: P. J. Kenedy & Sons, 1939.

Way to Inner Peace. Garden City, New York: Garden City Books, 1955.

Whence Come Wars. New York: Sheed & Ward, 1940.

Thoughts for Daily Living.

The Fulton J. Sheen Sunday Missal.

Sources

Agnosticism, *Old Errors and New Labels*, 33–35.

Amputation, Mortification, Limitation, *Life Is Worth Living* (first series), 140–145.

"Behold Thy Son," *The Seven Last Words*, 25–26.

"Blessed Are the Clean of Heart," *The Cross and the Beatitudes*, 39–40.

"Blessed Are the Meek," *The Cross and the Beatitudes*, 4–6.

"Blessed Are the Merciful," *The Cross and the Beatitudes*, 22–24.

"Blessed Are the Peacemakers," *The Cross and the Beatitudes*, 86–87.

"Blessed Are the Poor in Spirit," *The Cross and the Beatitudes*, 53–55.

"Blessed Are They That Hunger and Thirst After Justice," *The Cross and the Beatitudes*, 72–74.

"Blessed Are They That Mourn," *The Cross and the Beatitudes*, 99–101.

"Blessed Are They That Are Persecuted," *The Cross and the Beatitudes*, vii.

Broad-Mindedness, *Old Errors and New Labels*, 95–98, 100–101, 115–116.

Brotherhood, *Love One Another*, 103–105.

Buddha, Confucius, Lao-Tse, Socrates, Mohammed, *The Eternal Galilean*, 84–87.

Charity and Philanthropy, *Old Errors and New Labels*, 233–253.

Communism, *Life Is Worth Living* (first series), 62–70.

Conscience, the Interior Sinai, *The Moral Universe*, 13–16.

Creation, *The Divine Romance*, 41–46.